MYTHS, MODELS, & METHODS

IN SPORT PEDAGOGY

Editors

Gary T. Barrette, EdD
Ronald S. Feingold, PhD
C. Roger Rees, PhD
Adelphi University

Maurice Piéron
University of Liège, Belgium

Human Kinetics Publishers, Inc.
Champaign, Illinois

Proceedings of the Adelphi-AIESEP '85 World Sport Conference held
August 19–22, 1985 at Adelphi University, Garden City, NY.

Library of Congress Cataloging-in-Publication Data

Adelphi-AIESEP '85 World Sport Conference (1985:
    Adelphi University)
    Myths, models, and methods in sport pedagogy.

    "Proceedings of the Adelphi-AIESEP '85 World Sport
Conference, held August 19–22, 1985, at Adelphi
University, Garden City, NY"—T.p. verso.
    Includes bibliographies and index.
    I. Barrette, Gary T. II. Adelphi University.
III. International Association for Physical Education
in Higher Education. IV. Title.
GV205.A33 1985   613.7'07   86-20094
ISBN 0-87322-085-4

Developmental Editor: Laura E. Larson
Production Director: Ernie Noa
Assistant Production Director: Lezli Harris
Copy Editor: John Edwards
Typesetter: Sonnie Bowman
Proofreader: Jennifer Merrill
Text Layout: Leah Freedman
Printed By: Braun-Brumfield, Inc.

ISBN: 0-87322-085-4

Printed in the United States of America

10 9 8 7 6 5 4 3 2 1

Human Kinetics Publishers, Inc.
Box 5076, Champaign, IL 61820

Contents

Contributors

William G. Anderson
Dept. of Movement Sciences and
  Education
Teachers College, Columbia
  University
New York, NY 10027
U.S.A.

Ree K. Arnold
Dept. of Physical Education,
  Recreation and Leisure Studies
Montclair State College
Upper Montclair, NJ 07043
U.S.A.

Wolf-Dietrich Brettschneider
University of Paderborn
Sportwissenschaft
D-4790 Paderborn
WEST GERMANY

Bart J. Crum
Interfaculty of Human Movement
  Sciences
Free University
P.O. Box 7161
1007 MC Amsterdam
THE NETHERLANDS

Ronald S. Feingold
Adelphi University
Garden City, NY 11530
U.S.A.

Graham J. Fishburne
Dept. of Elementary Education
University of Alberta
Edmonton, Alberta T6G 2G5
CANADA

Paul Godbout
Dept. of Physical Education
PEPS—Laval University
Ste-Foy, Québec G1K 7P4
CANADA

Susan L. Greendorfer
Room 3 CRC
51 Gerty Drive
Champaign, IL 61820
U.S.A.

Udo Hanke
Institut für Sport und
  Sportwissenschaft
  der Universität Heidelberg
Im Neuenheimer Feld 710
6900 Heidelberg
WEST GERMANY

Wilma M. Harrington
Dept. of Physical Education
University of Georgia
Athens, GA 30602
U.S.A.

Andrew H. Hawkins
West Virginia University
School of Physical Education
P.O. Box 6116
Morgantown, WV 26506-6116
U.S.A.

Ann E. Jewett
Dept. of Physical Education
University of Georgia
Athens, GA 30602
U.S.A.

Kathryn L. Kisabeth
Dept. of Health, P.E., and
  Recreation
Hampton University
Hampton, VA 23668
U.S.A.

Lawrence F. Locke
Dept. of Professional Preparation
University of Massachusetts
Amherst, MA 01003
U.S.A.

Madeleine Lord
University of Montreal
Physical Education Department
C.P. 6128, succ. A
Montreal, Quebec H3C 3J7
CANADA

Victor H. Mancini
Ithaca College
School of Health, Physical
  Education, and Recreation
Ithaca, NY 14850
U.S.A.

Paul C. Paese
Southwest Texas State University
Dept. of HPER
A145 Jowers Center
San Marcos, TX 78666-4616
U.S.A.

Claude Paré
Départment des sciences de
  l'activité physique
Université du Québec
  à Trois Rivières G9A 5H7
CANADA

Maurice Piéron
Institut Supérieur d'Education
  Physique
Université de Liège, Bât. 21
au Sart Tilman par B-4000 Liège
BELGIUM

Judith E. Rink
University of South Carolina
Columbia, SC 29210
U.S.A.

Peter Röthig
Inst. für Sportwissenschaften
Ginnheimer Landstr. 39
6000 Frankfurt am Main
WEST GERMANY

George H. Sage
University of Northern Colorado
Greeley, CO 80639
U.S.A.

Michael A. Sherman
Dept. of Health, Physical, and
  Recreation Education
Teacher Behavior Laboratory,
  113 Trees Hall
University of Pittsburgh
Pittsburgh, PA 15261
U.S.A.

Daryl Siedentop
Ohio State University
Columbus, OH 43210-1221
U.S.A.

Risto Telama
Dept. of Physical Education
University of Jyväskylä
40100 Jyväskylä
FINLAND

Richard I. Tinning
School of Education
Deakin University
Geelong, Victoria 3217
AUSTRALIA

Marielle Tousignant
PEPS, local 2115
Université Laval
Sainte-Foy, Québec G1K 7P4
CANADA

Pauli Vuolle
Dept. of Sociology and Planning
  for Physical Culture
University of Jyväskylä
40100 Jyväskylä
FINLAND

Foreword

Adelphi-AIESEP '85 World Conference
An International Dialogue on Research in Sport and Physical Education

In recent years, when colleagues attempted to assess the present state of sport pedagogy research and to evaluate the outcomes of a conference in this area, it was common to speak about outstanding achievement and continuous growth. For many reasons, these plaudits are surely not an exaggeration or a *figure de style* (polite formality) in the case of the Adelphi-AIESEP '85 World Conference held in August in Garden City, New York, U.S.A.

AIESEP (Association Internationale des Ecoles Supérieures d'Education Physique) organized its first international meeting on the study of teaching in physical education in Madrid, Spain, in 1977. The subsequent yearly meetings of the association reflected significant growth in both the interest and quality of research in sport pedagogy. The sport pedagogy section of the Olympic Scientific Congress held in 1984 in Eugene, Oregon, was considered by many as the total achievement in the field for AIESEP. But records are made to be broken. When I met with the organizers from Adelphi University, I was immediately impressed with their enthusiasm and organizational skills and was confident that they were ready to take on the challenge of organizing a world conference. Now that the conference has come and passed, I can attest to its success and confirm that my confidence in them was certainly well placed.

The theme, "An International Dialogue on Research in Sport and Physical Education: Myths, Models and Methods," was challenging enough to make the conference a truly international meeting with 30 countries represented. The best researchers and speakers in the field of sport pedagogy presented outstanding papers, and it was easier to count those who were absent than those who attended. The findings presented and ideas debated during the 4-day meeting were challenging and promoted intense discussions and meaningful professional interaction.

The areas of research included were: process-product studies, teaching behavior modification, the decision-making process employed by the teacher, and qualitative research, among others. The subject foci of the research presented were also quite variable including elementary and secondary school classes, student teachers, mainstreamed populations, sports groups, and in-service staff development. In addition, an effort was made to link the data with interpretation by social scientists and learning process theory.

The success of any major conference remains limited without the publication of a high quality proceedings. Human Kinetics has shown its interest in the advancement of sport sciences and has already published numerous quality volumes in the field of sport pedagogy. It continues to pursue its commitment to the field by publishing this refereed proceedings and thus is contributing substantially to the extended success of Adephi-AIESEP '85.

As general secretary of AIESEP, I wish to express my sincerest thanks to the Adelphi University team: Ron Feingold and Gary T. Barrette, Conference Codirectors; C. Roger Rees, Conference Program Director; Ruth Skinner, Conference Manager; and the many wonderful volunteers who made Adelphi-AIESEP '85 a remarkable achievement and our trip to New York, U.S.A. a truly memorable experience.

Maurice Piéron
University of Liège, Belgium
General Secretary/AIESEP

Preface

The theme of the Adelphi-AIESEP '85 World Conference was "An International Dialogue on Research in Sport and Physical Education: Myths, Models and Methods." This particular theme was selected because the conference organizers were intent on producing a conference design that would provide real opportunities for the sharing of information and discussion of ideas. Furthermore, the topical research categories—teaching, teacher education research, and the sociology of physical education related to teaching and coaching—were intended to attract research and opinions on sport pedagogy from the many subdisciplines of physical education. It was a bold step for us and for AIESEP, and it seemed to work. The conference itself was well attended and reflected the energy of multidisciplinary representation and critical scholarly analysis.

This proceedings captures both the quality and diversity of the conference itself. It is organized along the major conference themes, Myths, Models, and Methods, and hopefully it will continue to promote international dialogue in sport pedagogy. Selection of papers for this text was very difficult because so many quality manuscripts were submitted. What appears in this volume are the study findings and scholarly analyses of a prestigious group of physical education researchers representing numerous cultures and disciplines and many differing points of view. It speaks about the past, is cognizant of the present, and suggests prospects for the future in sport pedagogy research. Our hope is that it serves you well.

Gary T. Barrette
Ronald S. Feingold
C. Roger Rees
Maurice Piéron

Opening Address

Research and the Improvement of Teaching: The Professor as the Problem

Lawrence F. Locke

How sweet it is to be together again, international friends from around the world and colleagues from across North America. Given the number of new names in the program and unfamiliar faces in the audience, it is clear that AIESEP is healthy, growing, and alive in Garden City.

My job is only to get things started, to help people refocus their intellects after a summer of happy indolence. With a homogeneous and task-oriented group of conferees such as ourselves the opening address need not be especially profound or particularly entertaining. In fact, as the organizing committee was at some pains to point out, it should not even be very long. Apparently someone from Adelphi has heard me speak before.

As suggested by the title, I want to examine the performance of professors not as producers of knowledge, but as consumers and users. Because a clear majority of the people at this conference are professors, scholar/educators of one kind or another, this will be a highly personal rather than a highly abstract presentation. This is going to be about "us," not about "them."

The outline has three main parts:

1. Some comments on the significance in the timing of this meeting,
2. Some simple definitions of words, so that we shall understand each other, and
3. A set of six naive questions about professors, research-based knowledge, and the work of teacher education.

History

For the hosts today, physical educators at Adelphi University and throughout the U.S.A., the occasion has special significance. August marks the centennial of events that were to impel and shape the course of sport and physical education in our nation. Those events began with a man who understood the need for communication among professionals, and thereby the power of the conference.

William G. Anderson (the elder) did not invent either physical education as a subject of the school curriculum or teacher education as a training enterprise. His unique contribution was the simple realization that it would be helpful if the people who directed "hygenic exercise" in schools, colleges, and agency settings could get together and talk about their work and problems. The idea was such an immediate and popular success that we really are commemorating not one meeting, but in fact three invited conferences which took place in 1885. That simple idea of a conference for teaching specialists in physical education provided the soil in which our sense of shared vocation and common cause was to root and, ultimately, the place from which our national organizations, both The American Alliance and The National Association, were to grow.

So it is that we remember and celebrate the vision of an early leader. Given the professorial proclivity for having mixed feelings over almost anything, however, it will surprise no one to discover that August 19 can also be the occasion for some ambivalence, or at least for some somber reflection. It was in 1885 that the small list of subscribers to the then fledgling journal *Education* opened their latest copy to discover an article titled "The Normal School Problem" authored by William Howard Payne (1885) of Michigan University. As a translation for our guests from abroad, the "normal school" was an early, 2-year version of collegiate teacher training.

From his Olympian position in what may have been the first professorship of education in the U.S.A., Payne argued three points. First, far too much attention was paid to practical methods of instruction in the preparation of teachers. Second, what would serve teachers far better would be immersion in the liberal arts and foundational subjects such as psychology and the history of education. Third, the study of education was not the study of pedagogy (how to teach) that, as a technical intrusion into higher education, threatened rather than supported the production of effective teachers. To Payne, method was merely a stylistic expression of the far more important intellectual qualities of the teacher. He clearly doubted that pedagogy could be the object of serious study and his opinion concerning its study in the normal school was unambiguous. "In proportion as the technical element [methods of teaching] is brought into prominence, the course of study will lose its value, and by so much will diminish the real teaching-power of the pupil" (p. 391).

From that opening salvo it was little time until pedagogy became for some the maligned "bag of tricks" and for others the heart of an emerging profession. In a single swift stroke, Payne had opened a Pandora's box of contentious disputation. As the actions of state legislatures (Corrigan, 1985; Friedman, 1985), national commissions (Haberman, 1984), and prominent physical educators (Siedentop, 1985) will attest, 100 years has not been enough to resolve that tangled snarl of issues.

It is appropriate, then, that we begin our week together in 1985 by remembering the heritage bequeathed by both Anderson and Payne: on the one hand a self-conscious profession organized to advance its own interests and those of the clients it serves and, on the other hand, disquieting questions about the legitimacy of pedagogy both as a proper subject for study in the teacher-preparation curriculum and as a suitable object for scientific inquiry.

Definitions

With our professorial ambivalence now properly established, we can turn to a short lexicon of terminology and the meanings arbitrarily assigned by me. The terms occur in four pairs, the first of which is *research on teaching* and *research on teacher education*. The two are not the same. Research on teaching includes investigations that examine the impact of what teachers do upon what students learn. In contrast, research on teacher education includes investigations that examine the impact of what teacher educators do upon what teachers learn about their work. There are hundreds of methodological and paradigmatic variations on those oversimplified definitions, but they make the distinction sufficiently clear for our needs.

The second pair is *doing research* and *using research*. Although making a distinction between the two may seem so obvious as to be gratuitous, it is surprising how often we mix them in ordinary speech. Doing research requires the actions of systematic inquiry, whereas using research involves both contemplation of prior findings and their employment in some act or decision.

The third pair juxtaposes the words *process* and *content* as used to designate different aspects of a teacher education program. Content designates collectively the knowledge, skills, and dispositions that the teacher educator intends the teacher (novice or veteran) to acquire. The processes of the program are the various activities and arrangements they employ to accomplish that goal.

For example, if you have read some of the recent research on teacher clarity (Cruickshank, 1985; McCaleb, 1984; Smith & Cotton, 1980) that includes study of strategies that can help teachers make themselves understood by avoiding vagueness and verbal mazes, you might be inspired to add a new module on teacher clarity to your methods class. In sorting through the literature to determine what to teach your students you would be using research to determine the content of your program.

With the new module in place, however, you might remember reading the Joyce and Showers (1980, 1981) reviews of the literature dealing with the component parts of teacher training. Rereading them might well inspire you to invent a discrimination test that would make sure that after modeling clear and vague instructions for your students they could reliably tell the difference when given some audiotaped examples. In this case, research helped you to decide not the content of the module, but how to use it—the process of your program.

Fourth, and finally, it is convenient in this context for me to distinguish between *teaching* and *doing the stuff teachers commonly do*. This gives the word *teaching* a more restricted definition than we ordinarily use. I do so here to underscore the difference between acting like a teacher and performing the critical function of a teacher. To do the stuff teachers commonly do, in the absence of any discernable consequence for student learning, is different from orchestrating those things in the special ways that lead regularly to the changes we call learning. The former I call *doing teacher stuff* and the latter I call *teaching*. The distinction is the same one used in resolving that old chestnut from your philosophy class, "If a tree falls in the forest, but no one is there to hear it, was there any sound?" When someone does teacher stuff all day, but without any consequent change in what pupils know, feel, or can do, there was no teaching done—only someone acting like a teacher but not performing the critical function.

We have George Bernard Shaw to thank for that venomous quip that can raise a teacher's fur at any time, "He who can, does, and he who cannot, teaches" (*Man and Superman*, Act IV), to which some of us might add, "and those who can neither do, nor teach, become university administrators." But I digress. Shaw's nasty jibe is a canard, something patently untrue, but used to malign or, as in Shaw's case, to have sport at the expense of the innocent victim. It is untrue because it is obvious to even the casual observer that anyone holding a job as a teacher spends the entire day *doing* all manner of things. To the close observer, at least, it even is doing hard and difficult work. Notwithstanding, unless the teacher organizes and selects the stuff of daily work so as to form the precursors of learning, Shaw is quite correct—they indeed are people who "can't do," for by my definition they are not doing teaching.

In contrast, some teachers learn how to put stuff together, doing the right thing at the right time for the right students and consistently getting the desired result. They have a sense of the rules that govern the transactions that lead to learning. Often those rules are tacit, private, idiographic, and difficult to communicate or extract, but once the rules begin to accumulate in a teacher's repertoire, real teaching becomes possible. Those who lack such a road map of events in classroom or gymnasium are just traveling on. Sometimes they get somewhere and sometimes they don't, and they rarely know why.

Understanders and Improvers

With that short dictionary in hand, we can now turn to an examination of professors and what is going on in the world of research and teacher education. For the study of teaching these have been vintage years. If you are interested in understanding how teachers do the work of instruction, this has been a good time to be alive. When I go into the gym or onto a playing field there is so much more to watch and so much more that now makes sense. Just in terms of concepts and technical language, probably half of what we will talk about at this confeence would have been impossible to discuss in 1965.

I wish it were possible to say the same thing about research on teacher education, but we are only beginning to ask sophisticated questions concerning how teachers learn to do their work (Evertson, Hawley, & Zlotnik, 1985; Feiman-Nemser, 1983; Koeler, 1985; Lanier, 1984b; McDonald, 1977). It is clear, however, that the long dry wait is over. We are about to learn more than we ever wanted to know about teacher education. Not all of the news will be happy, I fear, but it will be fascinating nonetheless.

All of this vintage-year talk, of course, reflects one point of view. It is the vantage point of a person who enjoys learning about how things work—the understander. But what about practical benefits? For most of us just understanding is not enough; we expect research to do more. Whether by explicit personal commitment, or simply by unconscious adoption of a cultural assumption, many of you in this room expect research to have the power to make practice better. Such is the improver's point of view.

For the real improvers among us these have been years of frustration and hard lessons. Instead of the heady wine of satisfaction too often there has been the bitter beer of failed expectations. The dissemination of new ways to teach derived from what we have learned from research on teaching turned out to be far more complex than just scattering the seeds of wisdom among practitioners. In fact, using traditional modes of spreading the good word from research turned out to be more like Johnny Appleseed sowing the Gobi Desert.

The reason that research on teaching has had little easy influence on the conduct of education in the gymnasium or in the classroom turned out to have a stark kind of simplicity once it was understood. What teachers do in schools is usually done for good and sufficient reason—it works. It works in the sense that it is rationally responsive to the social system in which the teacher must operate day by day. Good, bad, or simply indifferent relative to the goals of education, what teachers do is a response to the prime factors of school life: (a) numbers—teachers are one and the pupils are many; (b) time—there is never enough, and the pace of work is externally driven rather than following the needs of the inhabitants; and (c) power—teachers have extensive rights to intrude on the lives of their charges, but unless they can win a measure of compliance and collaboration from pupils, teaching is impossible.

Any so-called improvement must respond first to those prime factors. Many recommendations for improvement based on research have not been well tuned to the facts of school life because they were derived by logical operations in the aseptic world of the university. Successful improvers have not been those who simply espouse powerful innovations in pedagogy, but they have been those who learned how to help teachers adapt new ideas to the hard realities of numbers, time, and power.

That is not the topic here, however, for if we are interested in professors then it is the employment of research-based knowledge to improve teacher education programs that is our central concern. This is where we might have expected great things, in theory at least. Professors have immediate access to research. Professors understand the complex language of research reports. Professors are ideally situated to see practical implications of new knowledge for their own work. Professors have relatively high levels of control over content and process in their programs. Professors are always exhorting others to use research as the rational basis for everyday decisions. Fertile ground for revolution, indeed.

Research could have had any of several kinds of utility. It could have informed decisions about content. It could have suggested powerful processes and ways of organizing training programs. Research, in the forms of reports and reviews, could even have been used as program materials (Griffin, 1984). There is no lack of ways in which to use research in teacher education. It should not be difficult to track the influence of research, if there is any to detect, so we can proceed in a straightforward manner.

Six Naive Questions

I will pose some simple questions of the kind that naive outsiders would ask. If you went home from Adelphi to rejoin your colleagues and announced that having heard a lot of research you have decided to improve the teacher education program by using your new knowledge, people would ask things such as, Why and how?, Will it work?, Do you really know enough?, and, How will you get other people to try your ideas? Those questions may sound naive, but they are not unreasonable.

Question 1: Why and how? Why do you look to research for practical help and how do you expect it to be provided?

The best place to begin is to indicate what *not* to expect from research. If you ask research reports to tell you what to do, in the sense of providing instructions for action, you are asking for disappointment. Most educational research provides *findings* from the process of inquiry, not solutions to problems. If a study shows that physical education teachers use 34% of their class time on management tasks (which is a finding), it is unlikely that the report will contain any instructions for getting teachers to use only 5% (which is a solution to the problem).

You, or even the researcher, might elect to do some careful thinking and field testing to produce a handbook for use in helping veteran teachers change their unfortunate management behavior. That, however, would involve developing an intervention based on an idea drawn from research, not the discovery of a solution in the research literature. The idea that research reports are supposed to give solutions to school problems, answers to teachers' questions, and decisions about what is best to do is a mischievous misunderstanding and the cause of enormous confusion and disappointment.

Research can do one thing in addition to providing findings. What reading research does is make you smart. You can make yourself better informed about almost any topic you pursue in the literature. The significance of such pursuits rests in the fact that people who are smart about the area in which they have to solve problems sometimes possess a clear advantage. They are able to see more detail in a situation, some of which inevitably is missed by the less well informed. They often see more options for action, frequently of the kind not imagined by those who have not used research to help in understanding how things work. Finally, the research-smart practitioner is more likely to select or devise a powerful, rather than a weak, course of action. There are, of course, no guarantees for success, but the benefits of being smart are not inconsiderable advantages to have on your side.

The reality of using research is complicated because, as everybody knows, being smart is just a small part of what goes into doing a good job of anything. The familiar "applications" model of research utilization (the notion of technical rationality that permeates all of the physical education literature dealing with research), now is widely regarded as an oversimplification (Buchmann, 1983; Egbert, 1984; Emans, 1982; Feiman-Nemser & Ball, 1984). Only rarely is it possible for teachers or teacher educators to solve problems simply by using knowledge in a straightforward, unproblematic fashion (Fenstermacher, 1983; Spaulding, 1977; Tom, 1980). At the least, there are fundamental problems caused by the fact that research knowledge is *not* created for teachers to use in classrooms and by the fact that real-world problems rarely fit scientific categories.

In the professor's world there is an even more serious defect in the simplistic idea of research application. It ignores other vital sources of knowledge and warrants for action. To take an example from teacher education, when you design a new course many different things have to be considered besides whatever knowledge you may possess. At the least, there are

- personal commitments—what you happen to value in the content;
- consensual moral standards—what is considered ethical in your profession;
- personal style—what way of teaching is effective for you;
- local constraints—realistic options given time and context;
- experience—student evaluations from your last attempt;
- knowledge—what research has taught you about process and content in that area.

In practice, all these elements are mixed together to produce a course outline and a set of teaching behaviors. Clearly, research did not tell you what to do. It was one resource among many considerations. With regard to some questions, of course, research has to be given by far the greatest weight, but it is rarely the final and solitary arbiter in any educational decision.

There are some sound reasons to make research-based knowledge a regular part of the considerations used in deciding how to teach. It has a special advantage over other ways to arrive at what is known. First, research on teaching can help to make explicit, public, and accessible information that ordinarily is implicit, idiosyncratic, or unstructured (for example, the personal rules that permit some teachers to be teaching nearly all the time). Research can identify, separate, sort, codify, and generalize the often intuitive sources of effective instruction, thus forming a bridge between the observer and the inner worlds of teachers and students. Second, research can detect regularities that teachers or coaches are unlikely to notice. Some important things are invisible to the teacher (for example, details of the student subculture) or are too complex to detect as natural events (for example, the interaction of trials, task difficulty, and entry-skill level among students learning to swim). Third, research can make us see what we don't expect or don't wish to know.

Have you looked recently at the research dealing with the effects produced by correcting written homework, carefully marking student errors in the margins with your red pencil and handing it back at the next class? Don't do so if, like me, you have invested thousands of such laborious hours over a professional lifetime. The truth may make you free, but it sure can hurt in the process.

To sum up the answer for our first naive question, Why and how?, it can be argued that research is a valuable (sometimes superior) addition to experience and common sense. Although there are occasional instances in which it provides the best answer to a question of practical import, most of the time it functions best as a way to make ourselves smart about the problems we have to face.

Question 2: Will it work? Is there any evidence to suggest that the program will produce better teachers if the faculty uses research in revising content and process?

The honest answer is that with regard to programs, nobody really knows. There aren't any relevant data to examine. There are no studies using a deliberate program variation design in teacher education. There are very few program evaluation studies that follow graduates into the field to assess their performance—and none that I know of in physical education. There is nothing in the research literature to guarantee that any one program paradigm (Zeichner, 1983) or any one structural model (Schalock, 1983), whether research-based or not, will be more effective than any other. What we do know something about are individual program components. It is at the level of process elements, not whole programs, that research offers some utility.

Pause for a moment and think about the factors that cause teachers to do whatever they do on any Monday morning. Much of the enormous variety in teacher behavior (in technical terms, the "variance") would come from endogenous factors such as intelligence, personality, and physical characteristics, as well as from situational factors such as the explicit physical conditions and implicit social norms of each workplace.

We can set those aside because they are outside the immediate influence of any teacher education system. The rest of the variance in teacher behavior is accounted for by what teachers have learned to do as teaching acts. These are the things teachers acquire when they learn how to teach.

Teaching is learned from four primary sources. The experiences of presocialization, those 12 years of apprenticeship served as pupils in schools, provides the first source of what teachers know. Lawson (1983) tells us that recruits to college teacher training enter with elaborate subjective warrants about their chosen vocation. Novices already know and believe a great deal about physical education long before they ever encounter a professor.

The second venue for learning to teach is formal teacher training in an undergraduate program. Because programs rarely employ formal assessments that require the demonstration of specific teaching skills or pedagogical knowledge at exit, it is difficult to know what actually has been acquired by novice teachers (that they did not possess at entry). As for attitudes and values, those dispositions required if graduates are to employ and persevere with whatever pedagogy they have learned, research is mute—the cupboard is bare.

The third source of teacher behaviors is experience, particularly that acquired during the first several years when the process of induction into the school culture provides a potent period for teacher learning. That is when the "other" teacher educators—pupils, peers, administrators, and parents—tell and model what a good teacher must be like. The fourth and final source of teacher behavior is in-service education in the form of teacher development activities. In the case of physical education teachers, however, this presently is an inconsequential source of influence (Placek, 1985a).

Taken collectively, this is an extensive set of sources for teacher behavior. Transposing a term from curriculum theory, the truly functional curriculum (Dodds, 1983, 1984) of teacher education extends across as many as 18 years (presocialization, training, and induction). Clearly, it is a serious semantic error to define the term *teacher educator* as though it were coterminous with the word *professor*. In that long process of socialization into the role of teacher/coach there is a great deal that we have yet to understand, much less control.

Teacher preparation programs represent one source of influence within a network of influences. At its best, teacher education can never be more than one strong element among many. When we talk about using research to strengthen teacher education programs we are not dealing with trivial tinkering. A realistic perspective, however, warns us that there are some limits to what can be accomplished.

Returning now to the question, Will it work?, the logic of the improvers runs as follows:

> Teacher education programs in physical education mostly are weak treatments. The effects, if any, just get washed away when graduates enter full-time teaching. Thus, the task is to make the program strong enough to have a lasting impact. The way to make undergraduate programs strong is to help

professors become committed to the proposition that their job is to change
novice teachers in specific and verifiable ways. Graduates will then persevere with the kinds of effective practice strong programs can give them, and
the quality of school physical education programs will rise over time.

As you can detect, improvers believe that there are such things as effective teaching behaviors and that teacher educators should be accountable both for their transmission and for verification of their acquisition.

Given all the previous discussion about sources of teacher behavior,
the improver has to face a further question. Could formal teacher preparation in its present format ever be made powerful enough to overcome
wash-out effects caused by already potent sources in the schools? Here
again the improver's reasoning is straightforward:

> The question betrays a misleading assumption. Presocialization and induc-
> tion experience have been made to look *relatively* powerful only because we
> have done such a poor job of helping teachers learn in preparation programs.
> Teacher educators typically lecture at undergraduate majors for several
> semesters, feed them a smorgasbord of disconnected facts and experiences,
> and then hand them over to cooperating teachers who proceed to teach them
> the real facts of life. Under conditions like that almost anything would look
> stronger than the formal teacher preparation program.

From this it is clear that improvers believe programs that demand *par-
ticularized* demonstration of teaching competence could produce lasting
effects. Further, it is presumed they can do so even if the skills and dispositions acquired are in direct conflict with what teachers ordinarily learn
in school, either before or after collegiate training.

My own guess is that creating programs with such power will rest on
something more than just building better pedagogical training components. Professors will have to come directly to grips with the effects of
presocialization. This means taking seriously what undergraduates already
have learned about schools, teaching, and sport. Professors also will have
to come to grips with the qualitative problems associated with all the clinical training experiences embedded in the program. Both research and
experience make clear that, as exercises in dissonance, many clinical experiences serve to weaken, rather than strengthen, program effects.

Finally, the most fundamental impediment to development of powerful, research-informed teacher preparation programs may rest with a factor
not addressed until recently by anyone, either understander or improver.
How professors define what they are about influences both structure and
process in teacher education. Despite labels such as methods and student teaching, preservice education is neither organized nor conducted
as professional training. In a terse and incisive analysis, Weil (1985) put
her finger on the professorial role as the root cause of weak programs.

> In most situations, content is still delivered in much the same way as it is
> in other college courses, and the goals of the education curriculum are still
> informational, not behavioral. *On the whole, professors do not conduct themselves*

as trainers but as knowledge disseminators [emphasis mine]. Thus, one fundamental obstacle to research use in preservice education is a lack of understanding of the distinction between education and training. (p. 67)

That was a long answer to the simple question, Will it work? In one sense, it reflected the fact that we are dealing with elements that are far more complex than physical educators ordinarily care to admit. In another sense, however, the lengthy response reflected the true nature of the final answer, which is, It might work.

Question 3: Do you really know anything about effective teaching? Is there enough substance in the knowledge base to provide a reliable source of program content?

Here, at least, the answer is more than just a judgment call. Certainly we know enough to make a strong start. Members of AIESEP have more reason to know that fact than any other group of professionals in the world. The best testimony might be the Samaranch Prize–winning textbook, *Developing Teaching Skills in Physical Education*, authored by Daryl Siedentop (1983). If you prefer to be overwhelmed with research evidence, you can purchase a copy of the new *Third Handbook of Research on Teaching* (Wittrock, 1986), or if you like things a bit more predigested there is the incisive logic of Gage's Phi Delta Kappa Award monograph, *Hard Gains in the Soft Sciences* (1985).

Do we know enough about effective teaching? The answer by any reasonable standard is yes, and it is long past time to stop equivocating and dithering about how much is enough! It was Smith who was right in the 1980s, not Payne in the 1880s. Schools and departments of education need first and foremost to be schools and departments of pedagogy, and the extant body of knowledge about teaching should be the root source of the work they do (Smith, 1980, 1985; Smith, Silverman, Bors, & Fry, 1980).

Question 4: Do you really know anything about teaching teachers? Beyond the laying on of hands, is there a training technology sufficient to make reform in teacher education even a possibility?

Unlike the previous question, the answer here must be more restrained. Last year's *Journal of Teaching in Physical Education* summer monograph (Locke, 1984) at least demonstrated that it is possible to run on at great length on the topic of research on teacher education for physical educators. More to the point, as convincingly demonstrated by Siedentop in his Pre-Olympic Congress paper, "The Modification of Teacher Behavior" (1984), there is a solid body of evidence demonstrating that it is possible to change what teachers (veterans or new recruits) do in the gymnasium. In fact, we may need a moratorium on such special intervention studies so that we may turn to a simpler but now more directly relevant question, What's really going on in those method courses? (Placek, 1985b).

In addition to the existing body of research, there are examples of research-based teacher training programs that suggest that there are workable process components that might be imported into physical education

(Crawford & Gage, 1977). The teacher learning laboratories and short courses first demonstrated at the Far West Regional Lab in San Francisco (Berliner, 1984a, 1984b, 1985) have an imposing record of success. Substantially based on exportable materials (simulations through VTR, case study protocols, learning games, and microteaching exercises), most of them are aimed at immediate skill development in the training context. Within the limits of their intent, which is usually acquisition rather than transfer, and their content, which usually involves relatively discrete units of pedagogy rather than larger scale teaching strategies, they are both cost-effective and well regarded by teachers. Although ambitious proposals have been made (Locke, Mand, & Siedentop, 1981) nothing of the kind exists in physical education.

At the level of theory, there is Joyce and Showers' model of teacher training (1980, 1981). Based on a body of evaluation research on in-service education gathered over a 20-year period, the proposed program makes few technical demands and consists only of a suggested sequence for program components. There is no question that it could contribute directly to redesign efforts in preservice programs.

For myself, some of the most impressive evidence comes from an enterprise that is little recognized as a potential model for some aspects of teacher preparation. This is the commercial training industry that prepares people to use complex skills—and does so for profit. During the past year I have had the opportunity to examine commercial training course development in some detail.[1] In such educational modules, for a stiff tuition fee and the investment of some intensive effort, you can learn anything from how to cook a fine soufflé to new interpersonal skills for managing people in a corporate setting, all in a surprisingly short period of time. By any of the conventional measures of success (demonstrated skills at exit, expressed client satisfaction, and return customers) commercial training courses often work, and they do so in a context where *not* working is fatal. In the world of commerce, there is no tenure for the faculty.

From my observation notes I have extracted a list of characteristics that seem typical of training courses. It is instructive to match that list with the analogous traits that typify teacher education in physical education. All you need do is think of your student clients, your own faculty, and how your program operates and match those characteristics with the ones I found in commercial training courses.

- *There is heavy investment in research and development.* This is the primary cause of the typically stiff course fees. There is a large research literature shared among commercial training specialists (they have their own journals). All program components are field-tested, revised, and refined. Because the components can't afford failure, nothing goes to the customer until there is convincing evidence that it will work. I found it interesting to match that style of development for commercial training modules with the way methods courses are created in a typical undergraduate program.

- *Clients can walk out cold at any time and get their money back if not satisfied with what they are learning.* This seems to contribute substantially to the motivation of trainers to provide high-quality instruction.
- *For a small fee, clients can recycle through the entire module any time after graduation.* Further, they may do so as many times as needed (so long as they bring with them their original set of learning materials).
- *Most courses offer strong backup for graduates.* Telephone consultations are common and even field visits to help clients are included in some packages.
- *Most courses make heavy use of instructional media.* The need for stimulus variation exerts significant control over all classroom processes. As one trainer put it, "Never do any one thing in class for more than 10 minutes—especially lecture." That provides an interesting contrast with much that goes on in teacher education.
- *There is frequent opportunity for clients to respond.* The dictum that "the student has to do it to learn it" would provide exceptional ALT scores for most training courses.
- *Snacks, soft drinks, and coffee are continuously available during the training period.* Long, intensive sessions demand that learner needs be taken into account as a matter of reality, not rhetoric.
- *Courses tend to have carefully limited goals.* Despite plenty of flashy salesmanship, commercial trainers are at some pains not to make grand claims beyond what they can deliver. Here the contrast with department brochures and college catalogs may be interesting.
- *Two considerations always are evident at the planning stage: (a) get the skills into the client with enough background knowledge to prevent misuse, and (b) make the client feel good about the process of acquiring the skill.* This latter rule is critical in the training industry. When the customers feel good about learning, they tend to buy more of it. When they find learning painful or anxiety-arousing, clients may not come back even if they succeed in mastering the content. Juxtaposing that rule with the circumstances of my own test and measurement course has caused some somber reflection.
- *Students get armloads of take-home materials.* Much of this consists of usable items rather than reference lists, reprints, or instructional text. Emphasis is on providing material that is not available from other sources. Again, such tangible support for learning leans heavily on research and development processes that must precede marketing of the course.
- *The industry is capital-intensive rather than labor-intensive.* A single instructor may run an entire module with assistance only from a media technician. This contrasts with teacher education programs, which make heavy use of people and little use of technology in any sustained manner (Joyce, Howey, Yarger, Harbeck, & Kluevin, 1977).
- *Modules are packaged so as to be short in days, long in hours, and high in pedagogical intensity.* For the most part, the industry eschews programs that would require more than a few days of client development. While this may represent a genuine difference from the task of teacher education, the use of training modules with similar temporal dimensions

has been little explored in college programs (outside of CPR/first aid).

- *The task of course design is one of extraction.* Boiling down to basics from the mountains of things that might be learned is a fundamental service to customers. Training courses teach what is essential for practical action in the real world. Accordingly, in the process of curriculum development trainers must ignore a great deal that might be considered relevant as foundational material. This is technical training, not liberal education.
- *The instructors are unusual people.* Whereas ordinary employees work in course development and day-to-day operation of the industry, only highly selected and trained individuals operate the courses. The analogue of interest here would be how teacher educators commonly set about determining who will teach methods courses or supervise student teachers next semester. My observation suggests that the people selected to serve as instructors in the commercial world must meet the following criteria:
  a. Capacity to sustain high enthusiasm for extended periods
  b. Ability to handle both didactic and interactive modes of instruction
  c. High sensitivity to learner needs based on a large repertoire of pedagogical alternatives and adjustments
  d. Ability to provide rich, explicit examples from practice for any point or question likely to arise in the course
  e. Ability to model with confidence and precision any skill contained in the curriculum
  f. Great personal charisma

But, you ask, could they get tenure? Possibly not, but their income is commensurate with both the chanciness of the commercial world and their truly exceptional abilities. They would be very difficult to recruit for academe, even by dangling a full professorship.

Taken all for all, there appear to be a number of design and personnel characteristics in commercial training programs that might have application in teacher preparation. Our tendency to adopt the assumptions, processes, and format of the college academic course uncritically may have limited the chances for genuine breakthroughs in preservice teacher preparation. With that in mind, the training program industry and its research literature may offer a source of fresh options.[2]

Question 5: Don't professors already use lots of research in training teachers? Because teacher educators have access to the literature on teaching and teacher preparation, it should follow that recourse to such knowledge is a normal part of the program operation.

However much we might like to impress our naive questioner with a positive answer, the evidence points in the opposite direction (Clark & Guba, 1976; Ducharme, 1985; Judge, 1982; Wisniewsky, 1984; Yarger, Howey, & Joyce, 1977). Research simply is not part of the ethos of teacher education, whether the issue is production, consumption, or utilization.

A recent profile of the physical education professor indicates that we are no exception to this rule (Metzler & Freedman, 1985).

A report by Anderson (1982) provides a typical finding when research use is examined in the real world of teacher education. The subjects were five teacher-training faculty groups. Each consisted of a curriculum development or program revision committee assigned the task of designing scope, sequence, and content for an undergraduate program. All the committee members were professors, many of whom were themselves engaged in education research projects. Anderson simply tape-recorded all their meetings. An analysis of data extracted from over 100 hours of recorded committee dialogue revealed that less than 1% of the time was devoted to any discussion or process that made use of research. Instead of knowledge, it was state regulations, student enrollment, and faculty assignment to courses (who would get to teach what?) that occupied most of the time and controlled most of the curriculum decisions.

Each of you will have to contemplate your own experience, but Anderson's finding would, in honesty, be typical of events in most committees on which I have served. He hypothesized that the reason for such small attention to research rests in the fact that any recourse to the knowledge base invariably leads to long discussions and, often, to arguments. Because faculty members typically have little skill at confrontation, conflict reduction, and consensus building, they avoid the complexities of research and focus on areas in which the facts are established and agreements are easier to formulate.

This explanation has been given considerable credibility by both Nolan (1985) and Patriarca and Buchmann (1983), whose recent evaluation studies of curriculum development in teacher education revealed that fear of confrontation and its divisive consequences often prevents any genuine give and take among faculty members concerning what is known and believed about teaching. This behavior has two apparent consequences. First, where research-based knowledge is not allowed to play a strong part in attempts to make curriculum content and process more powerful, the resulting innovation often is nothing more than a rearrangement of tradition, supported by whatever folk wisdom is current among the designers. Second, where disagreements on fundamental issues of fact and belief are not addressed, the products produced by faculty efforts at program development simply are not implemented—irrespective of either their intrinsic merit or available resources. In the world of the professor, where the ethos of individualism rather than consensus is the dominant fact of life, acquiescence is not commitment.

Curriculum committees are not the only place to look for existing uses of research. A different, and possibly more fruitful, place is in teacher education courses themselves. Here, as you might expect, the picture is as complex as the professors who teach such courses. In a recent study of six programs, Champion (1982, 1984a, 1984b) found cause for both cheer and gloom. After interviewing faculty and administrators and examining mountains of course materials, the good news was that research *is* used by professors in teacher education courses. The bad news is that the way they use research is unlikely to impress anyone.

Citation, vocabulary building, brief mention of results, and assignment of readings that contain some reference to research constitute the primary form of research utilization in the classes surveyed by Champion. Only 30% of the professors indicated that they ever presented an actual study in class. Uses such as citing or word gathering are rather unsurprising and are certainly not powerful ways to use knowledge with students. When Champion asked professors why they use research in class, 70% said it was primarily for consumer protection (to help students avoid confusion *caused* by research), and only 30% responded that it had implications for teaching practice.

Reading through the material gathered in Champion's study of research utilization reveals a disturbing pattern. There are implicit, but nonetheless clear, messages communicated to students learning to teach:

- You can't trust research—be wary!
- Your own experience is a more trustworthy resource when making decisions about teaching.
- It is impossible to tell sense from nonsense in the research literature.
- Studies usually produce conflicting results.
- Researchers are impractical, naive people.
- Research is just too hard to understand.

With friends like that, research certainly does not need enemies. While each of those themes in the pattern of professorial communication is grounded in a grain of truth about the problems to be surmounted in using research, the overall picture is needlessly negative and cautionary. It is easy to understand why the teachers who come out of such experiences have little interest in research as a resource for understanding and improving practice.

What both Anderson and Champion found concerning the uses of research by teacher educators matches what others (Carter, 1984; Carter, Isham, & Stribling, 1981) have found about the nature of the professor of education. With blue-collar and middle-class social origins, teacher educators often are highly suspicious of theory and place great reliance on personal experience. Of the 46 professors in a recent sample (Carter, 1984), only three nominated a teacher preparation program when asked, "How did you learn to teach?" Forty-three either said "by doing it" or "by watching it." If that response were found to be typical of physical education professors, we would have a clue to the ambiguity that pervades so many programs and perhaps to the small amount of attention given research. That possibility leads nicely to the final question from our naive friend.

Question 6: What real hope is there that you can get your faculty to do it? Putting research to use would mean changing how things are done, which sounds both serious and controversial.

That final question brings us to the bottom line for this small homily. If there is nothing to say that could persuade you that people like you and I might actually do something, then all of this is just smoke. Because achieving collaborative action within groups of historically uncooperative and noncompliant people is the crux of this matter, the problem should be defined with great care before attempting a response.

At the outset, it is important to understand that it really doesn't matter what you or I do or do not do. Individual professors acting in individual ways in individual contexts can't make a significant impact on a problem of this complexity. The entire literature on training programs and organizational development unambiguously supports that judgment. The professor's relationship with each student is the functional unit of teacher preparation, but here we are dealing with a complex system of such units. Only a whole program, operated by a group of like-minded professors, in which people, process, and policy all push toward the same goals, can exert a reliable influence on students. Program consistency is the key to strong treatment effects. The bottom line is that *only* a faculty group can make truly effective use of research in a teacher education program.

In most cases our inability to achieve the level of programmatic consistency required to produce strong treatment effects is due neither to a lack of faculty commitment nor to a lack of insight into the defects of the present system. Most professors of physical education think what they are doing matters a great deal. They have strong personal commitments to sport and physical activity as content and to physical education as a school program. As to recognition of problems, when in public settings professors, like most people, are inclined to attribute their failures to external factors beyond their control (lower quality of student recruits, inadequate institutional support, or lack of time). In the safety of private conversation, however, many professors reveal a perfectly clear grasp of where the most serious and immediate problems lie. Most of those problems turn out to be internal and programmatic.

What, then, are the reasons for our inability to make significant improvement in undergraduate programs, and to do so by sustained and creative use of the knowledge base? In answering I speak only from my own experience and offer only the data of personal testimony.

The root impediment is the inability of most faculty groups to hammer out even limited consensus on program goals and needed reforms. The so-called democratic process used to make decisions and develop programs in the average department leaves half the faculty uncommitted to any decision, about a fourth prepared for active sabotage, and only the small remainder truly ready to live by the decision and do the required work.

Without process skills for dealing with disagreement and the building of commitment to decisions, much of what passes in the minutes of faculty meetings as progress on program development is illusory. Much that is decided is not implemented, or comes to operate in ways far different from what the designers intended. Neither research nor divine revelation can provide significant inputs to program development under those conditions. Research is power only in the hands of a faculty capable of decisive and cohesive action.

The second root impediment to effective utilization of research is less obvious but is no less a barrier. There is just below the surface a pervasive uneasiness among professors about research (Adams, 1976). The distaste and anxiety that attach to formal inquiry are revealed in the unguarded moments of everyday language and discourse with students and colleagues. Trauma from encounters with graduate school statistics, deep distrust of theory as impractical, guilt over not understanding complex and often poorly written research reports, resentment of other faculty members who brandish the magic jargon of science to browbeat their colleagues into submission on professional issues, profound uneasiness over the enormous gap between the intellectual world of theory in teacher education and the practical realities of teaching in a public school, and fear of admitting any of this to anyone else: research anxiety proves not to be just the student's disease—it is the endemic illness of the teacher educator.

What, if anything, can be done to help faculty groups achieve strong consensus? What, if anything, can be done to help individual professors become more comfortable with research (and thus more likely to make use of it)? The standard responses in higher education are to form a committee, run the copying machine, and engage in exhortation. This sort of bureaucratic response was modeled to perfection in the 1983 NIE Teacher Education Improvement Project (Lanier, 1984a). Even when backed by federal funds, those are not useful activities. Telling people what they ought to be doing and unsophisticated uses of top-down authority work as well with college professors as the same strategies have worked with public school teachers—they don't work at all.

Some of the regional research and development centers have been attempting more thoughtful approaches to help teacher educators (Gee, 1985). The difficulty there is that such efforts usually involve retraining key faculty members, significant inputs of outside money, and complex forms of collaboration with public school teachers. For most departments those are more likely to be the outcomes than the precursors of faculty development.

Self-help is the only viable option in most departments. At that point, however, we have closed the circle and are back at the starting place. If your experience has been like mine, you will have observed that most attempts to obtain consensus about faculty development schemes usually suffer the same fate as program revision. Despite the best of intentions, we rarely seem to get there.

One way to break into that closed circle is to develop a wider resource base for assistance *within the teacher education community*. At the University of Massachusetts, having had to find outside assistance to help us work on our own faculty development and program revision problems, we have been led to experiment with a new idea. We are providing individual or team consultants to help teacher educators in other institutions. We can't, of course, provide solutions for other people's problems, but we can help to identify critical questions and assist faculty members in discovering ways (and reasons) to work together.

To make it a truly available service we have to work at cost. To make it worth the effort we must limit involvement to departments where a sizable majority of the faculty can discover genuine commitment to the process. We are still learning how to be effective in working with professional peers, but two things already are apparent: (a) There is demand for the service, and (b) the feedback is positive even though real evidence of success is not yet available.

Carter's (1981, 1984) study of the teacher education professor again provides a clue to the positive reception given to interprogram assistance. In private interviews she found most professors confessing that they felt *more* support from, and colleagueship with, peers in other programs, or even in other institutions, than from faculty *in their own department*. The well-documented isolation of teachers may have some root in the ways teacher educators limit interaction among their students—and among themselves (Copeland & Jamgochian, 1985). No wonder professors seem pleased when intervention by a consultant provides little more than help in developing open dialogue with department colleagues. Alone in the midst of peers and an alien in the conventional world of higher education (Ducharme & Agne, 1982; Schwabel, 1985), the teacher educator may be far more lonely than anyone has yet appreciated.

The idea that renewal in teacher education demands that professors be participants in staff development already is upon us (Hall, 1985). The idea that problems of support and accessibility will make it necessary for education professors to provide staff-development services for each other may just be dawning. Even modest knowledge of strategies for staff and organizational development should permit teacher educators to play a useful consultant role in other programs. Whereas such cross-program collaboration clearly runs contrary to the prevailing political norms of inter-institutional behavior in higher education, it also is obvious that faculty groups can break the rule of isolation in ways that administrators dare not.

Finally, just to make sure that what is sauce for the goose is also sauce for the gander, the first required reading for anyone wanting to play a helpful role in someone else's program is the research literature on change and program development in teacher education. There is not a great deal to read (Brandt, 1981; Haney, 1981; Nelli, 1981; Nolan, 1985; Patriarca & Buchmann, 1983), but those who propose to urge the good medicine of research-based knowledge should first try some for themselves.

The problem of helping professors of physical education become more comfortable with research is best regarded as a matter of individual therapy and development (although staffwide approaches might be imagined). Again, our experience at the University of Massachusetts provides the only data at hand. Patt Dodds and I coteach a series of graduate-level research courses (in research on teaching and research on preservice and in-service teacher education) populated by school teachers and administrators, college faculty, and graduate students in education and physical education. Out of those experiences we have learned that traditional seminar and lecture/laboratory course formats are ineffective without prior attention to "research-anxiety-desensitization." People can't be angry or guilty about research if they are to work comfortably with research-based knowledge.

Methods that we have found helpful in desensitization include

- rewarding the behavior of saying, "I don't understand . . .";
- safe sharing of research consumption problems in small groups;
- learning how to explain simple research reports to another person;
- learning by examples and experience that 90% of consumer problems arise from the poor level of writing found in most research reports;
- learning that technical discrimination concerning the adequacy of method, design, and analysis need not always be the reader's primary concern; and
- learning that most inferential statistics are irrelevant to the needs of the practitioner-consumer of research.

Plenty of practice with rewards, avoidance of situations that make the student feel vulnerable, and modeling of positive examples of research in use taken together form a treatment package that seems to work for many of our clients. It is more difficult to provide testimony that, once desensitized, these teachers and professors return to work and make more use of research. If, however, the question is, Do they become distinctly more at ease with research as exemplified by such behaviors as seeking out research in their own areas of interest?, the answer is a firm (and happy) yes.

Conclusion

I am no more hopeful about revolutionary reform in teacher education than any of you. What I am optimistic about is our ability to do some useful things to help each other. The trick is to stop blaming people (others or ourselves) and start dealing with the human problems that limit what our programs might become.

In his presidential address at the national meeting of the American Educational Research Association this spring, Lee Shulman (1985) said something that takes us back to Mr. Shaw and his wonderful canard. After arguing with passion that research does give us the basis for improving the work of teaching and teacher education, Shulman observed that the canard might be reconstructed to tell the truth rather than a lie: Those who can will be destined merely to do things, but those who understand, shall become the teachers. To which we, with less eloquence, but no less validity, can add: Those professors who understand how teachers learn to teach shall truly become the teacher educators.

Notes

1. Appreciation is extended to Dr. Mary D. Jensen, formerly Associate Professor of Physical Education at The Ohio State University and now a consultant for the Institute of Business Seminars, Inc., who initiated me into the mysteries of commercial training programs.
2. An inexpensive publication that examines implications for teacher education of training programs in 10 corporations and agencies is *Mirrors of Excellence* by W.R. Howsam (1986, Association of Teacher Educators, Reston, VA).

References

Adams, R.D. (1976, April). *Strategies for more effectively interpreting and utilizing educational research findings: Implications for professional educators.* Paper presented at the annual meeting of the American Educational Research Association, San Francisco. (ERIC Document Reproduction Service No. ED 124 505)

Anderson, C.W. (1982). *The use of codified knowledge in five teacher education programs* (Research Series No. 118). East Lansing: Michigan State University, Institute for Research on Teaching.

Berliner, D.C. (1984a). Making the right changes in preservice teacher education. *Phi Delta Kappan, 66*(2), 94–96.

Berliner, D.C. (1984b). *Reform in teacher education: The case for pedagogy.* Paper presented at the annual meeting of the Association of Colleges and Schools of Education in State Universities and Land Grant Colleges, Las Vegas.

Berliner, D. (1985, March). *Laboratory settings and the study of teacher education.* Paper presented at the annual meeting of the American Educational Research Association, Chicago.

Brandt, N.C.S. (1981). A study of relationships between external factors, structure and organization, and innovativeness of teacher education programs. *Dissertation Abstracts International, 41,* 3054A. (University Microfilms No. 81-00417)

Buchmann, M. (1983). *The use of research knowledge in teacher education and teaching* (Occasional Paper No. 71). East Lansing: Michigan State University, Institute for Research on Teaching.

Carter, H.L. (1981). *Teacher educators: A descriptive study.* Austin: University of Texas at Austin, The Research and Development Center for Teacher Education.

Carter, H.L. (1984). Teachers of teachers. In L.G. Katz & J.D. Raths (Eds.), *Advances in teacher education* (Vol. 1, pp. 125–143). Norwood, NJ: Ablex Publishing.

Carter, H.L., Isham, M.M., & Stribling, R. (1981). *The relative force of selected environmental factors upon the professional activities of university-based teacher educators.* Austin: University of Texas at Austin, The Research and Development Center for Teacher Education.

Champion, R.H. (1982). The use of research in the teacher preparation curriculum. *Dissertation Abstracts International, 43,* 763A. (University Microfilms No. 82-16, 752)

Champion, R.H. (1984a). Faculty reported use of research in teacher preparation courses: Six instructional scenarios. *Journal of Teacher Education, 35*(5), 9–12.

Champion, R.H. (1984b). Going beyond lists of research findings: The next challenge to teacher educators. *Action in Teacher Education, 4*(1–2), 85–92.

Clark, D.L., & Guba, E.G. (1976). *A faculty self-report on knowledge production and utilization activities in schools, colleges, and departments of education* (Occasional Paper Series). Bloomington: Indiana University.

Copeland, W.D., & Jamgochian, R. (1985). Colleague training and peer review. *Journal of Teacher Education, 36*(2), 18–21.

Corrigan, D.C. (1985). Policy development and implementation as related to teacher education. In S.M. Hord, S.F. O'Neal, & M.L. Smith (Eds.), *Beyond the looking glass* (pp. 17–25). Austin: The University of Texas at Austin, The Research and Development Center for Teacher Education.

Crawford, N., & Gage, N. (1977). Development of a research-based teacher training program. *California Journal of Teacher Education, 4*(2), 105–123.

Cruickshank, D.R. (1985). Applying research on teacher clarity. *Journal of Teacher Education, 36*(2), 44–48.

Dodds, P. (1983). Consciousness raising in curriculum: A teacher's model. In A. Jewett, M. Carnes, & M. Speakman (Eds.), *Proceedings of the Third Conference on Curriculum Theory in Physical Education* (pp. 213–234). Athens: University of Georgia Press.

Dodds, P. (1984, July). *Are hunters of the functional curriculum seeking quarks or snarks?* Paper delivered at the 1984 Olympic Scientific Congress, Eugene, OR.

Ducharme, E.R. (1985). Establishing the place of teacher education in the university. *Journal of Teacher Education, 36*(4), 8–11.

Ducharme, E.R., & Agne, R.M. (1982). The education professoriate: A research based perspective. *Journal of Teacher Education, 33*(6), 30–36.

Egbert, R.L. (1984). The role of research in teacher education. In R.L. Egbert & M.M. Kluender (Eds.), *Using research to improve teacher education* (pp. 9–21). The Nebraska Consortium (Teacher Education Monograph No. 1). Washington, DC: The ERIC Clearinghouse on Teacher Education.

Emans, R. (1982). The role of professors of method in educational research. *Journal of Teacher Education, 33*(4), 16–21.

Evertson, C.M., Hawley, W.D., & Zlotnik, M. (1985). Making a difference in educational quality through teacher education. *Journal of Teacher Education, 36*(3), 2–12.

Feiman-Nemser, S. (1983). *Learning to teach* (Occasional Paper No. 64). East Lansing: Michigan State University, Institute for Research on Teaching.

Feiman-Nemser, S., & Ball, D. (1984, April). *Views of knowledge in the preservice curriculum.* Paper presented at the annual meeting of the American Educational Research Association, New Orleans. (Available from the senior author at the Institute for Research on Teaching, Michigan State University)

Fenstermacher, G.D. (1983). How should implications of research on teaching be used? *The Elementary School Journal, 83*(4), 496–499.

Friedman, M.S. (1985). Policies and policy making in New Jersey. In S.M. Hord, S.F. O'Neal, & M.L. Smith (Eds.), *Beyond the looking glass* (pp. 381–386). Austin: The University of Texas at Austin, The Research and Development Center for Teacher Education.

Gage, N.L. (1985). *Hard gains in the soft sciences: The case of pedagogy.* Bloomington, IN: Phi Delta Kappa Center on Evaluation, Development and Research.

Gee, E.W. (1985, March). *Applying effective instruction research findings in practice: A proposal for analyzing two implementation strategies.* Paper delivered at the annual meeting of the American Educational Research Association, Chicago. (Available from the Far West Laboratory for Educational Research and Development)

Griffin, G.A. (1984). Why use research in preservice teacher education? A proposal. *Journal of Teacher Education, 35*(4), 36–40.

Haberman, M. (1984). *An evaluation of the rationale for required teacher education: Beginning teachers with and without teacher preparation.* Paper prepared for the National Commission on Excellence in Teacher Education. (Available from the author at the Division of Urban Outreach, University of Wisconsin at Milwaukee, P.O. Box 413, Milwaukee, WI, 53201).

Hall, G. (1985). Beyond the looking glass: Policies, practices, and research in teacher education. *Journal of Teacher Education, 36*(1), 2–6.

Haney, B.J. (1981). A study of relationships between internal processes and innovativeness of teacher education programs. *Dissertation Abstracts International, 41*, 3057A. (University Microfilms No. 81-00428)

Joyce, B., & Showers, B. (1980). Improving inservice training: The messages of research. *Educational Leadership, 37*(5), 379–385.

Joyce, B., & Showers, B. (1981, April). *Teacher training research: Working hypotheses for program design.* Paper presented at the annual meeting of the American Educational Research Association, Los Angeles.

Joyce, B., Howey, K., Yarger, S., Harbeck, K., & Kluevin, T. (1977). Reflections on preservice preparation: Impressions from the national survey (Pt. 1, First impressions). *Journal of Teacher Education*, **28**(5), 14–15.

Judge, H. (1982). *American graduate schools of education*. New York: Ford Foundation.

Koehler, V. (1985). Research on preservice teacher education. *Journal of Teacher Education*, **36**(1), 23–30.

Lanier, J.E. (1984a). The preservice teacher education improvement project: A critical review. *Journal of Teacher Education*, **35**(4), 24–27.

Lanier, J.E. (1984b). *Research on teacher education* (Occasional Paper No. 80). East Lansing: Michigan State University, Institute for Research on Teaching.

Lawson, H.A. (1983). Toward a model of teacher socialization in physical education: The subjective warrant, recruitment, and teacher education. *Journal of Teaching in Physical Education*, **2**(3), 3–16.

Locke, L.F. (1984, Summer). Research on teaching teachers: Where are we now? *The Journal of Teaching in Physical Education* (Monograph No. 2).

Locke, L.F., Mand, C., & Siedentop, D. (1981). The preparation of physical education teachers: A subject-matter-centered model. In H.A. Lawson (Ed.), *Undergraduate physical education programs: Issues and approaches* (pp. 33–54). Reston, VA: American Alliance for Health, Physical Education, Recreation and Dance.

McCaleb, J. (1984). Selecting a measure of oral communication as a predictor of teaching performance. *Journal of Teacher Education*, **35**(5), 33–38.

McDonald, F.J. (1977). Research and development strategies for improving teacher education. *Journal of Teacher Education*, **28**(6), 29–33.

Metzler, M.W., & Freedman, M.S. (1985). Here's looking at you, PETE: A profile of physical education teacher education faculty. *Journal of Teaching in Physical Education*, **4**(2), 123–133.

Nelli, E. (1981). Program redesign in teacher preparation. *Journal of Teacher Education*, **32**(6), 39–42.

Nolan, J.F. (1985). Potential obstacles to internal reform in teacher education: Findings from a case study. *Journal of Teacher Education*, **36**(4), 12–16.

Patriarca, L.A., & Buchmann, M. (1983). *Conceptual development and curriculum change: Or is it rhetoric and fantasy?* (Research Paper No. 123). East Lansing: Michigan State University Institute for Research on Teaching. (ERIC Document Reproduction Service No. ED 234 042)

Payne, W.H. (1885). The normal school problem. *Education* **5**(4), 382–399.

Placek, J.H. (1985a, April). *Inservice education: What we know and what we use*. Paper presented at the Annual Conference of the American Alliance for Health, Physical Education, Recreation and Dance, Atlanta, GA.

Placek, J.H. (1985b, April). *Teacher educators and students: The communication gap.* Paper presented at the Fourth Curriculum Theory Conference, University of Georgia, Athens, GA.

Schalock, D. (1983). Methodological considerations in future research and development in teacher education. In K.R. Howey & W.E. Gardner (Eds.), *The education of teachers* (pp. 38-73). New York: Longman.

Schwebel, M. (1985). The clash of cultures in academe: The university and the education faculty. *Journal of Teacher Education,* **36**(4), 2-7.

Shulman, L.S. (1985, March). *Presidential address.* Paper delivered at the annual meeting of the American Educational Research Association, Chicago.

Siedentop, D. (1983). *Developing teaching skills in physical education* (2nd ed.). Palo Alto, CA: Mayfield Publishing.

Siedentop, D. (1984, July). *The modification of teacher behavior.* Paper presented at the meeting of the 1984 Olympic Scientific Congress, Eugene, OR.

Siedentop, D. (1985). The great teacher education legend. In H. Hoffman & J. Rink (Eds.), *Physical education professional preparation: Insights and foresights* (pp. 48-57). Reston, VA: American Alliance for Health, Physical Education, Recreation and Dance.

Smith, B.O. (1980). Pedagogical education: How about reform? *Phi Delta Kappan,* **62**(2), 87-91.

Smith, B.O. (1985). Research bases for teacher education. *Phi Delta Kappan,* **66**(9), 685-690.

Smith, B.O., Silverman, C., Bors, D., & Fry, H. (1980). *A design for a school of pedagogy* (U.S. Department of Education Publication No. E-80-42000). Washington, DC: U.S. Government Printing Office.

Smith, L.R., & Cotton, M.L. (1980). Effect of lesson vagueness and discontinuity on student achievement and attitude. *Journal of Educational Psychology,* **72**, 670-675

Spaulding, R. (1977). Problems faced by teacher educators in attempting to use results of research on teaching. *California Journal of Teacher Education,* **4**(2), 91-104.

Tom, A.R. (1980). The reform of teacher education through research: A futile quest. *Teachers College Record,* **81**(1), 15-29.

Weil, M. (1985). Research use in inservice and preservice education: A case study of California. *Journal of Teacher Education,* **36**(1), 65-68.

Wisniewski, R. (1984). The scholarly ethos in schools of education. *Journal of Teacher Education,* **35**(5), 2-8.

Wittrock, M.C. (Ed.). (1986). *Third handbook of research on teaching*. New York: Macmillan.

Yarger, S.J., Howey, K., & Joyce, B. (1977). Reflections on preservice teacher preparation: Impressions from the national survey (Pt. 2, Students and faculty). *Journal of Teacher Education, 28*(6), 34–37.

Zeichner, K.M. (1983). Alternative paradigms of teacher education. *Journal of Teacher Education, 34*(3), 3–9.

PART I

Myths

The papers in this section deal with myths that have been tacitly accepted by some scholars in the field of pedagogical research in physical education. The first deals with the neglect of the social sciences. Two of the leading researchers in the field of sport studies present suggestions about how this subdiscipline can be used in physical education. In the first paper George Sage makes a forceful appeal for the inclusion of social science information in the curriculum of the physical education student. Such content is important because physical education teachers and coaches deal with social issues on a day-to-day basis.

In the second paper Susan Greendorfer suggests that scholars need to draw on knowledge from sport studies and sport pedagogy when doing research in physical education. Because the subdisciplines embrace similar concepts they can each benefit from the other's perspective. Such cooperation will help to reduce the fragmentation of information and increase the development of an integrated body of knowledge within physical education. Following Greendorfer, Ronald Feingold reiterates the point that social science knowledge is an important aspect of the curriculum, but calls for the sociology of physical education rather than the sociology of sport.

In his provocative discussion of sport pedagogy, Peter Röthig criticizes the field for what he perceives to be too great an emphasis on technical questions dealing with how to improve athletic performance. This should be replaced, he suggests, by a greater emphasis on *verstehen*. This term is defined as an integration of research methodology and individual experience to investigate pedagogical problems that have their roots in real-life situations and focus on social interaction.

The myth of cultural simplicity reflected in the games and sports of different cultures is the theme of Wolf Brettschneider's paper. He asks us to remember the configurational relationship between games and culture. Sport in schools is not isolated from cultural reality. Our culture presents us with a complex array of models that must be reflected in the curriculum. For example, students should have the opportunity to develop a sense of fulfillment and enjoyment in games and sports as well as learn the value of competition and victory.

The final paper in this section deals with the spectra of technological control and the ethical problems that this control generates. Andrew Hawkins and Robert Wiegand describe their attempts to utilize technology in their teacher-education program. Although they show that the "big brother" syndrome is not yet a reality in pedagogical research, they warn against sacrificing humanism in an attempt to attain this technological control.

Although they deal with different topics, these six papers underscore the need for scholars in physical education and sport to take note of research that is occurring in related fields and to see physical education in particular, and education in general, as part of a complex and changing society, rather than in a social vacuum.

The Role of Sport Studies in Sport Pedagogy

George H. Sage

Several preliminaries must be attended to before I proceed with the main points of this paper. First, this is not another call to arms in the protracted discipline-versus-profession war. Too many missiles already lie harmlessly on the battlefields of this dispute (see, e.g., Bressan, 1982; Broekhoff, 1979, 1982; Kretchmar, 1980; Lawson, 1979, 1980, 1985; Lawson & Morford, 1979; Locke, 1977, 1980; Locke & Siedentop, 1980; Ulrich, 1982). My purpose is not to chastise sport pedagogues for insisting that pedagogical skills are important in preparing physical educators, nor do I claim that the various sport subdisciplines are the salvation of sport pedagogy.

The second preliminary has to do with the terms *sport pedagogy* and *professional preparation* in physical education. I shall consider them to be synonyms, recognizing that there may be subtle differences and personal preferences (Haag, 1978).

The third preliminary is a recognition that the world is a very large place. What I will have to say is framed in a North American context, but I think my comments will have relevance beyond North America.

My final introductory vignette is an acknowledgment that much of what I have to say has been said before by others—probably more eloquently (Lenk, 1973; Voigt, 1974; Widmar, 1977). My role may be like that of the 30-second television commercial that is shown repeatedly; ultimately it convinces many consumers to buy the product. For those who are not already converted to the importance of sport studies in sport pedagogy, perhaps being exposed to the arguments one more time will be convincing.

The main theme of this paper is really in the form of a modest appeal— an appeal to those who control the curriculum in sport pedagogy to rethink the role of sport studies in the preparation of physical educators and athletic coaches. An assumption that is linked to this appeal is that sport studies are not given sufficient recognition at the present time. Indeed, it is my contention that this paper could more aptly be titled "The Phantom Role of Sport Studies in Sport Pedagogy."

Between 1965 and 1975 courses in sport sociology, sport history, sport philosophy, and anthropology of play began to appear regularly in university schedules—in most cases under the aegis of departments of physical education. Simultaneously, national and international societies for each of these fields of study were created, and, in several cases, specialized journals began publication. These subdisciplines, as they have come to be called, tend to have their firmest roots in physical education departments. By that I mean that most sport studies scholars hold academic ranks in physical education.

One might infer from what I have said that the growth in sport studies was accompanied—even nurtured—for its value in the training of physical educators. Not so. In fact, an awkward (sometimes acrimonious) relationship has developed between sport studies specialists and sport pedagogues. On the one hand, specialists in sport studies often perceive their theoretical and empirical affinities to be in the parent disciplines, namely sociology, history, anthropology, and philosophy. On the other hand, however, they hold academic ranks in physical education, so many attempt to relate their subject matter to aspiring physical educators, reasoning that, because the students' future careers will involve them intimately with sports, course work in sport studies is important. This somewhat ambiguous state of affairs has strained relationships with pedagogically oriented colleagues whose major criterion for judging courses offered to aspiring physical educators tends to be how the course will improve teacher effectiveness. The result has been little support for sport studies in sport pedagogy.

Surveys of the status of sport studies in North America have found that the majority of preservice physical education programs do not require these courses (Southard, 1982). For example, of the 536 colleges and universities polled by Dan Southard, only 7% of the teacher preparation programs required sociology of sport, whereas some 19% combined its subject matter with some other subject. None of the sport studies were listed in the top 12 out of 20 competencies that sport pedagogues believed to be important for an aspiring physical educationist. Earle Zeigler (1980) reported that the number of philosophy of sport and physical education courses has declined since 1960.

Reasons for the Low Status of Sport Studies in Sport Pedagogy

Understanding the low status of sport studies in the preparation of physical educators must begin with an understanding of historical developments in physical education as well as contemporary visions of purposes of higher education. Academic preparation in physical education has traditionally included a substantial portion of study in the biological sciences, primarily human anatomy, exercise physiology, and biomechanics (at first called kinesiology). Today these courses are as firmly entrenched in the training of physical educators as they have ever been; indeed, in many cases the proportion of required bioscience has increased over the past 20 years.

Bioscience emphasis in physical education is a function of physical education's historical origins and professional demands. Early physical education leaders were themselves typically trained in medicine. As they developed curricula for the preparation of physical educators, they quite naturally emphasized their own academic strength in biosciences. But also, because physical educators must, in their on-the-job roles, work with students in dynamic movement settings, the relevance of information about human bodily systems and the applications of laws of force was recognized by these early leaders. Thus, anatomy, physiology, and bio-mechanics have been traditionally considered the essential "sciences" for the preparation of physical educators. Association with the biosciences carries with it a strong dosage of the natural science paradigm. Unfortunately, the infatuation with the natural science paradigm often discourages understanding of other ways of knowing and alternative research methodologies, many of which are foundational in the sport studies (Widmar, 1977).

From the beginning of the so-called New Physical Education at the beginning of the 20th century, social development has been an integral component of physical education objectives; but rarely have there been systematic learning experiences in seriously analyzing sport and physical activities from a sociocultural or humanities standpoint in programs of sport pedagogy. Subject matter dealing with the social science and humanities aspects of physical activity has been traditionally subsumed in catch-all courses titled "Principles of Physical Education" or "Foundations of Physical Education." In such courses, perhaps one or two weeks might be devoted to a smattering of history, philosophy, sociology, and anthropology of games and sports.

Another reason that sport studies probably have a low status in sport pedagogy is that the preparation of teachers of sport is dominated by the performance principle. This is manifested in biosciences that are taught to aspiring physical educators. Content in exercise physiology stresses understanding muscle and cardiovascular physiology for the development of strength and endurance. The implications and applications of this are that improved strength and endurance will make for improved sports performance. Biomechanical principles emphasize the importance of proper body position for the most efficient application of forces—for what?—for improved performance. At the same time, courses in sport pedagogy are concerned with teaching behaviors that are correlated with student learning. We see again the stress on performance; in this case, the relationship between teacher performance and student performance.

Immediate payoffs in the form of improved performance or enhanced rates of skill acquisition from sport studies courses are obviously less salient. In an age obsessed by relevance, applications, and "faster, higher, stronger," sport studies do not appear to have market value. C. Roger Rees (1984) observed that sport studies are "rejected by physical education for not being applied enough or concerned with problems in physical education" (p. 55). Sport sociology, for example, is accused by Melnick (1975, 1980) of being basic rather than applied and by Greendorfer (1977), Hanson (1982), and Ulrich (1979) as being mostly about elite sport, not physical education. John Loy (1980) observed that the legitimation of sport sociology in the physical education curriculum appears to be confronted with a "catch-22" problem. On the one hand, unless sport sociologists in physical education address themselves to applied research problems in order to produce useful professional knowledge, they will not be well received by fellow faculty in departments and schools of physical education. On the other hand, if sport sociologists in physical education strictly confine themselves to applied research, they are unlikely to establish a cumulative body of knowledge with a sociological base and thus fail to legitimate the sociology of sport as a subdiscipline of scholarly inquiry. (p. 104)

The same situation exists with the other sport studies (Miller, 1984; Zeigler, 1980).

At a broader level of analysis, we must recognize that the social sciences and humanities are in a precarious state in higher education. This is true because in 1986 higher education has precious little to do with our timeless struggle with ourselves and almost nothing to do with the connection of personal troubles and public issues. Official educational rhetoric emphasizes the necessity of equipping students with the skills to get a job and achieve "success" in postindustrial society. If it doesn't pay or can't be sold—if it doesn't have market value—it is worthless, or so the current conventional wisdom admonishes.

Limitations of Bioscience and Pedagogy in the Preparation of Physical Educators

So that there is no misunderstanding about my position toward the importance—nay, the necessity—of study in the biosciences for future physical educators, let me confirm my support for the sport biosciences. I have no quarrel with these disciplines, although some sport pedagogues question their relevance for teacher preparation (Locke, 1977). In my case, I view the education of a physical educator as more than learning a variety of motor skills and a set of techniques for keeping students busy and under control.

As for sport pedagogy, I declare my devotion to it as well. Certainly, aspiring physical educators must learn effective techniques—must acquire know-how—for promoting motor skill learning. Moreover, I am deeply sympathetic to the observation made recently by Locke and Dodds (1984) that pedagogical preparation for the work of teaching physical education has been cheated by time constraints. Not nearly enough time is given over to the preparation of physical educationists. Many trade occupations require more preservice education. So I am indeed "familiar with the tortured and elusive problems which beset the preparation of [physical education] teachers" (Locke & Siedentop, 1980, p. 36).

Having made these genuflections, I want to emphasize that I do not think subject matter in the biosciences and pedagogical studies is adequate preparation for teaching physical education and coaching sports. As important as the bioscience subject matter and techniques of teaching

are, what will be missing—tragically missing, in my view—is the possession of a quality of mind that is essential to grasping the interplay of humans and society, of biology and history, of self and world. This particular
perspective is what C. Wright Mills (1959) called "the sociological imagination." According to Mills,

> the sociological imagination enables its possessor to understand the larger
> historical scene in terms of its meaning for the inner life and the external
> career of a variety of individuals. . . . It is the capacity to range from the most
> impersonal and remote transformations to the most intimate features of the
> human self—and to see the relations between the two. (pp. 5, 7)

Although Mills used the word "sociological," he went to great pains to
emphasize that his use of it did not mean merely the academic discipline
of sociology; indeed, he meant it to apply to all of the social sciences and
humanities.

As valuable and necessary as the biosciences and pedagogy are to the
preservice preparation of physical educators, they do not address the connection between sport and the broader society, especially as it is manifested in ideological, political, and economic systems. Both tend to
completely ignore the sociocultural, historical, and political dimensions
of sport as a cultural activity. They tend to be systematically ahistorical
and noncomparative. Training in the biosciences emphasizes efficiency
and performance in sports; the teacher with a bioscience perspective will
be primarily concerned with how to make students perform better. Training in pedagogy emphasizes efficient use of time and space and the organization of groups of various ages and sizes. The current buzzword
in sport pedagogy is "academic learning time," that is, counting seconds
that students are actively practicing or performing the task to be learned.
The emphasis, then, of a teacher employing pedagogical skills is on being a technician. The focus is on student acquisition of motor skills as
a teacher's major goal (Graham & Heimerer, 1981). Siedentop (1982) asserted that "the subject matter that is of interest [in sport pedagogy] is
the behavior of the individual teacher" (p. 85). He said there is an emphasis on a "developing technology" in pedagogy. Locke (1977) noted
that "the principal 'valuable' that we have to give our client is motor skill"
(p. 35).

In the biosciences faith in the natural-science paradigm and abstract
empiricism is unconstrained. Sport pedagogy appears to be adopting this
approach as well. Siedentop (1982) claimed recently that in the past decade a "development of descriptive measurement systems in the tradition of the natural sciences" (p. 84) has emerged in pedagogy, and that
there is now a "natural science of teaching" that is concerned with teaching behavior that is correlated with student learning.

Now, do not misunderstand my remarks; they are not meant as criti-
cisms of biosciences or sport pedagogy as disciplines. Indeed, as I have
said before, they both have essential contributions to make in the preparation of physical educators/coaches. But they are not enough. Bioscience

and pedagogy have little feeling or sensitivity to the constitutive character of sports as an element of culture, nor do they deal with the class character of sports. Indeed, they implicitly validate dominant attitudes about the social character of sport—their approach is unreflecting and uncritical; they accept the dominant sport forms and behave accordingly.

What Can Sport Studies Contribute to Sport Pedagogy?

The first issue that must be confronted when attempting to stress the importance for sport studies learning experiences to sport pedagogy is the compulsive demand that sport studies convey specific applications of their subject matter to practitioners in physical education. For example, Locke (1977) has asked for "the mechanism by which the disciplines [including sport studies] propose to make themselves useful to the profession, the linkage between research and practice" (p. 41). He declared that there "are almost no documented and unambiguous instances of research directly causing any persisting change in the public school gymnasium" (p. 41). Greendorfer (1977) observed that "sociologists of sport have not focused on physical activity within the context of learning or acquiring motor skill" (p. 59). I want to suggest that these expectations for sport studies are misguided. The role of sport studies is not to provide specific prescriptions for teaching. Whereas exercise physiologists might discover a way of developing strength that may readily be translated into sport conditioning programs, biomechanicians may discover a better way to apply force in executing a sport skill, and sport pedagogues may find more effective methods for enhancing group learning—clear examples of "application for the practitioner"—sport studies research will not very often result in neat recipes for the practitioner (Sage, 1977). But that does not diminish their usefulness, for that is not primarily how they should be judged.

Let's face it, physical educators and coaches are notoriously socially naive. Professional preparation programs have traditionally been heavy in subject matter emphasizing how to teach motor skills, how to develop strength and endurance, and how to use the levers of the body to produce force (whether they have been effective in these matters is another issue), but they have been sadly lacking in making aspiring physical educators and coaches aware of the social consequences of their programs and socially conscious of the changing nature of modern society and the complexities and contradictions of contemporary sport. Preservice programs of most aspiring physical educators and coaches never once encourage students to question their own personal attitudes and values about sports or to make them explicit. Instead, students are fed a diet of traditional slogans, clichés, sacred cows, and ritualized trivia about sport. Sport and society are typically presented as discrete institutional arenas, with sport seen as a realm where character is built and virtue pursued. The main contribution to a mission-oriented perspective that sport studies can make is an expanded social awareness and an elevated social consciousness in relation to social order and change. One important outcome of such an approach is that the social world is viewed not as some given entity controlled by unalterable natural laws but as a social process capable of being transformed by human agents (Giddens, 1979).

From my 20 years of experience in teaching physical education majors I have consistently found that they have a blissful unsophistication about the social relations that control education, physical education, and sport. To a frightening degree there is a naiveté to the social context and material conditions underlying physical education. Most programs of sport pedagogy do not once confront students with questions about the larger social issues and the consequences of modern sport forms.

If physical educators are to understand themselves and their society, they must look beyond the individual and his or her immediate surroundings. There are larger issues to be addressed by physical educators than time on task, feedback schedules, and student discipline. Few things are more destructive to a sociological imagination than narrow instrumental and vocational concerns. Sport philosopher Donna Mae Miller (1984) posed an appropriate question: "In our zeal to prepare [physical education] students for job opportunities of a specialized nature, are we unduly narrowing their opportunities for achieving certain habits of mind and for examining the ends of living as well as the means?" (p. 28). One very real issue in this regard was raised by Neil Postman (1982): "Can a culture preserve humane values and create new ones by allowing modern technology the fullest possible authority to control its destiny?" (p. 145).

One of the greatest potentials of sport studies is the development of an understanding of the social and material basis of culture and consciousness and the way in which relations of power and authority structure various cultural products, such as sports and games. Sport is a cultural form rooted in problems of freedom and constraint, voluntarism and determinism, liberalism and domination. Sports are constitutive practices embedded in a whole range of social processes in which humans interact with one another (Gruneau, 1983; Voigt, 1974).

Mills' (1959) admonition 25 years ago is as valid today as it was then. He said:

> Man's chief danger today lies in the unruly forces of contemporary society itself, with its alienating methods of production, its enveloping techniques of political domination, its international anarchy—in a word, its pervasive transformations of the very "nature" of man and the conditions and aims of his life. (p. 13)

In a more recent statement, and one related directly to sport, Gruneau (1978) noted:

> The main thrust of the sociological analysis of sport should not be seen as the attempt to make isolated remarks about "what sport is like". . . . rather, it should be seen as the continuous effort to relate sport to general features

of social organization in order to gain a more coherent and comprehensive understanding of institutional arrangements and cultural values in the whole society and the place of sporting activities within them. (p. 82)

The cultural meanings of natural science are becoming doubtful. As an intellectual force, natural science is increasingly being seen as inadequate. As research findings accumulate, they have not provided solutions to any problems widely known and deeply pondered by intellectual communities and cultural publics. Instead, they are seen as the result of highly specialized inquiry, but they have raised more questions—both intellectual and moral—than they have answered, and the problems they have raised reside almost totally in the field of social, not natural, affairs. The range of issues addressed in sport studies goes beyond abstract empiricism to explore actual changes that occur in the logics and patterns of social and cultural organization in society; they also address interpretative and evaluative questions about the relationship of social change to differential life chances and various forms of consciousness characterizing different individuals and groups in society (Gruneau, 1983; Widmar, 1977).

If sport pedagogues are to maintain programs appropriate to the needs of students who will be working in physical education and sport environments, they must do much more than prepare students with management strategies, technical knowledge, and sport skills. Robert Hollands (1984) has articulately described the importance of solid preparation in sport studies:

There is much more to play, games, leisure, and sport than technical knowledge and practical skills. As elements of contemporary popular culture, these human activities have far more impact and importance than is readily acknowledged. . . . The practical implications of a sociocultural understanding of play, games, and sport are broad and far-reaching. For it is only by coming to terms with the production, reproduction, and representation of cultural forms, and how these processes link up to the broader features of a society, that change becomes possible and alternatives become realities. (p. 76)

Before concluding this presentation, there is a final point I wish to make. Although I have tried to show that sport studies should not be judged by the applications they can make to helping physical educators and coaches with their specific day-to-day tasks, I want to emphasize that sport studies do have good potential for applied, policy, and evaluation research that can help schools, sport programs, teachers, and coaches. Elaboration on this issue would require another paper. Hal Lawson (1983a, 1983b) and Hans Lenk (1973) have given some illustrations of this, and I suggest you consult their work if you are interested.

Conclusion

The form and content of preservice programs in physical education and coaching are in the hands of sport pedagogues. The theme of this paper is that courses in sport studies need to be an integral part of such programs. What is suggested is a rethinking of the organization of preservice programs in physical education. I realize that the politics of curricular change have become a zero-sum game, in which contenders for scarce resources battle over faculty positions. Given the politics and constraints with which we all must contend, the polarization of curricula into biosciences and pedagogy and sport studies is a sheer loss to us all, and especially to the students whom we are preparing for a career in physical education and coaching. Understanding and cooperation are what is needed. It seems to me that we have all spent too much time warring against each other. If we had spent the same amount of time in the past 15 years cooperatively trying to find ways to improve the preparation of physical educators as well as the advancement of the various subdisciplines, rather than spending hour after hour preparing missiles to be fired past one another at conventions and via journal articles, we would have all been better off, and it is likely that we would have made a greater contribution to physical education and to our own specialities.

The sport studies are still grappling with their own identities. Although the preparation of teachers and coaches is not the sole mission of sport studies, sport studies scholars, like sport pedagogues, would like to see improved physical education programs, and if their work helps they will be pleased about it.

Note

1. At least in the United States, the number of physical education majors who report that they selected this major because they want to teach is surprisingly small. Most physical education majors want to coach sports (Chu, 1981; Segrave, 1981).

References

Bressan, E.S. (1982). An academic discipline: What a fine mess! In L.L. Gedvilas (Ed.), *National Association for Physical Education in Higher Education Annual Conference Proceedings: Vol. 3* (pp. 22–27). Champaign, IL: Human Kinetics.

Broekhoff, J. (1979). Physical education as a profession. *Quest, 31,* 244–254.

Broekhoff, J. (1982). A discipline—who needs it? In L.L. Gedvilas (Ed.), *National Association for Physical Education in Higher Education Annual Conference Proceedings: Vol. 3* (pp. 28–35). Champaign, IL: Human Kinetics.

Chu, D. (1981). Functional myths of educational organizations: College as career training and the relationship of formal title to actual duties upon secondary school employment. In V. Crafts (Ed.), *National Association for Physical Education in Higher Education Annual Conference Proceedings: Vol. 2* (pp. 36–46). Champaign, IL: Human Kinetics.

Giddens, A. (1979). *Central problems in social theory.* Berkeley: University of California Press.

Graham, G., & Heimerer, E. (1981). Research on teacher effectiveness: A summary with implications for teaching. *Quest, 33,* 14–25.

Greendorfer, S. (1977). Sociology of sport: Knowledge of what? *Quest, 28,* 319–328.

Gruneau, R. (1978). Conflicting standards and problems of personal action in the sociology of sport. *Quest, 30,* 80–90.

Gruneau, R. (1983). *Class, sports, and social development.* Amherst: University of Massachusetts Press.

Haag, H. (1978). *Sport pedagogy.* Baltimore: University Press.

Hanson, D. (1982). Applications. In H.M. Eckert (Ed.), *The Academy papers: Synthesizing and transmitting knowledge, research and its applications* (pp. 67–70). Reston, VA: American Alliance for Health, Recreation, and Dance.

Hollands, R.G. (1984). The role of cultural studies and social criticism in the sociological study of sport. *Quest, 36,* 66–79.

Kretchmar, R.S. (1980). In search of structure: Perspectives of the discipline. In L.L. Gedvilas & M.E. Kneer (Eds.), *National Association for Physical Education in Higher Education Annual Conference Proceedings: Vol. 1* (pp. 85–95). Champaign, IL: Human Kinetics.

Lawson, H.A. (1979). Paths toward professionalization. *Quest, 31,* 231–243.

Lawson, H.A. (1980). Beyond teaching and ad hocracy: Increasing the sphere of influence and control for physical educationists. *Quest, 32,* 22–30.

Lawson, H.A. (1983a, Spring). Toward a model of teacher socialization in physical education: The subjective warrant, recruitment, and teacher education. *Journal of Teaching in Physical Education, 2,* 3–16.

Lawson, H.A. (1983b, Fall). Toward a model of teacher socialization in physical education: Entry into schools, teachers' role orientations, and longevity in teaching (Pt. 2). *Journal of Teaching in Physical Education, 3,* 3–15.

Lawson, H.A. (1985). Knowledge for work in the physical education profession. *Sociology of Sport Journal, 2,* 9–24.

Lawson, H.A., & Morford, W.R. (1979). The crossdisciplinary structure of kinesiology and sports studies: Distinctions, implications, and advantages. *Quest, 31,* 222–230.

Lenk, H. (1973). The pedagogical significance of sport sociology. *International Journal of Physical Education, 10,* 16–20.

Locke, L.F. (1977). From research and the disciplines to practice and the profession: One more time. In L.L. Gedvilas & M. E. Kneer (Eds.),

Proceedings of the NCPEAM/NAPECW (pp. 34–45). Chicago: University of Illinois, Chicago Circle Publication Services.

Locke, L.F. (1980). Reaction to Kretchmar paper disciplines by declaration: Verities and balderdash. In L.L. Gedvilas & M.E. Kneer (Eds.). *National Association for Physical Education in Higher Education Annual Conference Proceedings: Vol. 1* (pp. 96–100). Champaign, IL: Human Kinetics.

Locke, L.F., & Dodds, P. (1984). Is physical education teacher education in American colleges worth saving? Evidence, alternatives, judgment. In N.L. Struna (Ed.), *National Association for Physical Education in Higher Education Annual Conference Proceedings: Vol. 5* (pp. 91–107). Champaign, IL: Human Kinetics.

Locke, L.F., & Siedentop, D. (1980). Beyond arrogance and ad hominem: A reply to Hal Lawson. *Quest, 32,* 31–43.

Loy, J.W. (1980). The emergence and development of the sociology of sport as an academic speciality. *Research Quarterly for Exercise and Sport,* **51,** 91–109.

Melnick, M.J. (1975). A critical look at sociology of sport. *Quest,* **25,** 34–47.

Melnick, M.J. (1980, Fall/Winter). Towards an applied sociology of sport. *Journal of Sport and Social Issues,* **5,** 1–12.

Miller, D.M. (1984). Philosophy: Whose business? *Quest,* **36,** 26–36.

Mills, C.W. (1959). *The sociological imagination.* New York: Grove.

Postman, N. (1982). *The disappearance of childhood.* New York: Delacorte Press.

Rees, C.R. (1984). Applying sociology to physical education: Who needs it? In N.L. Struna (Ed.), *National Association for Physical Education in Higher Education Annual Conference Proceedings: Vol. 5* (pp. 54–59). Champaign, IL: Human Kinetics.

Sage, G.H. (1977). Sport sociology: The state of the art and implications for physical education. In L.L. Gedvilas & M.E. Kneer (Eds.), *Proceedings of the NCPEAM/NAPECW* (pp. 310–319). Chicago: University of Illinois, Chicago Circle Publications Services.

Segrave, J.O. (1981). Role preferences among prospective physical education teacher/coaches. In V. Crafts (Ed.), *National Association for Physical Education in Higher Education Annual Conference Proceedings: Vol. 2* (pp. 53–61). Champaign, IL: Human Kinetics.

Siedentop, D. (1982). Recent advances in pedagogical research in physical education. In H.L. Eckert (Ed.), *The Academy papers: Synthesizing and transmitting knowledge, research and its applications* (pp. 82–94). Reston, VA: American Alliance for Health, Physical Education, Recreation, and Dance.

Southard, D. (1982). A national survey: Sociology of sport within American college and university physical education professional preparation programs. In A.O. Dunleavy, A.W. Miracle, & C.R. Rees (Eds.),

Studies in the sociology of sport (pp. 365–372). Ft. Worth: Texas Christian University Press.

Ulrich, C. (1979). The significance of sport sociology to the profession. In M.L. Krotee (Ed.), *The dimensions of sport sociology* (pp. 11–19). Champaign, IL: Leisure Press.

Ulrich, C. (1982). Pomp and circumstance. In L.L. Gedvilas (Ed.), *National Association for Physical Education in Higher Education Annual Conference Proceedings: Vol. 3* (pp. 11–20). Champaign, IL: Human Kinetics.

Voigt, D. (1974). Sociology in the training of the sport teacher and the teacher in general. *International Journal of Physical Education, 10,* 26–40.

Widmar, K. (1977). Social sciences of sport and sport pedagogy as part aspect of sport science. *International Journal of Physical Education, 14,* 21–35.

Zeigler, E.F. (1980, October). Without philosophy, coaches and physical educators are "unguided missiles." *The Physical Educator, 37,* 122–127.

The Role of Sport Studies in Sport Pedagogy: Who Needs It?

Susan L. Greendorfer

In many respects what I have to say merely extends some of Sage's (1987) remarks and reinforces his appeal to those who control curriculum in sport pedagogy. The message is not new, nor is this the first time it has been delivered publicly at a large conference. Essentially, it seems that we all need to rethink the role of sport studies in sport pedagogy and rise to the challenge of initiating more communication and dialogue between the two fields, despite the years of strained relations. As I see it, the problem is not simply insufficient recognition of sport studies; rather, it is the total eclipsing, isolating, and ignoring of these subdisciplines. The situation at the present time is not dissimilar to the plight of an aged relative who has been allowed or tolerated in the house, but for all practical purposes is not truly a member of the household. Although his or her presence may be acknowledged on occasion, no one in the family seriously considers this individual. Such is the state of affairs with sport studies. However, this situation need not continue because there is something we all can do to bring about change.

Although several have recognized and discussed the uneasy relationship that has existed between physical education and the social science of sport (Greendorfer, 1975, 1977; Melnick, 1975, 1981; Sage, 1977, 1979), there have been few attempts to trace the source of these difficulties. Yet, if we are to understand the nature of the problem, this would be a logical starting point.

The trend toward subdisciplinary specialization in the 1960s brought with it a set of false expectations within the field of physical education. In some respects sociology of sport was viewed as the professional's way to "prove" the social objective of physical education. Unfortunately, however, what early physical educators called for and what they got relative to the social sciences (Cowell, 1960) were extremely different. The schism created then planted the seeds of misunderstanding that seem to grow in greater profusion today than ever before. When the new subdiscipline defined the scope of its knowledge, it eschewed the social development objective and opted for a discipline/research approach in order to understand the social phenomenon of sport (Kenyon & Loy, 1965). In retrospect, perhaps sport pedagogy felt somewhat betrayed by the new generation of specialists who not only refused to identify with mission-oriented goals but also separated themselves from the "educational" or professional teaching model. Sociology of sport and related areas of sport studies emphasized research and discipline-based curricula rather than teacher preparation. This position is no more understandable today (to sport pedagogues) than it was then, despite the fact that sport pedagogy now espouses a more discipline-based orientation.

Essentially, the development of social scientific approaches should have been accompanied by drastic social change with respect to the way we structure our thoughts about our subject matter. Instead of resynthesizing, reorganizing, or reformulating the body of knowledge by attempting to incorporate what these new subdisciplines had to offer, however, past tradition dominated sport pedagogy. As a result, the new subdisciplines were expected to fit into the prescriptive model that was already operating in physical education/sport pedagogy. When sport studies demonstrated a disinclination to study social issues or solve problems related to sport, sport pedagogy virtually disowned, without dismantling, the social sciences. As a consequence, the type of specialization that evolved in the social sciences created a subdiscipline whose narrow research focus resulted in an independently operating system within the field. This resultant fragmentation has fostered an avoidance of cross-disciplinary fertilization within the field and has retarded development of any semblance of an integrated body of knowledge (Hoffman, 1985).

Indeed, we speak different languages, ask different questions, and have devised such a convoluted system of jargon that we impart different meanings to commonly shared words, thereby creating greater confusion and further division. Most attempts at communication become virtually impossible because we tend to translate questions and answers in light of our own perspectives, rarely allowing for credibility or respect for alternative points of view. As a result, there has been little, if any, attempt to address what the logical and functional relationship is between sport pedagogy and sport studies.[1] Consequently, there has been a virtual lack of concern with the potential contributions offered by the social sciences.

The challenge, then, is to build bridges, not simply those between researchers and practitioners, but those between the existing fragments of the field. This plea is not simply a call for more applied or relevant research. Rather, it is a plea for a widespread communication that calls for a sensitivity to alternative perspectives and an unbiased translation of such points of view. In this respect, the social sciences have much to offer sport pedagogy. Recognizing that statements of this type could foster further misunderstanding, let me hasten to add that some compromise is needed on all fronts. Those in sport pedagogy who dismiss sport studies because they feel the social sciences don't deal with "real-life" topics or mainstream issues are simply going to have to reevaluate their bias. By the same token, those who see sport studies as focusing only on a very narrow institutionalized connotation of formalized "sport" need to recognize that the subdisciplines have evolved to include more broad-based phenomena, such as physical activity and exercise, as well as sport. In a similar vein, sport scientists who believe that calls for action-oriented or applied research (Gruneau, 1978; Melnick, 1981) represent abandonment of sociological perspectives or capitulation of basic tenets of the subdisciplines also need considerable attitude modification. A plea for communication is not synonymous with subscription to prescriptive practice.

Both of these perspectives represent extremes and both err in their failure to recognize the vast middle ground that remains virtually unexplored—that of mutual concern, compromise, and understanding. Unfortunately, differences in orientations or perspectives foster differences in approach. When such differences create divergent purposes in the nature and content of knowledge systems, the result is incompatibility. The challenge now for both sport studies and sport pedagogy is to make the other discipline aware of the nature of each one's interests, concentrating on those questions and issues that represent mutual concern. How do we construct well-rounded curricula in professional preparation if we ourselves are not receptive to new information or perspectives? Why should future professionals be receptive to research and its implications for teaching if we who prepare them have little understanding or tolerance of such research?

There is more involved in this enterprise than simply asking how the data will solve a specific teaching or coaching problem. What is needed is a better understanding of mutual goals and a more cooperative attitude that will provide a supportive context for pursuing shared interests. This requires a restructuring of what and how we think about our general body of knowledge. Reshaping belief systems and instituting changes in curricula are required. In short, reshaping involves reconstituting our conception of knowledge and types of factors that influence physical activity. The role and relevance of sport studies research in sport pedagogy need to be understood, as do the significance, meaning, and implications of research questions.

One essential change that must take place is an alteration of value systems because value systems are responsible for the obstacles and barriers that exist. They have inhibited the development of any cross-disciplinary fertilization by creating false dichotomies and splintering the field. The type of research topics pursued and questions asked are shaped by value systems that need to be expanded to include a holistic approach to issues that confront the field as an entity. Although there are many contributors to disparity, the most insidious has been the abandonment of the totality of the field and a retrenchment toward a natural science model that has ignored an intellectual wholeness (Miller, 1984). Even though the issue of fragmentation has been discussed elsewhere recently (Hoffman, 1985), Hoffman's question pertaining to what we do and where we belong is most appropriate for our consideration here. The question implicitly suggests that all the subdisciplines might be better placed in departments other than physical education. Furthermore, his questions seem as appropriate for sport pedagogy as they are for the exercise and sport sciences. Specifically, What is the focus and nature of knowledge in sport pedagogy? Secondly, Has it been incorporated into a more general body of knowledge, or has it also remained distinct and isolated from "physical education"?

To repeat, the underlying issue is a change in attitude—one that permits us to function in more than one dimension. The relevance of research, the classical criticism leveled by practitioners, is not truly the issue here. In contrast, the issue has become far more encompassing because, on the one hand, it involves the receptivity and understanding of the significance of research questions. Yet, on the other hand, it also includes the recognition of implications of research findings for both curriculum instruction and direct practice.

Specific to this point are the ways that social science principles and insights can enhance analysis and understanding in the field of sport pedagogy. This point has not escaped notice of sport pedagogue researchers; much of what is studied and discussed in their investigations leans heavily on underlying social and psychological forces. Such forces, which comprise the essential foundation of knowledge in sport studies, are in fact recognized by sport pedagogues as powerful influences. Those observable behavioral products that make up the core of sport pedagogy research—whether they be teaching effectiveness, on-the-field performance, teaching/learning of motor skills, or behavior modification—seem to have overlapping conceptual links with much of the micro-research in sport studies.

In fact, a perusal of all the published issues of *Journal of Teaching Physical Education* reveals that well over 50% of the articles published are concerned with observation or measurement of causes and consequences of social behavior. In many instances the only distinction between sport studies and sport pedagogy research seems to be in the social context analyzed or in the specification of who the subjects are. Psychological, social, and cultural forces have been recognized as important factors relative to the learning or performance of motor skills, teacher effectiveness, teaching/coaching strategies, and professional socialization. Despite the strong similarity in perspectives or overlapping themes of research, communication across the areas has been virtually nonexistent. Attempts to synthesize knowledge have been virtually nonexistent, and there have been few attempts to holistically "package" information to embellish curricula.

It is amazing that such short shrift has been paid to sport studies when we consider the growing body of knowledge that has accumulated over the past 20 years. Not only should a liaison be provided to increase communication between sport studies and sport pedagogy, but it seems that more collaborative research and synthesis of information are also needed. We need a vehicle to help us more fully recognize the significance and implications of existing research.

Imagine how much more we would know were findings pertaining to self-efficacy and perceived competence, achievement motivation, personal investment, and role commitment combined with findings relative to movement confidence, adherence to exercise, and teacher effectiveness. Imagine the dimensions of enhancement in teacher effectiveness if more information pertaining to racial and sex-role discrimination could be integrated into professional preparation programs such that teacher sensitivity to various forms of bias was heightened. Instruction could be based on principles emanating from social learning theory rather than from nonconscious stereotypes. Similarly, imagine the modification of both student performance and teacher behavior if there were more complete awareness of how playing styles and objectives of games are shaped by cultural values. More complete understanding of cultural differences would add tremendous insight into the design and offerings of curricula, so that knowledge relevant to curriculum planning as well as cultural value systems could be integrated and resultant programs would be more meaningful and consonant with the value orientations of the participants.

Because much of what is researched and discussed in sport pedagogy relies on observation or measurement of behavioral products, the absence of research findings or a social science context in which to place them could easily lead to misunderstandings. Thus, the issue is not one of quality of evidence but rather of attitude toward research (Locke, 1984). Although I agree with Locke that relevance or implication of information essentially depends on how readily information and innovation are accepted, I wonder why the attitude of sport pedagogy has been rather narrow with respect to the contributions that can be made by sport studies. In my opinion, the greatest problem has been one of resistance to change and refusal to alter practice, because doing so would require a massive rethinking and possible restructuring of what we are doing and why.

The challenge for the future is to recognize the similarities rather than the differences in research interests and to communicate sufficiently with each other so that the significance and implications of research are understood. The true challenge is whether we can more effectively pursue questions that seem to be remarkably similar in concept and approach by acknowledging the commonality of interests. More important, once committed to such an endeavor, will we incorporate and synthesize new knowledge into curricula and professional preparation even if it means radical departure from the fragmented kaleidoscope that currently exists?

Note

1. Although sport pedagogy and physical education have been used interchangeably up to this point, I feel this assumption is unwarranted because the former shows every indication of becoming an independent subdiscipline *sui generis*. Thus, the second question cannot be ignored and should be explicitly stated: What is the logical and functional relationship between sport pedagogy and physical education?

References

Cowell, C.C. (1960, May). The contributions of physical activity to social development. *Research Quarterly*, **31**, 286–306.

Greendorfer, S.L. (1975). The social science of sport: Need for further knowledge. In *Proceedings of 78th Annual Meeting National College Physical Education Association for Men* (pp. 319–328).

Greendorfer, S.L. (1977). Sociology of sport: Knowledge of what? *Quest,* **28,** 58–65.

Gruneau, R.S. (1978). Conflicting standards and problems of personal action in the sociology of sport. *Quest,* **30,** 80–90.

Hoffman, S.J. (1985, August). Specialization + fragmentation = extermination: A formula for the demise of graduate education. *Journal of Physical Education, Recreation and Dance,* pp. 19–22.

Kenyon, G.S., & Loy, J.W. (1965, May). Toward a sociology of sport. *Journal of Health, Physical Education & Recreation,* pp. 24–25.

Locke, L. (1984). Research on teaching teachers: Where are we now? *Journal of Teaching in Physical Education* (Monograph No. 2), 3–11.

Melnick, M. (1975). A critical look at the sociology of sport. *Quest,* **24,** 34–47.

Melnick, M. (1981). Toward an applied sociology of sport. *Journal of Sport and Social Issues,* **5,** 1–12.

Miller, D.M. (1984). Philosophy: Whose business? *Quest,* **36,** 26–36.

Sage, G.H. (1977). Sport sociology: The state of the art and implications for physical education. In *Proceedings of the NAPECW/NCPEAM National Conference* (pp. 310–319).

Sage, G.H. (1979). The current status and trends in sport sociology. In M.L. Krotee (Ed.), *The dimensions of sport sociology* (pp. 23–31). Champaign, IL: Leisure Press.

Sage, G.H. (1987). *The role of sport studies in sport pedagogy.* In G.T. Barrette, R.S. Feingold, C.R. Rees, & M. Piéron (Eds.), *Myths, models, and methods in sport pedagogy* (pp. 29–40). Champaign, IL: Human Kinetics.

Why Can't the Sport Sociologist Teach Sociology of Physical Education?

Ronald S. Feingold

"Sociology is the scientific discipline that describes and explains human social organization. . . . The sociologist is interested in the patterns that emerge whenever people interact over periods of time" (Eitzen & Sage, 1982, p. 3). Massengale (1984) in the last National Association for Physical Education in Higher Education (NAPEHE) proceedings noted that "traditional American physical education is based upon many foundations, and one of those foundations, regardless of the exact title or definition, always featured a strong general relationship to the social process" (p. 69). He also notes that "the successful integration of social science into the physical education curriculum at all levels, especially as it relates to behavior and/or learning, remains paramount in the eyes of many physical educators. . . . Yet, the social process in traditional physical education remains vague and ambiguous, but most important, it remains pervasive."

The Missing Emphasis in Physical Education

Although the significance of the social process is recognized as a basic foundation, the practice of incorporating courses related to the social process in physical education, as well as the study of the social process, still lacks serious significance and acceptance. According to Massengale (1984), even the sport sociologists refrain from studying the social process in physical education. "A casual review of the scholarly efforts in sport sociology will reveal an overemphasis on those topics that tend to be exciting and sensational, namely competitive athletics and the protest of the status quo" (Massengale, 1984, p. 69).

Greendorfer (1977), in her *Quest* article, tried to explain why the sport sociologist tended to ignore physical education. She felt that Kenyon and Loy (1965) established the separation when they established sociology of sport as a subdiscipline. The objective was to understand sport per se—to identify the regularity of underlying patterns of behavior in a sport context—with the help of sociological theory and method (Greendorfer, 1977). Thus, the earliest position espoused by Kenyon (1966) claimed that research in sport sociology would contribute both to an understanding of sport as a particular social phenomena and to knowledge about social systems in general (Greendorfer, 1977). Most of the research since 1966 has tended to support this original position of Kenyon (1966).

Typical of this position, one finds an objective of a doctoral program "in the sociocultural perspective" to be the search for an understanding of man engaged in sport and the phenomenon of sport itself (Duthie et al., 1976). Why not man and woman engaged in movement or activity?

Greendorfer (1977) also points to the second phenomenon that may have contributed to this separation of the sport sociologist from physical education; the structure and organizational patterns established in higher education, that is, the total separation between athletics and physical education. However, that would make more sense if the sport sociologists were in the athletic department—usually they are in the physical education department.

Thus in the literature dating back to the 1920s we have the social and cultural impact on children in sport and physical education as a basic foundation. But only since as late as the mid-1960s has there been a serious endeavor to study physical activity from a social perspective by trained sociologists or sport sociologists. It is interesting, however, that those same specialists have chosen to channel their energy into the study of sport. It is also interesting how few colleges and universities require sociology of physical education, or even a course relative to it, yet most have a course in sociology of sport. Thus, as late as the mid-1980s, for the most part, teacher preparation programs do not address the social and cultural perspective of physical education, and if they hit upon it at all it is in an introductory course taught by a nonspecialist in sport sociology or in a course in sociology of education. Incredibly, this basic foundation of physical education, certainly as important as the scientific foundations, exercise physiology, and kinesiology, is not addressed. It would be similar to requiring anatomy without kinesiology, or allowing any physical educator to teach exercise physiology or kinesiology. How have we come to this state of affairs? This same question was raised almost 10 years ago, and again most recently at the 1984 NAPEHE conference (Rees, 1984). Why have the sport sociologists ignored physical education, and why have the physical educators ignored the sport sociologists?

Modern Study of Sport

It might appear that the study of sport became popular during the time of civil strife, black athletes, freedom for athletes, and female athletes because it was interesting, newsworthy, and popular. It was also a time when research on teaching was in its infancy. Today, however, the study of sport is still interesting to many, but many departments have had to cut back. The study of sport, although interesting, has been perceived as a fringe elective. Also, as the research on teaching has matured, we find research from the social, psychological, and cultural perspectives missing, or only present at a level that may be compared to the study of the teaching act 20 to 30 years ago. The sport sociologists and sociologists are investing their energy in the study of sport, instead. Thus, we find the sport sociologist without a significant role within the physical education department or university and the teaching methodology/analysis people without strong theoretical backgrounds in the psychosocial aspects of activity.

The students lose, of course. It is a necessity that we bring the sport sociologist into the physical education department; it is a necessity that we look at the teaching act from the psychosocial perspective afforded by specialists; it is a necessity that we do scholarly research on the psychosocial perspective of physical activity; it is a necessity that teachers and coaches be prepared and understand the social interaction of their students. I am not suggesting that we give up the study of sport, but only that there be a refocusing of energy onto the study of physical education and physical activity.

In looking through some sport sociology texts, I modified a few chapter headings to better reflect titles and topics that would be more relevant to the teacher.

- Physical education (rather than sport) as a microcosm of society
- Physical education (rather than sport) and American values
- Physical education and role stereotyping
- Dehumanizing practices in physical education
- Physical education class: Cooperation or competition?
- The ritual of the physical education class
- Physical education class as a socializing agent
- Racism in physical education
- Social class and physical education
- Segregation in physical education
- Reward systems in physical education
- Sportsmanship in physical education
- Integrating the handicapped, the black, and the female in physical education
- Psychosocial impacts on the participant in physical education

I do not think that the sport sociologists/scholars will be demeaning themselves by altering the focus of their research or by looking at a different subject. Both parties must realize that we need each other. Physical education needs the social scientist. We need the research, we need the courses, we need their expertise, and the sport sociologists need faculty positions. Although the study of sport is interesting, it is not critical to the preparation of the teacher; sociology of physical education is essential, however.

References

Duthie, J.H., Galasso, P.J., Metcalfe, A., Moriarity, R.J., Olafson, G.A., & Salter, M.A. (1976). The socio-cultural perspective in a human kinetics doctoral program. *Quest,* **25,** 58–66.

Eitzen, D.S., & Sage, G.H. (1982). *Sociology of American sport.* Dubuque, IA: W.C. Brown.

Greendorfer, S.L. (1977). Sociology of sport: Knowledge for what? *Quest,* **28,** 58–65.

Kenyon, G.S. (1966, March). *A sociology of sport: On becoming a subdiscipline.* Paper presented at the American Alliance for Health, Physical Education, Recreation, and Dance National Convention, Chicago.

Kenyon, G.S., & Loy, J.W. (1965). Toward a sociology of sport: A plea for the study of physical activity as a sociological and social psychological phenomenon. *Journal of Health, Physical Education, Recreation, and Dance,* **36,** 24–25, 68–69.

Massengale, J.D. (1984). Social process and traditional physical education. In N.L. Struna (Ed.), *National Association for Physical Education in Higher Education Annual Conference Proceedings: Vol. 5* (pp. 69–74). Champaign, IL: Human Kinetics.

Rees, C.R. (1984). Applying sociology to physical education: Who needs it? In N.L. Struna (Ed.), *National Association for Physical Education in Higher Education Annual Conference Proceedings: Vol. 5* (pp. 54–59). Champaign, IL: Human Kinetics.

Reflections on Researching Sport Pedagogy

Peter Röthig

The difficulties in the theoretical clarity of sport science are reflected in sport pedagogy. If we perceive sport science to be an aggregate of different disciplines, then sport pedagogy is only a part of it. But such a construct has no central theme that connects the parts. One proposal for a combination or integration can be to utilize the knowledge of sport pedagogy as such a core, because historically sport and pedagogy have always been connected.

My understanding is that sport science today is not satisfied with the discipline-oriented model, but it has not yet developed an efficient or useful opposite construct.

Structures Within Sport Pedagogy

Sometimes organizational solutions replace the rigid discipline orientation with the construction of specific areas in the work of sport science. Therefore, some institutions or departments at universities have such organized courses as the following:

- "Sport Lessons and Education," "Body and Movement," and "Sport and Society"
- "Sport and Education," "Movement and Action in Sport," "Sport and Health," and "Sport and Society"
- "Physical Education," "Recreation," and "Human Performance Science"

One of the reasons for such organizational and structural arrangements is the hope that this would positively influence the interdisciplinary research on sport scientific problems. But in most cases this hope is unfulfilled. The contradictions in the traditional understanding of the social roles of scientists or researchers are large. Following Kirsch and Preising (1985), the scientific systems at the university define the carrier models of the scientists to a relatively high degree. That means that if it is not necessary, they don't give up the connection to the so-called mother science. That connection also affects methodological decisions.

In addition, the initiation, perception, and development of problems are mostly oriented by the mother science (Heinemann, 1985). Experience shows us that we can only realize the so-called interdisciplinary relationship in teaching and research through the cooperation of interested scientists, and not through organizational models.

Sport pedagogy is to be interpreted as an integrated science. The traditional focal points and contents of sport pedagogy are:

- philosophy of education, anthropology of education;
- history of education;
- curriculum theory (goals of education);
- teacher/student interaction;
- teaching and learning processes (media in teaching and learning; learning environment—functional, interpersonal, organizational); and
- theory of school and educational institutions (organizational structure, staff, management, etc.).

The task of sport pedagogy is to develop the theories that guide actions in education. In order to heighten perception and understanding, sport pedagogy needs results and information from other fields (e.g., medicine, psychology, training theory, biomechanics, and sociology). The utilization of such information is manifested on three different levels:

- Theoretical level (social-anthropological discussion, educational and learning goals, etc.)
- Technical level (learning and teaching methods, communication methods, organizational models, etc.)
- Practical level (situative interaction, understanding of actions in education, etc.)

Research Proposals

With this background and description of sport pedagogy I will now discuss several propositions or theses about research in this field.

Thesis 1—Not all methods are usable for pedagogical problems.

Because the spectrum of pedagogy is so large and differentiated that generally all research methods are usable in it, I have to defend this thesis. Designs of inquiries with a high aspiration to exactness normally reduce the educational reality (or the ordinary praxis of lessons) and are therefore less useful in the field of pedagogy. Their results do not copy the life reality in education. Such data fail to enlighten the problems; they are only detailed results with a limited affirmation. Because of their delimitations and their often unattractive mechanisms of processing the data (look at some of the specific language of research papers), they cannot offer a deeper understanding of the pedagogic area.

Thesis 2—The focus of pedagogical research has to be the social interaction of man.

That means that the focal point of empirical research should be on the practice level, focusing on the problems of human relations. Much of the detailed research on the technical level underlines the flight of the researchers from the pedagogic reality. Where are the practical applications of the learning models, what utilization does the interesting information about the reinforcement of rats, doves, or geese have, when such results do not influence pedagogical actions and the human interaction in the classroom? If I see correctly, teachers need more information about solving human relations in the family, the school, and society. (In this context it might be interesting to ask, Is it possible to research such questions?)

Thesis 3—The German term *Handlungsrelevanz* is an important key word. It means that results of research must enhance the understanding of pedagogic situations.

This key word is in reality a "superterm," and most of the research can use it. Because many research results can be declared as so-called *handlungsrelevant*, it should be explained how to reach the *Handlungsrelevanz* in the pedagogic area. I would like to describe this through the term *verstehen* in Thesis 4.

Thesis 4—The important term *verstehen* in pedagogy means to understand the empathetic relations of the actors.

In the past the term has had a high value in German pedagogy (Dilthey) and psychology (*Ganzheitspsycholigie, Gestaltpsychologie*). When the empirical understanding of sciences became more and more important (especially in psychology) the term lost its relevance. It was (and is) seldom used. But in the meantime we have recognized that the results of the empirical analytical research are not so productive for pedagogical questions. Therefore I suggest that it is absolutely sensible, if not necessary, to give more attention to the term *verstehen* in the pedagogical discussion.

What is the meaning of *verstehen*? Which kind of awareness is that? One definition of the pedagogic dimension *verstehen* can be to integrate and to value adequately the experiences and findings. Instead of adapting hypotheses, theories, and constructs from outside to the pedagogic reality, it should be better to develop these from inside. That means realizing the real-life problems, and this requires primarily empathy to the problems, to the persons, and to the situations. *Verstehen* requires, on the one hand, a sensibility to the internal problems of the pedagogic subjects, an approach to these, and a ciphering of the real pedagogic complexity. On the other hand, it requires an act of cognitive and simultaneous creative interpretation of the fragmentary stocks of knowledge. And this, indeed, is a different process from the functional and isolated research of separate questions.

For example, it is not necessary to investigate all tints of color of a painting to learn something about the value or importance of this painting (although some are doing that). More important is to realize and understand the structures and constellations, and this means to imagine the internal relationships and contexts of the total work.

It is similar with pedagogic action. Indeed, it is necessary to have singular findings, but they are more disturbing if they cannot be integrated into the total context. Both must work together. This *verstehen* gives pedagogical research a qualitative dimension, and this is called *handlungsrelevant*.

Thesis 5—Research in sport pedagogy is restricted to the ethics of education.

The task of research in the area of education is not only to be involved in construction of theories, differentiation of methods, and quantification (with all criteria of objectivity, reliability, validity, norms, and economy), but research is also obligated to deal with the following:

- To behave within the educational reality
- To offer an effective contribution to a deeper understanding of the basic questions (such as goals, obligations, persons, interactions, environment, political situations, etc.) and to highlight these questions
- To accept the moral horizon of education (goals, values, historical meanings, etc.)
- To accept that pedagogical research is not independent of influences; it is not a neutral field.

Indeed, this makes researching in pedagogy very difficult.

Thesis 6—The qualitative aspect of research in sport pedagogy must focus on the question of anthropological, cultural, and historical realities. The results of the research must enlighten and inform the perception of these realities.

Education and educational research that are not based on philosophical and anthropological principles are only busywork. A responsible pedagogic research has to describe the human picture to which education has to lead; this makes necessary historical, anthropological, and cultural considerations and reflections.

Thesis 7—The research methods must be in line with the perception of the studied phenomena. Appropriate methods for studying sport pedagogy would include interview, narrative analysis, and case study.

Each of these merits its own paper. Here, however, only a few points can be made. Often, by reason of a scientific reputation, the empirical analytical research methods are favored in the field of pedagogy. But mostly the measured data do not correspond to the pedagogic subjects. Methods that do not break the complexity of pedagogic subjects are more suitable for the *verstehen*, even if the research methodology might not always be highly objective and precise.

Thesis 8—Sport is susceptible to technical understanding because sport performance is easily measured through technical facts. These facts have become the main goal of education at the expense of other important goals such as human relations, well-being, health, aesthetics, and so forth.

Indeed, the main problem of research in sport has been to increase the motor abilities. From my perspective, it is desirable that the goal of our efforts be to improve quality of movement, interpersonal relationships, and well-being in human life.

The need to increase sport abilities and achievements of athletes has been emphasized by pressure groups and lobbyists outside the pedagogical area. The contribution of sport pedagogy must focus on the totality (*Ganzheit*) of humans. That is an educational process and not a technical procedure. Movement engineers need information; movement educators need to understand the whole situation of an acting person. In that aspect the pedagogical research should support our educators.

References

Heinemann, K. (1985). Entwicklungsbedingungen der Sportwissenschaft [Conditions of development of sport science]. *Sportwissenschaft*, 1, 33–36.

Kirsch, A., & Preising, W. (1985). Interdisziplinare Forschung als Problem der Wissenschafts-Organisation [Interdisciplinary research as a problem of science organization]. *Sportwissenschaft*, 1, 46–50.

Analysis of Games and Sports in Cultural Contexts and Its Significance for Physical Education

Wolf-Dietrich Brettschneider

In the contemporary debate on play, games, and sport, certain contributions both in the German as well as in the American literature argue that games from other cultures should be integrated into our world of games. From the perspective of a "search for lost nature" they recommend above all an orientation toward the so-called primitive societies. This is frequently justified on the basis of a model presenting a linear development with the following phases (Bausinger, 1983):

> Phase 1: Paradise. Cooperative games without competition or winners. Isolated ethnological remains from "primitive" societies serve as evidence for the assumption of a perfect games-world.

> Phase 2: Paradise lost. A peaceful social life is persistently disturbed in the industrial society. Success, competition, rivalry, and records dominate the pattern of games.

> Phase 3: Paradise regained. Postindustrial society with a changed value system and a different set of norms. New and cooperative forms characterize the world of games, in which there is no place for competition and gain. (p. 47)

Such a model is questionable for a number of reasons. The utopian world of perfect games does not bear up to historical scrutiny. The model, rather, is the result of an ideological idealization of games. Above all, it does not take account of the interrelatedness of games with other cultural forms of thought and action and also with the given natural environment. It implies that games are arbitrarily interchangeable across historical periods and cultural frontiers. In the process the cultural relativity of the games is lost sight of. The completely legitimate aim of relativizing one's own world of games and of developing new and complementary perspectives cannot be based on such a model.

My aim is to reveal the interrelatedness between culture and game, in other words, to represent games as elements of cultural configurations. From this point of view the consequences of games and sport may be presented from an educational perspective. I attempt to do this in three steps:

1. Analyze in the first section medieval games in central Europe as well as traditional Inuit and Indian games from cultural-historical and cultural-anthropological perspectives.
2. Apply the chosen configurational approach to the contemporary situation in our society. The aim is to demonstrate that also today the deep structures of our culture are reflected in games and sport.
3. Constructively apply the consequences of this analysis, in particular those relevant to physical education.

Games as Elements of Cultural Configurations: Traditional Games

It is relatively simple to demonstrate that medieval folk games in Europe bear little resemblance to the idyllic pastorals suggested, for example, in the paintings of Breughel or other Flemish masters. Rather, they were characterized, to mention superordinate features, by robust physicality and strength and an associated tendency toward excess. Games were often rituals, though by no means monotonous, because the pattern of the game was strongly influenced by natural and social differences. The games were firmly embedded in customs or even in religious feasts. They were not excluded from the normal circle of social life. Numerous examples of this can be found in Bausinger (1983) and Dunning (1973), among others. The games were characterized by features that from our modern point of view seem to be barbaric and uncivilized. Experiencing, causing, or witnessing pain must have constituted one of the main sources of enjoyment for those who took part in them. Examples of this behavior include the ritual beatings of fools, cruelty toward the blind, bull and bear baiting, and the social spectacle of burning witches.

The interrelationship of games and culture suggested by the preceding example is demonstrated on the basis of an intercultural investigation. The traditional games of the natives of modern Canada are examined in their respective cultural contexts on the basis of 19th-century ethnographic data. Included are the games of three closely neighboring populations, namely the Inuit, the Kwakiutl, and the Cree. The analysis takes place within the grid of relationships between natural environment, social form of organization, and economic conditions.

Without going into detail, it can be said that the three populations under investigation live by hunting. However, the common ground between them ends there. As far as geographical and climatic conditions are concerned, in part extreme differences exist, as can be clearly seen from the arctic, northwest coast, and prairie territories where they live. These differences are reflected in the social organization. The arctic environment forces the Inuit to live a nomadic existence. They survive by fishing and by hunting seals, whales, and reindeer. Products of this nomadic existence are igloos, sledges, and kayaks, as well as the social organization of families or smaller local groups based on family relationships. Larger groups are only formed for the purposes of hunting and the ritual activities associated with this.

The Kwakiutl, too, on the whole, live from fishing in the coastal waters. The wealth of this stretch of coast ensured the development of settlements and of institutions based on affluence, status, and prestige. The social phenomenon of the chiefs came into being, involving a complex political organization in which each individual from the chief to the common people had his place within the hierarchy. Social status and its associated prestige is revealed above all in the Potlatch ceremony, the principal aim of which is to demonstrate one's own material wealth and to humiliate others.

The Cree could count as the prototype of native prairie culture, the main feature of which is the horse, which reached the North originally from Mexico. It made possible the bison hunt, which ensured an abundance of food and wealth. The social order of these natives is governed by the yearly cycle of the bison, which were scattered across the wide land but which moved across the prairies in huge herds in summer during the breeding period. The lifestyle of the natives was accordingly nomadic; they lived in small tribal groups except for the purposes of hunting, coming together to form so-called mixed tribes whose homogeneity was determined mainly by ritual and quasimilitary activities.

Structural comparison of the games in terms of similarities and differences reveals features that show parallels to other elements of the cultural system. By concentrating on categories such as the apparatus, time and space, participant constellation, and motor demands of games one can establish that Inuit games involve mainly one or two participants and a minimum of apparatus and space. They are brief and usually take place in the core family. Their aim is mainly for the individual to test him- or herself, and they are characterized by strength of will, physical strength, stamina, and dexterity (Ager, 1977; Glassford, 1976, 1981; Zuk, 1970).

The Kwakiutl games are richer in material, make more use of space, last longer, and generally involve several participants. They are more concerned with dexterity and strategy than with physical and mental strength (Boas, 1966; Johns, 1972).

In the case of the Cree it is of central importance that, apart from numerous games that require precision and dexterity, highly varied ball games have been described, such as shinny, double-ball, and lacrosse. The dimensions of the playing fields are larger, but flexible, as is the case for the number of participants and the duration of the games. Reports exist of games with hundreds of participants that lasted several days (Catlin, 1903; Culin, 1907/1975; Mandelbaum, 1979).

These features, however, concern the surface structure of the games and say little about *how* the games were played or *what* cultural significance they had. It seems as if the Inuit games were more concerned with the individual's testing his or her own capacities. Defeat or victory do not appear to have played much of a role, possibly because self-validation was not required within the family itself. The Kwakiutl games may signify the pervasive competitive spirit of this tribe. Here victory and defeat play a major role. The large number of participants in the Crees' ball games suggests that these also had an organizational function related to the mixture of tribes and acted as an intelligent mechanism for the establishment of social homogeneity and group solidarity, which the mere parallel existence of the tribes did not offer.

As far as the relationship between ecological and cultural factors, on the one hand, and specific games, on the other, is concerned, it can be said that the structure of the games cannot be explained solely by reference to single factors—neither by the physical environment nor by specific cultural elements. The games are firmly embedded in the relational network of environment, social organization, and economic conditions. They reflect social structures and cultural behavior patterns in the same way that these are reflected by the relationship of the people to their environment. The games can only be explained from the viewpoint of this configurational interrelatedness with the culture—not as isolated phenomena but in its entirety (Eichberg, 1982, 1983).

Even though such conclusions may seem plausible, there are two reasons why I would nevertheless like to demonstrate the configurational connection between games and cultural context on the basis of a further concrete example:

- Reservations about the reported studies, as well as those of Roberts, Arth, and Bush (1959) and Sutton-Smith (1978), are justified from the ethnographic point of view.
- So far, culture has been understood as a mechanism of adaptation, by means of which ethnic groups have guaranteed their survival. The aim of the next example is thus to demonstrate that culture is to be seen as a system of thought defining a framework of orientation for human action.

Different Configuration:
Western Culture and Competitive Sports

Taking certain ideas of Galtung (1982) as a starting point, I would like to establish a relationship between modern games and sport and what might be called "Eurocentric culture" or "Western culture." In other words, games and sport can be interpreted as vehicles of a specific deep structure and culture.[1] The thesis here is that a large proportion of sport in its present structure can be interpreted as an expression of central features of Western culture, particularly the orientation of the latter toward competition, the aim of which is to establish an order of rank for individuals as well as for teams (see Rees, 1985).

To demonstrate this, an analytical framework is used consisting of five concepts that are to be treated as a configurational whole (Galtung, 1982):

- *The conception of space.* The West conceives of space in terms of center-periphery, with the West in the center, seen as the source of what matters. Most of the sports that exist across the world originated in Europe, mainly in Greece and England. The multiplicity of other forms of sport, from African dances and various Asian forms of sport and games to noncompetitive forms of sport, in contrast, plays only a subordinate role.
- *The conception of time.* In Europe or the West time is conceived of as something dramatic: beginning, progression, crisis, catharsis, downfall. Above all, concepts such as "to save time" and "Time is money" can be seen as guiding principles of the industrial society. This concept can be recognized also in sport and in institutionalized games. Everything is focused on the competitive event—Heaven or Hell, win or fail.
- *The conception of knowledge* (epistemology). Western knowledge results from individual, measurable dimensions rather than from the perspectives of holism. Precisely this pattern is reflected in sport. Achievement is mainly operationalized in the dimensions of time, distance, and weight. Spiritual, aesthetic, or ethical factors are less important. Competitive sport is above all c-g-s sport: Everything is measured according to centimeters, grams, and seconds. A hierarchy is established even among comparable achievements. Even such sports in which the result is determined by the relationship between individuals or teams are concerned ultimately with ranking.
- *The conception of the relationship to nature.* The relationship of humans to nature in Western culture can be characterized as one of dominance and control rather than one of partnership. This position is reflected in modern sport, principally in the attempt to eliminate natural possibilities of variation in sports and games by the use of increasingly artificial spacial conditions and to control the factors conditioning the sport or game.
- *The conception of interpersonal relationships.* These relationships can be characterized above all by two distinctive features that can also be combined, namely, the vertical and the individual. These are the properties that determine the nature of competition. The more complex the society, the richer the hierarchy in its social system. Society makes the defeat of others legitimate, and this is reflected in sport.

This necessarily simplified presentation is meant neither as an argument for cultural pessimism nor as an attack on competitive sport—my respect for individual and collective cultural achievement is too great for that. My basic point is that the dimensions stated above, including their reflection in sport, constitute a configuration. This configuration expresses a central feature of Western culture, namely, a stronger orientation toward competition than toward cooperation.

The preceding image of sport can be taken as the established one. However, there is increasing evidence of a rejection of this inherited form of games and sport in favor of new, alternative forms that deviate from the deep structure and culture of Western civilization. I refer here to the development in Germany. However, there are clear indications that this movement is taking place at the very least across Europe and the North American continent.

Meditative physical techniques of non-European origin, such as Yoga, Tantra, or Zen exercises, are becoming increasingly popular, as are the East-Asian martial arts such as karate, kung fu, and Tae Kwon Do. Modern dance is characterized by elements taken from the Afro-American form (Eichberg, 1982). In addition to this, new currents constantly appear; it is impossible to say, initially, whether they will be short-lived fashions or long-term phenomena. To this category belong, for example, jogging, aerobics, bodybuilding, and the varied forms of new games in which the emphasis is in cooperation, improving oneself but not at the expense of others, mutual help instead of interpersonal competition, and having fun instead of winning. The reasons for such expansive and dynamic movements, which lead to such a diffuse image of movement, sport, and games, are complex and in part contradictory (Rittner, 1983). A basic supposition would be that this area of sports and games-culture also reflects social changes, which find expression in those oft-quoted, handy formulae coined in the transition from the values of the industrial society to those of postmaterialism: competition/cooperation, economic/ ecological, achievement/need, efficiency/participation, hierarchy/ humanization, and technical perfection/creativity.

This impressionistic and generalized presentation of the established image of sport and games and its structural transformation demonstrates again the configurational relationship between sport and games and culture. The more complex the society is, the richer is its cultural scene; the more contradictory the situations experienced by individuals, the more they orientate themselves toward alternative values and the more flexible are their "politics of identity." This is a process that sociologists observe in many areas of daily life and that, with reference to sport, can be incorporated without difficulty in Csikszentmihalyi's (1975) "flow-experience hypothesis."

Consequences for Physical Education

The question now arises of what the relationships that have been described between games and sport and culture mean for the field of physical education. Note, first of all, that sport in school does not take place in isolation from cultural reality. Rather, it is tied to the social forms of the culture. Resulting from this, the central task of physical education is to analyze games and sport as cultural variables from the perspective of their future relevance and the value of their transmission. How this can be realized in the concrete sports lesson will be made clear in the following four points (Mollenhauer, 1983):

- Physical education is always—and can never be anything other than—an encounter with everyday reality, a *presentation* of what children and adolescents experience in the field of sport and games as part of their world. At the same time, however, it is a transmission of what the adults find important; in their rules those games and sports reflect the cultural norms that are relevant in the contemporary world.
- The more complex the social world becomes, and the greater the differences between the individual biographies of young people, the less the worlds of sport will contain all that children need for their future lives. Then the second task of physical education becomes more important, namely, to make accessible to the young people those elements of games and sport-culture that so far have been outside their experience. In this way, the second task of physical education is the *representation* of sport and games forms.
- The fact that we are concerned with the connection between culture and physical education entails the presupposition that young people are educable. *Educability*, however, can only be discovered in active behavior. To this extent, physical education entails the arrangement of situations aimed at reducing the complex reality of games and sport and at presenting these as a field of different units of significance (for example, health, communication, vertigo, competition, cooperation, risk, and relaxation), for which independent action is required.
- In this way elements can be discovered that enable a structure to be developed that is concerned with the field of sport and games and that today is often discussed under the heading of "identity."

Awareness of the relationship between games and culture requires becoming aware again of relationships that have been forgotten. The educational problem in the dialectic of preservation or improvement is not solved by this. However, a greater awareness of these relationships could contribute to a more differentiated understanding of the contemporary reality of sports and games (and, as a result of this, of our whole culture), to more appropriate explanations, and to a more responsible approach to making changes.

Note

1. These ideas of Galtung have been adopted by Roger Rees in a recent issue of *Quest* (see References).

References

Ager, L.P. (1977). The reflection of cultural values in Eskimo children's games. In D.F. Lancy & B.A. Tindall (Eds.), *The study of play: Problems and prospects* (pp. 92–98). Champaign, IL: Leisure Press.

Bausinger, H. (1983). Spiel unter Dummen. Anmerkungen zur Kulturgeschichte von Spiel und Sport [Play among fools. Observations on the cultural history of play and sport]. In O. Grupe, H. Gabler, & U. Göhner (Eds.), *Spiel, Spiele, Spielen*. Schorndorf: Hofmann.

Boas, F. (1966). *Kwakiutl ethnography* (H. Codere, Ed.). Chicago: The University of Chicago Press.

Catlin, G. (1903). *North American Indians* (Vol. 2). Edinburgh: John Grant.

Csikszentmihalyi, M. (1975). *Beyond boredom and anxiety*. San Francisco: Jossey-Bass.

Culin, S. (1975). *Games of the North American Indians*. New York: Dover. (Original work published in 1907)

Dunning, E. (1973). The structural-functional properties of folk-games and modern sports: A sociological analysis. *Sportwissenschaft*, 3(3), 215–232.

Eichberg, H. (1982). Die Kulturrelativität des Spiels. Ansätze ethnologischer Spielforschung [The cultural relativity of games. Assessments of ethnological play research]. *Jahrbuch Deutsch als Fremdsprache* (8).

Eichberg, H. (1983). Einheit oder Vielfalt am Ball? [Unity or multiplicity at the ball?] In O. Grupe, H. Gabler, & U. Göhner (Eds.), *Spiel, Spiele, Spielen*. Schorndorf: Hofmann.

Galtung, J. (1982). Sport as carrier of deep culture and structure. *Current Research on Peace and Violence*, 5(2–3), 133–143.

Glassford, R.G. (1976). *Application of a theory of games to the transitional Eskimo culture*. New York: Arno Press.

Glassford, R.G. (1981). The life and the games of the traditional Canadian Eskimo. In G. Lüschen & G. Sage (Eds.), *Handbook of social science of sport*. Champaign, IL: Stipes.

Johns, D.P. (1972). *The role of play activities among the Kwakiutl Indian*. Unpublished master's thesis, University of Alberta, Edmonton.

Mandelbaum, D.G. (1979). *The plains Cree: An ethnographic, historical and comparative study* (No. 9). Regina: Canadian Plains Studies.

Mollenhauer, K. (1983). *Vergessene Zusammenhänge. Über Kultur und Erziehung* [Forgotten coherence. On culture and education]. München: Juventa.

Rees, C.R. (1985). The Olympic dilemma: Applying the contact theory and beyond. *Quest*, **37**, 50–59.

Rittner, V. (1983). Strukturwandlungen des Sports in der modernen Gesellschaft [Structural transformations of sports in modern society]. *Olympische Jugen,* **28**(11), 4–7.

Roberts, J.M., Arth, M.J., & Bush, R.R. (1959). Games in culture. *American Anthropologist,* **61**(4), 597–605.

Sutton-Smith, B. (1978). *Die Dialektik des Spiels* [The dialectic of games]. Schorndorf: Hofmann.

Zuk, W.M. (1970). *Eskimo games of the western Arctic.* Edmonton: Boreal Institute of Northern Studies.

Where Technology and Accountability Converge: The Confessions of an Educational Technologist

Andrew H. Hawkins
Robert L. Wiegand

The second half of the 20th century will very likely be characterized as an age of technological revolution. Whereas the effects of technological change on traditionally scientific, technical, and industrial fields have been well chronicled, the effects on education in general, and on teacher education in particular, have registered more slowly. Indeed, only the most sensitively perceptive observer would be able to detect any technologically generated differences between the teacher education programs of the 1980s and their counterparts of, say, the 1920s.

Among the areas of rather profound technological advancement that could have obvious potential applications in teacher education are the measurement of educationally related variables (usually behavior) and the control of behavior through environmental contingencies. That a more sophisticated understanding of the variables that affect teaching and learning should enable more efficient and effective pedagogical training is self-evident. The argument that teacher educators should apply the principles emerging from the science of behavior to influence the quality of teaching is more than compelling. It approximates a moral imperative.

During the past 4 years we have experimented with relatively sophisticated measurement technologies for didactic, evaluative, and research purposes. Further, we have employed our measurement system as one basis for the accountability systems in the pedagogy portion of our program. Unfortunately, the adoption of technologically progressive practices is not without its problems. We perceive the problems as falling into two classifications: empirical and ethical. The primary questions arising from these classifications may be stated as (a) *Can* we technologically do what we think we can do? (empirical), and (b) *Should* we do all that we are technologically capable of doing? (ethical). The purpose of this paper is to explore answers to these questions.

We begin by providing a cursory historical overview of the major technological trends that have influenced our adoption of technologically progressive strategies. Next, we describe the strategies that we have adopted. Finally, we consider the empirical and ethical questions through an analysis of some of our own data and a discussion of the major philosophical trends that currently underlie ethical decision making.

Technological Trends

The notion that behavior can (a) be measured and (b) be controlled through environmental contingencies (including performance/grade exchanges) has its roots, of course, in experimental psychology. Measurement technology in those early days of infrahuman subject research usually was not problematic. Most of the behaviors analyzed were selected due to their ability to generate mechanically a permanent product of responding (as in key pecks and bar presses resulting in cumulative frequency recordings on a kymograph). Thus, behaviors in such research were selected more for measurement convenience than for adaptive significance. Nonetheless, the rudiments of a science of behavior began to emerge from such research.

The quality and sophistication of measurement systems became more problematic as less convenient behaviors became the foci of investigations. Experimental psychologists began to study behaviors in infrahuman subjects that had considerable adaptive significance. The field of applied behavior analysis was born, focusing on socially important behaviors of, usually, retarded or seriously developmentally disabled human subjects. Such behaviors often proved impossible to transduce mechanically on a recording device, and the employment of human observers was necessitated.

Still, significant breakthroughs in measurement technology were not necessary because the behaviors of interest, both of infrahuman subjects and of the severely developmentally disabled, tended to be rather simple. Paper-and-pencil recording regimens were reliably utilized by human observers during this period, and questions of validity were rarely raised. One could accurately say, "I'm measuring what I'm measuring—out of seat is out of seat." Principles of behavior continued to emerge and the rudiments of a *technology* of behavior began to appear.

It was inevitable that the field of applied behavior analysis would extend into more mainstream applications. The human subjects employed in research have become more normal, and the behaviors of interest have become not merely socially significant, but culturally important. Behavior analysts are now less interested in "out of seat" behavior and more interested in such complicated educational problems as those chronicled in *A Nation at Risk* (Sulzer-Azaroff, 1985). The result has been the recent conception of the multifaceted field of behavioral assessment.

It is at this point that technological advancements in measurement are so desperately needed. Behaviors are no longer the subject of inquiry. Rather, complex response classes comprised of numerous and presumably functionally related behaviors provide the units of analysis. No longer can the simplistic paper and pencil coding systems provide grist for the mill.

Fortunately, the microchip revolution is upon us (Metzler, Burton, Magliaro, & Hawkins, 1985; Metzler & Reif, 1985). Microcomputers and microprocessors are not needed merely to more efficiently collect and manage the same kinds of simple paper and pencil data we've been collecting, though that is certainly an advantage. They are necessary to produce a richer, more complex understanding of the naturalistic setting.

In a sense, the highly productive field of applied behavior analysis, riding high on the wave of the optimistic humanism of the 1960s, has hit the beach. This is no great tragedy for behavior analysts—just time to start swimming again and look for another wave. Don't misunderstand the point: Behavior analysis has been highly productive, its principles very effective, and its technology socially useful—as far as it goes.

Even B.F. Skinner, I believe, foresaw this particular crossroad. As early as his *Verbal Behavior* (1957) he alluded to higher order human behaviors that were not controlled by their consequences but by an individual's ability both to generate and to be affected by descriptions of contingencies. The term "rule governed behavior" was coined in his *Contingencies of Reinforcement* (1969) to represent this phenomenon (Michael, 1985). The notion of rule governed behavior is receiving considerable attention today in psychology, not because we know a lot about it, but because we don't. At this writing many use the term "rule governed behavior" as a label to describe behaviors the origins of which are not well understood. In such cases it falls into the category of an explanatory fiction (a presumed cause, which is another name for the effect).

The point is that, in spite of the productive nature of applied behavior analysis, there is much that we don't know about the determinants of more complex forms of human behavior. Furthermore, it is likely that these more complex forms of behavior are the very kind we are supposed to be developing in our teacher education programs. Thus, the need is apparent for more sophisticated measurement technologies employed in teacher education programs to discover how we can more effectively enhance the behaviors of prospective teachers and their students. This brings us to a description of our nascent attempts at employing such technologies in our teacher education program.

Technological Applications in Teacher Education

Students of physical education take a series of four courses that entail field-based training: (a) Instructional Systems, (b) Generic Teaching Skills, (c) Special Physical Education, and (d) Student Teaching. It is in these courses that technology applications have been implemented. The first application, the measurement system, includes a comprehensive, mutually exclusive teacher behavior category system with 11 response classes and another comprehensive, mutually exclusive student behavior category system comprised of the 8 learner-involvement response classes in the ALT-PE system (Siedentop, Tousignant, & Parker, 1982).

The primary technological innovation employed is the collection of data on an electronic microprocessor. These instruments allow the collection of both frequency and duration data in real time (rather than modified frequencies as in interval recording), thus producing an ostensibly more accurate representation of actual behavior. The microprocessors also provide a richer data display because numerous dimensions are assessed for multiple-response classes and response class sequences.

Students are evaluated using this system approximately 12 times throughout their pedagogical training, usually over a 3-year period. In the four courses observations take place in microteaching settings, field experiences, peer teaching sessions, on-campus clinics, and in elementary and secondary student teaching placements.

The second technological application involves the use of the measurement system as a basis for the performance/grade exchange in the courses. Usually first in the sequence, it is in the instructional systems course that the measurement system is introduced. Students are taught the system from a didactic standpoint, evaluated in their practica, but not held accountable for any data-based performance results. Generic teaching skills, the second in the sequence, provides a highly structured peer teaching experience with a formal accountability system. Twenty percent of the grade in that class is based on the data-based performance as determined by the measurement system. A formal accountability system is also employed in the special populations class, again with a substantial percentage of the grade based on data-based performance. In student teaching the data-based analysis provides the basis of the supervisor's written descriptive evaluation. However, because student teaching employs a pass/fail scheme the accountability system is best described as informal.

The Empirical Question

With an elementary understanding of the measurement and accountability applications in our program it is now possible to consider the empirical question: Can we technologically do what we think we can do? Stated with more relevance to our program applications, the question may be phrased, Do performance/grade exchange accountability systems based on a complex measurement system influence the teaching performance of trainees?

In order to begin to answer this question we have analyzed graphically the teaching performance of most of the program's graduates during the past 3 years. The graphical analyses were displayed primarily across accountability conditions (i.e., across courses). Unfortunately for the integrity of our program, but fortunately for our research agenda, students don't always take the courses in the advised order. This resulted in a variety of single-subject designs that at times resembled reversals, at other times alternating treatments, and at still others complex combinations of the two.

The number of observations may leave something to be desired because sometimes as few as two or three observations per condition appear. Thus the affirmation of any substantive consequents must remain tentative. On the other hand, with the collection of teaching performance data over such a long period of time, across so many varied conditions, with so many teacher trainees, we therefore believe we are at least entitled to some clues.

Subject DM (Frame 1 of Figure 1) produced a fairly prototypic response pattern, indicating the potency of accountability systems. Those courses that involved clear performance/grade exchanges seemed to produce higher levels of motor appropriate patterns (the most common focus of

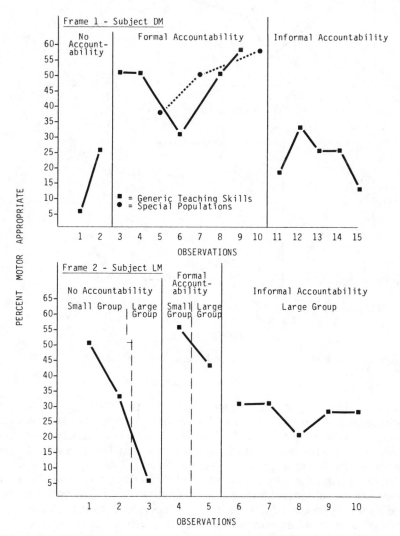

Figure 1 Possible effects of accountability system and class size: Subjects DM and LM.

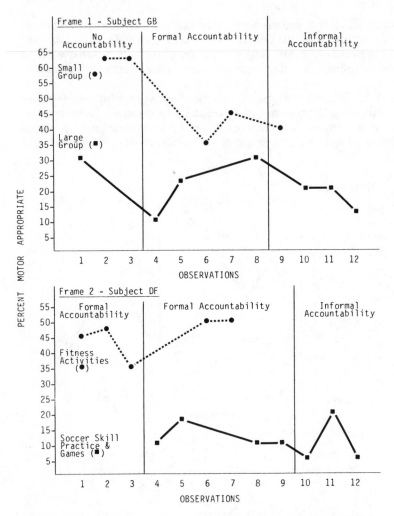

Figure 2 Possible effects of class size and activity: Subjects GB and DF.

accountability systems). Class size and the type of activity don't seem to influence these data. Subject LM (Frame 2 of Figure 1), however, produced a different pattern. At first glance the accountability conditions seem to control the performance, but closer examination reveals that class size may also be influential. Subject GB (Frame 1 of Figure 2) departed even more from the typical pattern, and the activity and class size seem to have more influence than the accountability systems. Subject DF (Frame 2 of Figure 2) produced a more activity-dependent response pattern, in spite of accountability conditions; only two activity types were taught across three accountability conditions.

There is much more that could be said about these graphs, and other alternative syllogisms could be considered. It is sufficient at this point to conclude that whereas accountability systems seem to be controlling some trainee performances, other influences, like activity and class size, may have an even more potent effect for others. The message for our teacher educators is twofold: (a) We need to be flexible and sensitive about how our accountability systems are applied, and (b) we need to examine the didactic portions of our training program to discover why increased class size and certain activities seem to cause performance decrements for some.

The Ethical Question

It is clear from our own data and from the current status of behavior analysis that behavior control technology is not yet sophisticated enough to substantially control the more complex response classes of human subjects. But what if it were? The question would then become, Should we do what we are capable of doing? It would be relatively easy to remain on the level of particulars in attempting to answer this question. We could debate which physical education ends would justify which technological means and attempt to come to some consensus. However, if our profession desires to play a significant role in the culture, then the larger question of the effects of technology must be seriously considered.

It is our contention that the question of the effects of technology have not so much to do with the technological revolution as with the philosophical frame of reference of the 20th century. How one views the world has much to do with how one views technology.

During the last 100 years, first in the Northern European culture and then in North America, a basic shift from the absolute Judeo-Christian view of moral and ethical values to the relativistic values of humanism (in its many forms) can be detected. In other words, 100 years ago, even though perhaps a majority of the populations were not individually Jewish or Christian, the values that permeated the culture, including education, law, and government, were based on Judeo-Christian principles. Today, the shift is complete—"man" is indeed the measure of all things.

While hailed originally by the early optimistic humanists as tremendously liberating, this shift is having a devastating impact on any humane view of the relationship between technology and society. If "man is the measure of all things," then justice is "the majority vote of that nation that could lick all the others" (Holmes, 1918, p. 40). Thus, technological power becomes God (Ellul, 1954/1964), and the liberating humanist revolution is another name for idolatry. This is true whether the technology involves nuclear weapons, terrorist tactics, or even behavioral control. In such an intellectual climate science ceases to be the basic process for the discovery of truth and degenerates into the means for the development of technological power.

Humanism, oddly enough, provides an ultimately inadequate basis for a humane view of technology. The limits of technology are thus determined by whatever individual or group controls it. Indeed, the optimistic humanism of the 1960s has given way to the pessimistic humanism of the 1970s and 1980s (Brown, 1966; Calder, 1970; Russell, 1962; Taylor, 1970; Teilhard de Chardin, 1964), and the death of absolutes may indeed have inaugurated the degeneration of the culture (Nietzche, 1892/1978).

Highly technological approaches to physical education are thus vestiges of a dying optimistic humanism. While concentrating on means we have lost sight of ends, both professionally and culturally. We must know who we are and where we are going, even if we are physical educators. This notion was poignantly expressed by Lewis Carroll in his philosophical treatise, *Alice in Wonderland*. Alice approaches a fork in the road, and uncertain about which way to go, peers heavenward as if to receive some divine guidance. Unfortunately, she finds only the smiling Cheshire Cat. She asks the cat which way she ought to go. "That depends . . . on where you want to get to," replies the Cat. "I don't much care where," says Alice. The cat very perceptively sums it all up: "Then it doesn't matter which way you go" (Carroll, 1966, p. 59).

Thus, as the technological revolution approaches us (finally), let us not be characterized by sloppy thinking (or no thinking at all) on these issues. Rather, let us carefully consider the empirical and ethical limits of technology founded in a clear understanding of who we are. Otherwise, it won't matter which way we go.

References

Brown, N.O. (1966). *Life against death*. Middletown, CT: Wesleyan University Press.

Calder, N. (1970). *Technopolis: Social control of the uses of science*. New York: Simon and Schuster.

Carroll, L. (1966). *Alice's adventures in wonderland and through the looking glass*. New York: Macmillan.

Ellul, J. (1964). *The technological society* (J. Wilkinson, Trans.). New York: Knopf. (Original work published 1954)

Holmes, O.W. (1918). Natural law. *Harvard Law Review, 32*, 40–44.

Metzler, M., Burton, J., Magliaro, S., & Hawkins, A. (1985, May). *Designing microcomputer programs for data collection, analysis, and storage*. Workshop conducted at the Association for Behavior Analysis Annual Meeting, Columbus, OH.

Metzler, M., & Reif, G. (1985, August). *Microcomputers for research in physical education*. Workshop conducted at the Association Internationale des Ecoles Supérieures d'Education Physique Annual Meeting, Garden City, NY.

Michael, J. (1985). Behavior analysis: A radical perspective. In B.L. Hammonds & C.J. Scheirer (Eds.), *Psychology and learning* (Master lecture series, Vol. 4). Washington, DC: American Psychological Association.

Nietzche, F.W. (1978). *Thus spake Zarathustra* (W. Kaufman, Trans.). New York: Penguin Books. (Original work published 1892)

Russell, B. (1962). *Has man a future?* New York: Simon and Schuster.

Siedentop, D., Tousignant, M., & Parker, M. (1982). *Academic learning time —Physical education: Coding manual.* Columbus: School of Health, Physical Education, and Recreation, Ohio State University.

Skinner, B.F. (1957). *Verbal behavior.* New York: Appleton-Century-Crofts.

Skinner, B.F. (1969). *Contingencies of reinforcement.* New York: Appleton-Century-Crofts.

Sulzer-Azaroff, B. (1985). A behaviorist's response to the Report of the National Commission on Excellence in Education. *The Behavior Analyst, 8,* 29–38.

Taylor, G.R. (1970). *The doomsday book.* New York: World Publishing.

Teilhard de Chardin, P. (1964). *The future of man* (N. Denney, Trans.). New York: Harper and Row.

PART II

Models

The papers included in this section are reports representative of models for future direction and action.

Daryl Siedentop's paper integrates curriculum and instruction. Through his sport education model, Siedentop follows an extension of play education. His model integrates the excitement and context of sport into the physical education class. Analysis of play and sport culture, including the psychosocial impact, is essential. Similarly, Ann Jewett's paper integrates curriculum and instruction, whereby she provides a model for program evaluation and development based on analysis of participant purposes and motives. Ree Arnold, on the other hand, promotes a model for learning that combines motor learning and teaching analysis theory, as well as begs the question of the value of research on teaching without pursuing the question relative to student learning. She indicates that the appropriate model for teaching is consideration of the learning process. Graham Fishburne utilizes a motor-learning model by investigating the role of imagery. Richard Tinning presents views on teacher preparation for the purpose of moving teachers beyond the utilitarian and toward a critical-reflective perspective. His model of teachers as researchers refutes the notion that simply by knowing how to increase learning time one will learn more. He notes that we have tended to embrace a technical-scientific model that promotes simple solutions to a complex problem. In support of the complex problem and in pursuit of grass roots research and program development, William Anderson describes his experiences in the implementation of a public-school teaching center.

As additional reinforcement of the complexity of the teaching act and cross-disciplinary research, Udo Hanke, Bart Crum, and Michael Sherman present concepts relative to student/teacher interaction and cognition. Hanke notes that past research to a great extent has been "teacher-centered," with students being considered only as the passive, recipient element of teacher behavior. The students' perceptions, intentions, and evaluations seldom have been the focus of analysis. He further notes that, when conducting research on teaching, one must consider the socio-psychological perspective as well, including perceptions, thoughts, aims, and emotions of the interacting partner. Crum presents an interesting analysis on program effectiveness when considering the relationship between the teacher's perception of physical education and student learning. Sherman's paper shows that a major difference in planning between experienced and inexperienced teachers is familiarity and knowledge about the students being taught, that is, the student/teacher interaction from past experience.

The importance placed on the student as a social interacting person with the teacher, peers, and self is further reinforced in Kathryn Kisabeth's and Pauli Vuolle's papers. Kisabeth concludes that the development of self-confidence may be as crucial for continued participation as the development of competence in movement programs. Vuolle synthesizes the results of several studies to ascertain the significance of and fluctuations in social motives associated with physical recreation in the life cycle.

In all the papers in this section, the investigators reinforce the necessity for a closer view and understanding of the interaction between teacher, student, and peers. Also, each reinforces the complexity of the teaching act and the notion that teaching and program development are more than counting ALT (academic learning time) or the number of times positive reinforcement is given. Thus, each in his or her own way suggests that the future models call for more cross-disciplinary study, education, and research.

The Theory and Practice of Sport Education

Daryl Siedentop

The purpose of this paper is to describe and explain briefly a curriculum and instruction model, the primary objective of which is to help students become competent, literate, and enthusiastic sport participants and consumers. By competent, I mean that students acquire skill, learn to understand and be able to execute strategy, and become more knowledgeable gamesplayers. By literate, I mean that students learn to understand and to value the many roles, rituals, and traditions in sport and learn to discriminate between good and bad sport practices. By enthusiastic, I mean that students learn to want to participate in sport, that is, they acquire approach tendencies toward sport, and they behave toward sport in ways that serve to preserve, protect, and enhance the sport culture.

I do not have time to articulate fully the theory underlying sport education and to describe in detail what sport education looks like when put into practice. What I have chosen to do is to sketch briefly the background of sport education and then to describe it using soccer in the fifth and sixth grades in an American elementary school physical education program as an example.

I began to outline the theoretical and practical implications of sport education in my keynote address to the physical education section of the Commonwealth Games Conference in Brisbane in 1982. Since that time, the model has been more fully developed, tested in schools, revised somewhat, and extended. It is now a model that I believe to be informed by theory, research, and practice.

The Background of the Model

There are two interests in my own professional work that coalesced several years ago to form the foundation for sport education as a curriculum and instruction model. As some of you know, I have had an abiding interest in play and play theory. My own doctoral work, in fact, was a curriculum model in which the subject matter of physical education was defined as a species of play. In 1972, much of that work was included in the first edition of my work *Physical Education: Introductory Analysis*, the later chapters of which define and explain what has come to be described as the "play education" curriculum model.

Drawing heavily on the work of Johann Huizinga and the French sociologist Roger Caillois, I defined physical education as any process that increases human abilities to play competitive and expressive motor activities. I argued that play is the proper classification for physical education in that it places physical education (sport and dance) alongside music, art, and drama as the primary institutional forms of play.

I believe now, as I did then, that what we do in physical education is best explained by reference to play. I also believe, as I did then, that sport is a manifestation of play and, when done well and properly, is, as Brian Sutton-Smith argued in Brisbane at the Commonwealth Games Conference in 1982, the apotheosis of play. The play education model described in that text has survived, has been slightly refined in each of its subsequent editions, and is often referred to now in curriculum texts as one among several competing theoretical perspectives in physical education. What I'm going to describe to you as sport education is the logical extension of play education—it finally has a *concrete form*.

The second interest that has led me to sport education is more recent and is rooted in the experimental research on teacher effectiveness that we have done at Ohio State. This work is more familiar to you, and I will allude to it only briefly. Suffice it to say we have had a great deal of experience and some success in helping teachers to change their own teaching behavior and to alter their managerial and instructional strategies in ways that create more learning opportunities for students. The early portion of the research program focused almost exclusively on preservice teachers, but in 1979 we began a series of studies that focused on inservice teachers.

The more we did this kind of work, the more it struck me that far too often a teacher could utilize reasonably effective managerial and instructional strategies and still have a lesson or a unit that somehow had less impact on students than it ought to have had.

It was during that time that the question arose that eventually led me to sport education. Put simply, the question was: Why is interscholastic and youth sport so relatively exciting and school physical education so relatively dull? And why is it sometimes dull even when it is taught effectively, given teacher skills or student engagement as effectiveness criteria?

The linking, for comparative and analytic purposes, of sport and physical education was the key step that quickly led me to the basic notions that underlie sport education. It was conceptual territory I had covered before, so the answers were fairly straightforward. I simply needed to ask the right questions.

The question comparing the relative excitement found in sport as opposed to physical education had an immediate and straightforward answer. In physical education we saw many sport *activities* and sport *skills* being taught and occasionally even competed, but they were done in isolation—that is, they were sport activities done without the contextuality that provides the framework within which a sport is defined and derives part of its meaning as an institutionalized form of play.

It was this search for contextuality that gave birth to sport education and the search rather quickly raised an even broader question: What is the relationship (or what should be the relationship) between physical education and the larger sport culture? It was my judgment that physical education had tacitly and often overtly distanced itself from the sport culture. It did this in two ways. First, it developed theoretical models for explaining the subject matter and for curricula based on those explanations that hardly made mention of sport. Secondly, physical education too often has turned its collective organizational back on problems in sport so as not to be tainted by them.

When the question was asked in the "should be" rather than the "is" form, the answer, at least for me, was immediately apparent. Physical education *should* educate students in the sport culture (skills and strategies being the main component here), socialize students as sportsmen and sportswomen, preserve and protect the best in the sport culture, and advocate, both by rhetoric and behavior, good sport practices. As I saw it, physical education should be partially responsible not only for the next generation of sportspersons, but also for the health of the sport culture itself. This view, of course, makes sport central to physical education and puts sport education within reach of all students, not just those who are *good enough* to be on school teams or *interested enough* to be involved in community programs.

This was the necessary link to invest the emerging curriculum-instruction model with a larger cultural meaning. There is a sport culture. It is obviously important to the larger social milieu. It is a culture in evolution, as are all cultural practices. It, therefore, can grow in positive directions providing a contribution to the growth of social life, or it can deteriorate and in so doing contribute to the deterioration of social life.

It was in this way, then, that the model for sport education emerged gradually out of my interest in defining the subject matter of physical education in relationship to play and, in my more recent involvement, in teacher effectiveness research in school physical education.

The Sport Education Model

As I mentioned earlier, the curriculum-instruction model I call sport education emerged as a solution to what I saw as a major problem in school physical education: the teaching of sport activities and sport skills in ways that removed them from their contexts as institutionalized forms of motor play.

I then began to ask myself, How can the contextuality of sport be defined in ways that lead, in a fairly straightforward way, to a curriculum-instruction model that could be implemented in most school physical education programs? At the outset, I was determined to develop a model that was both *understandable* to school personnel and *doable* in school situations. I have never had much respect for curriculum theories that were understandable only to other curriculum theoreticians nor with instructional models that can only be implemented in schools with unlimited resources.

This search for contextuality culminated in two underlying propositions: (a) that understanding the nature of competition would provide leads to understanding the needed contextuality, and (b) that institutionalized sport had certain distinct features.

Competition

Competition is, of course, the very essence of sport. Caillois had used agnostic activity to define one of the fundamental categories of play. In our own field many have speculated about the nature of competition and its role in sport. I needed to know what there was in the meaning of competition that might inform a curriculum-instruction model. Again, I knew the conceptual territory fairly well but was still a bit surprised when, in consulting the dictionary, I found a simple, yet very satisfactory, set of meanings.

To compete, according to *Webster's New Collegiate Dictionary*, means first of all *to come together*. I took this meaning to refer to the festival nature of competition. Competition involves tradition, ritual, celebration, intimacy, and the sharing of significant experiences. It is this festival characteristic of competition that is least understood and, therefore, most often neglected or violated. Organizing a game in a physical education class at the end of a 3-week unit does not do justice to the festival nature of competition.

The second meaning given is to strive consciously for an objective. I took this to refer to the pursuit of competence in sport. Sport, as an institutionalized form of play, creates forums within which persons can demonstrate competence, can reach goals that have been set, and can learn what new goals might await them. The forum, with its rules, standards, judgments, and records, is crucial to the pursuit of goals and, in turn, to the pursuit of competence. Forums for competition give definition to that pursuit in the individual sense and provide frameworks that infuse the quest for competence with a larger, collective meaning. I knew that to succeed, sport education had to create such forums for all students in their regular program.

A third meaning of competition is to be in a state of rivalry. You all know the many different kinds of rivalries that exist within sport, and you also know that such rivalries seldom involve zero-sum contingencies. Indeed, rivalry tends to have its strongest meaning when it is seen as part of the festival nature of competition and in terms of the standards and traditions that create the forum within which competence is pursued. It is this view of the meaning of competition that underlies sport education.

Distinct Features of Sport

It remained, then, to sort out the main features of institutionalized sport, to see how typical physical education classes matched these features, and to design a curriculum-instruction model that created a better match.

It seemed to me that institutionalized sport has five main features. First, it is done in *seasons*, and seasons typically have some length to them. Physical education is typically done in units, and these are often of very short duration.

Sport typically involves an *affiliation*—players are members of a team or a club and then tend to retain that membership for at least the length of a season. In physical education it is more likely that affiliation changes from class to class and students can often be on different teams even within one class.

Sport involves a *formal competition*—a conference or league schedule with a round-robin format, a series of dual meets. This schedule is typically fixed prior to the season. In physical education formal competition in this sense is atypical. Because affiliations change, a schedule wouldn't mean much anyway.

In sport, a season typically closes with a *culminating event*. It is in the nature of sport to find out who is best for a particular season. Physical education units often have culminating events of a type, but they have little meaning because they are not part of an established forum, the forum that is partially vested with meaning as a result of affiliation and a schedule of formal competitions.

Finally, sport most often involves the keeping of *records*—batting averages, kicks on goal, shooting percentages, scores of judges. The records provide feedback for individuals and groups, they constantly help to redefine standards, and they become an important part of the tradition and ritual associated with sport. In physical education, the record keeping is more likely to start and stop with attendance.

Implementing Sport Education

Sport education, then, would aim to develop players—sportsmen and sportswomen. It would emphasize skilled performance and socialization into the role of player. It would be characterized by the creation of forums within which competence could be pursued, by the intimacy to be associated with affiliation, by the creation of meaningful competitions, and, as a developmental school program, by gradual socialization from the characteristics of lower forms of ludic activity to the characteristics of higher forms of ludic activity, namely, practice, subordination to rules, increased complexity, and appreciation for the forum itself.

To do that, sport education would be taught in seasons, students would be on teams, there would be formal competitions with culminating events, and records would be kept. Students would practice and compete together on their teams, and they would also learn the other roles that are necessary for institutionalized sport to take place, among them the roles of coach, manager, referee, and record keeper.

In the longer term, after many years of sport education, one might expect that students would be more prepared to seek out meaningful lifetime sport involvement and also to participate in the larger sport culture in ways that improve the conduct and practice of sport within the society. In so doing, they might eventually build a higher level of sport literacy within the culture.

There are many ways in which sport education can be implemented and still be faithful to this basic model. I will show you one way, using as an example a fifth-grade soccer season with a group of students who were having their first experience in sport education. The 26 students in the class were divided into three teams; the teacher made the team membership selections with a primary aim of equalizing competition. The teams practiced and competed together throughout the season. The indoor space was divided into three "soccer fields." Each team was assigned one field for practice.

The initial competition for the soccer season was a 2-on-2 modified soccer game. Students not competing in any given game (all games on the three "fields" started and stopped at the same time) were assigned roles as referees or scorekeepers. Games were short in duration, and several games could be completed during each class session. The several 2-on-2 teams from any one of the three parent teams contributed to their parent team totals for that particular competition.

The 2-on-2 season was followed by a 4-on-4 competition. Students were more prepared (in terms of skills and strategies) for the more complex modified game. Again, a formal competition was held, with each parent team providing two teams for the 4-on-4 competition. Students continued to serve as officials when they were not competing. Captains were in charge of organizing their teams for competition, getting officials to the right place at the right time, and organizing the equipment.

Students continued to practice each day and practice routines were shown. Captains played a significant role both in organizing their teams' practices and in providing leadership during practice. The teacher continued to act as a teacher, supervising and providing guidance and feedback during practice time. A high degree of managerial competence by the teacher is also necessary to implement the sport education model successfully in a way that provides for efficient use of time and optimal practice/competition time for students.

After the 2-on-2 and 4-on-4 seasons were concluded, an overall seasonal champion was determined, combining points won in the various competitions along with sportsmanship and officiating points.

Students began to learn the roles appropriate to the sport of soccer, not only the skill and strategy roles but roles like (a) being a team leader,

(b) being a team member and cooperating by following instructions, (c) being an official and calling violations fairly and assertively, and (d) being a scorekeeper and keeping not only scores but also some simple statistics such as shots on goal.

This program illustrates how the theoretical aspects of sport education were made concrete. Students had begun to learn a sport, to be responsible for the context within which the sport was pursued, and to understand and value the many roles necessary for the sport to be successful.

Participant Purposes for Engaging in Physical Activity

Ann E. Jewett

In 1977, the Purpose Process Curriculum Framework (PPCF) was presented by the American Alliance for Health, Physical Education, Recreation and Dance as a conceptual framework for curricular decision making in physical education (Jewett & Mullan, 1977). The PPCF is composed of two dimensions: human purposes for moving and the processes through which persons learn movement. The primary components, key purpose concepts and a movement category system, provide for the selection of curricular content in terms of its meaning for individual persons.

The research on purposes has been more extensive than the research on processes up to the present time. The purpose of this paper is to provide a systematic overview and an update of the research on participant purposes. Comments are structured in the broad context of the overall findings relating to participant purposes for engaging in movement activities, without reporting the particular research investigations in complete detail. The framework identifies three key concepts of individual development, environmental coping, and social interaction, including 22 purpose elements conceptualized as unique ways of finding or extending personal meaning through movement activities (see Figure 1). This report is organized in terms of nine statements summarizing the research findings.

Figure 1 Key Purpose Concepts

I. INDIVIDUAL DEVELOPMENT: I move to fulfill my human developmental potential.
   A. Physiological Efficiency: I move to improve or maintain my functional capabilities.
      1. Circulorespiratory Efficiency. I move to develop and maintain circulatory and respiratory functioning.
      2. Mechanical Efficiency. I move to develop and maintain range and effectiveness of motion.
      3. Neuromuscular Efficiency. I move to develop and maintain motor functioning.
   B. Psychic Equilibrium: I move to achieve personal integration.
      4. Joy of Movement. I move to derive pleasure from movement experience.
      5. Self-knowledge. I move to gain self-understanding and appreciation.
      6. Catharsis. I move to release tension and frustration.
      7. Challenge. I move to test my prowess and courage.

Figure 1 (Cont.)

II. ENVIRONMENTAL COPING: I move to adapt to and control my physical environment.

  C. Spatial Orientation: I move to relate myself in three dimensional space.

    8. Awareness. I move to clarify my conception of my body and my position in space.

    9. Relocation. I move in a variety of ways to propel or project myself.

    10. Relationships. I move to regulate my body position in relation to the objects or persons in my environment.

  D. Object Manipulation: I move to give impetus to and to absorb the force of objects.

    11. Maneuvering Weight. I move to support, resist or transport mass.

    12. Object Projection. I move to impart momentum and direction to a variety of objects.

    13. Object Reception. I move to intercept a variety of objects by reducing or arresting their momentum.

III. SOCIAL INTERACTION: I move to relate to others.

  E. Communication: I move to share ideas and feelings with others.

    14. Expression. I move to convey my ideas and feelings.

    15. Clarification. I move to enhance the meaning of other communication forms.

    16. Simulation. I move to create an advantageous image or situation.

  F. Group Interaction: I move to function in harmony with others.

    17. Teamwork. I move to cooperate in pursuit of common goals.

    18. Competition. I move to vie for individual or group goals.

    19. Leadership. I move to motivate and influence group members to achieve common goals.

  G. Cultural Involvement: I move to take part in movement activities which constitute an important part of my society.

    20. Participation. I move to develop my capabilities for taking part in movement activities of my society.

    21. Movement Appreciation. I move to become knowledgeable and appreciative of sports and expressive movement forms.

    22. Cultural Understanding. I move to understand, respect, and strengthen the cultural heritage.

Figure 1 (Cont.)

Note. From *The Curriculum Process in Physical Education* (pp. 329–330) by A.E. Jewett and L.L. Bain, 1985, Dubuque, IA: W.C. Brown.

Purposes for Participation in Physical Activity

What do we know about participant purposes for engaging in physical activity as a result of PPCF research?

- *We know that the 22 purposes identified in the PPCF are all-inclusive.*
  Purposes identified by male and female participants, by participants of different ages, and by participants in different geographic locations can all be identified within the 22-purpose framework. LaPlante (1973) validated this set of purposes initially in 1973, using a modified Delphi technique with a panel of approximately 100 physical educators. LaPlante investigated the total range of potential purpose meanings, using three rounds of judgment responses. These professional educators demonstrated substantial consensus on the importance of these

purposes as directed student learning outcomes. The research to date continues to confirm the inclusiveness of this set of purposes for engaging in physical activity.

- *These 22 purposes, as ways in which participants may seek personal meaning through physical activity or as potential objectives of physical education, have not changed significantly in 12 years.*

Although certain improvements in the wording of the definitions continue to be needed, the purpose concepts themselves continue to be valid. A 1985 investigation by Speakman found this same set of purposes to be inclusive. Participants in the Speakman (1985) study were 50 physical education curriculum specialists and teacher educators in England, Japan, and the United States.

- *Although the set of purposes has been found to be constant, the relative importance placed on individual purposes does vary with different populations of participants.*

Two investigations focused on the purposes of secondary school students for engaging in physical activity. Chapman (1974) evaluated the responses of 420 7th-, 9th-, and 11th-grade students in Madison, Wisconsin. Mangham (1979) conducted a similar study, using a randomly selected sample of 87 9th- through 12th-grade students in Turner County High School, Ashburn, Georgia. The findings of the two studies demonstrated both common priorities and differences between the two groups. Five of the 22 purposes were ranked among the top 7 by both groups: circulorespiratory efficiency, neuromuscular efficiency, mechanical efficiency, joy of movement, and teamwork. The Georgia high school students ranked leadership, competition, and cultural understanding higher than did the Wisconsin students; they gave lower rankings to relocation, spatial relationships, and maneuvering weight. It should be noted that differences in responses of these two groups may be related to the 5-year time span or to the quality of physical education background experiences as well as to the geographic location.

Investigations of adult purposes for participation in movement activities indicate that similar high priorities are held for fitness outcomes and enjoyment, that teamwork receives low rankings, and that catharsis is assigned relatively high rankings, compared to the responses of secondary school students. Some of these studies have used a PPCF Purpose Rating Scale; others have used instruments based on the PPCF purposes. Norton (1982) developed the Fitness Activities Purposes Inventory and administered it to 197 university students enrolled in Fitness for Life classes. The most meaningful purposes were identified as musculoskeletal efficiency, attractiveness, mechanical efficiency, circulorespiratory efficiency, weight control, vitality, and enjoyment. Neikirk (1985) administered the Personal Purposes and Meanings in Movement Inventory (PPMMI) to 136 university students randomly selected from the list of undergraduate female students 25 years of age and older. The purposes rated most important were aliveness, circulorespiratory efficiency, musculoskeletal efficiency, weight control, attractiveness, catharsis, and mechanical efficiency. James (1984) administered the PPMMI to 189 older adult participants in senior citizen centers in a South Georgia area planning district and to 124 Elderhostels enrolled at South Georgia College. The top four purposes among the Elderhostels were circulorespiratory efficiency, weight control, mechanical efficiency, and movement efficiency. The older adult group rated circulorespiratory efficiency, self-integration, catharsis, and participation as the top four purposes. Five purposes were ranked among the top eight by both groups: circulorespiratory efficiency, self-integration, weight control, enjoyment, and participation (see Table 1).

Speakman's (1985) investigation was the first in this series that permitted purpose comparisons across countries. Participants in this study were 50 physical educators, 20 in England, 20 in the United States, and 10 in Japan. A Delphi technique was used with the purposes validated by LaPlante in 1973. Using a 7-point scale, 17 of the 22 purposes were rated significantly different between countries as presently desired physical education outcomes. The Americans gave the three highest rankings to circulorespiratory efficiency, joy of movement, and participation. The English rated joy of movement highest, followed by teamwork and neuromuscular efficiency. The three purposes ranked highest by the Japanese educators were mechanical efficiency, catharsis, and teamwork.

- *The relative importance of the 22 purposes as perceived by participants may vary in at least two dimensions.*

Chapman (1974) developed the Movement Purposes Attitude Inventory (MPAI) to evaluate the affective responses of students to the purposes of human movement as identified in the Purpose Process Curriculum Framework. The MPAI is a semantic differential instrument in which each purpose statement is followed by eight bipolar scales, four representing the utility dimension and four representing the likability dimension. It yields two scores for each purpose, a utility score and a likability score (see Table 2).

Participants responding to the MPAI perceive some purposes as very useful, although they are not well liked. For example, Chapman's subjects perceived catharsis, maneuvering weight, and spatial relationships as more useful than likable. On the other hand, they perceived expression, clarification, and movement appreciation as more likable purposes for moving than useful. A separate assessment of likability and utility is an effective way to determine attitude toward movement concepts.

- *The relative importance of the purposes as perceived by participants and prospective participants in sport, dance, and exercise programs may differ from the perceptions of physical education professionals.*

LaPlante's (1973) judges were asked to rate the importance of each purpose as a desired student outcome. Chapman (1974) suggested that the relative value of individual purposes as perceived by students could also be highly relevant to physical education curriculum planning. She developed the MPAI to assess student perceptions of the likability and utility of the individual purposes. Comparison of the findings of Chapman (1974) and Mangham (1979) and those of Neikirk (1985) (who

Table 1 Adult Purposes: Personal Purposes and Meanings in Movement Inventory

Rank	University students (FFL) Norton (1982) (n = 197)	Reentry women (25+) Neikirk (1985) (n = 136)	Elderhostels James (1984) (n = 124)	Senior citizens James (1985) (n = 189)
1.	Musculoskeletal efficiency	Aliveness	Circulorespiratory efficiency	Circulorespiratory efficiency
2.	Attractiveness	Circulorespiratory efficiency	Weight control	Self-integration
3.	Mechanical efficiency	Musculoskeletal efficiency	Mechanical efficiency	Catharsis
4.	Circulorespiratory efficiency	Weight control	Movement efficiency	Participation
5.	Weight control	Attractiveness	Participation	Weight control
6.	Vitality	Catharsis	Self-integration	Self-knowledge
7.	Enjoyment	Mechanical efficiency	Enjoyment	Communication
8.	Movement efficiency	Movement efficiency	Attractiveness	Enjoyment

Table 2 Rankings of Purposes by Grade and Sex

Purpose	Grade 7				Grade 9				Grade 11			
	Likability		Utility		Likability		Utility		Likability		Utility	
	Male	Female	Male	Female	Male	Female	Male	Female	Male	Female	Male	Female
Circulorespiratory efficiency	7	7	3	1	1	3	1	1	3	12	1	1
Mechanical efficiency	14	9	11	11	4	7	3	4	19	3	7	4
Neuromuscular efficiency	4	6	6	7	2	5	2	2	2	10	2	8
Joy of movement	12	2	9	4	7	9	7	10	1	1	6	5
Self-knowledge	13	11	13	10	14	11	17	12	13	7	11	6
Catharsis	21	19	14	17	19	17	15	5	18	13	4	3
Challenge	5	4	4	5	11	10	11	16	7	14	13	19
Awareness	17	16	17	13	18	19	16	18	15	9	15	14
Relocation	1	1	2	2	5	1	4	3	6	6	5	2
Relationships	19	18	7	6	12	16	5	7	4	18	3	9
Maneuvering weight	16	20	5	19	20	21	9	8	14	21	9	13
Object projection	3	12	8	9	9	15	12	9	9	20	17	20
Object reception	6	8	12	12	10	14	8	15	10	15	14	15
Expression	10	15	19	16	15	6	19	11	8	2	12	10
Clarification	18	10	21	20	17	12	21	20	16	4	20	12
Simulation	22	22	22	22	22	22	22	22	22	22	22	22
Teamwork	2	3	1	3	3	4	6	6	5	5	8	7
Competition	15	17	18	15	6	13	14	17	11	16	10	21
Leadership	8	21	16	21	16	20	18	21	20	19	18	18
Participation	11	13	15	14	13	2	13	14	17	8	16	11
Movement appreciation	9	5	10	8	8	8	10	13	12	11	19	16
Cultural understanding	20	14	20	18	21	18	20	19	21	17	21	17

Note. From *Evaluation of Affective Responses of Students to a Selected List of Purposes for Human Movement* (p. 93) by P.A. Chapman, 1974, unpublished doctoral dissertation, University of Wisconsin, Madison.

utilized the PPMMI to investigate participant attitudes) with those of LaPlante (1973) provides evidence that both common priorities and differing perspectives characterize the values associated with these purposes by professional educators and the participants themselves. Ratings are consistently high for the physiological efficiency purposes and for joy of movement. Discrepancies are typically the greatest for participation, competition, and leadership. Educators ranked participation fourth highest in the LaPlante (1973) study (and similarly in the Speakman [1985] study); participants ranked it 11, 14, and 11 in the Chapman (1974), Mangham (1979), and Neikirk (1985) studies, respectively. Competition was ranked 8 and leadership 10 by the physical educators in the LaPlante (1973) study; competition ranked 18 and 14, leadership 19 and 21 in the investigations of participant attitudes by Chapman (1974) and Neikirk (1985) (see Table 3).

- *Perceptions of present importance differ from perceptions of future importance in making judgments concerning purposes for engaging in physical activity.*

Both LaPlante (1973) and Speakman (1985) sought professional judgments on the importance of each purpose as a valued outcome for present students and for the future. Both researchers found significant differences between present and future ratings. LaPlante's respondents, ranking the purposes in 1973 for future importance, rated circulorespiratory efficiency, joy of movement, self-knowledge, and participation as the top four (see Table 4). The American educators in Speakman's (1985) study gave top rankings for both present and future to circulorespiratory efficiency, joy of movement, and participation. Speakman's English respondents assigned the highest future value to teamwork, circulorespiratory efficiency, and joy of movement. Purposes rated highest for the future by the Japanese were circulo-respiratory efficiency, joy of movement, and catharsis (see Table 5).

Pasternak completed an investigation in 1981 in which 145 adults

Table 3 Selected Purpose Rankings

Purpose	Physical educators	Secondary students	Secondary students	Reentry college women
	LaPlante 1973	Chapman 1974	Mangham 1979	Neikirk 1985
Circulorespiratory efficiency	1	1	1	2
Mechanical efficiency	5	4	4	7
Neuromuscular efficiency	2	2	2	3
Joy of movement	3	7	5	9
Participation	4	11	14	11
Competition	8	18	8	14
Leadership	10	19	3	21

Table 4 Rankings of Desired Student Learning Outcomes

	Ranking	
Purpose	Present importance	Future importance
1. Circulorespiratory efficiency	1	1
2. Mechanical efficiency	5	7
3. Neuromuscular efficiency	2	5
4. Joy of movement	3	2
5. Self-knowledge	6	3
6. Catharsis	9	6
7. Challenge	14	15
8. Awareness	11	8
9. Relocation	18	17
10. Relationships	15	13
11. Maneuvering weight	21	21
12. Object projection	13	19
13. Object reception	16	20
14. Expression	17	10
15. Clarification	20	18
16. Simulation	22	22
17. Teamwork	7	9
18. Competition	8	14
19. Leadership	10	11
20. Participation	4	4
21. Movement appreciation	12	12
22. Cultural understanding	19	16

Note. From *Evaluation of a Selected List of Purposes for Physical Education Using a Modified Delphi Technique* (p. 106) by M.J. LaPlante, 1973, unpublished doctoral dissertation, University of Wisconsin, Madison.

Table 5 Ranking of the Purposes

Purpose	Present			Future		
	U.S.A.	England	Japan	U.S.A.	England	Japan
1. Circulorespiratory efficiency	1	5	4	1	2	1
2. Mechanical efficiency	4	8	1	4	8	8
3. Neuromuscular efficiency	5	3	7	7	10	5
4. Joy of movement	2	1	4	2	3	2

(Cont.)

Table 5 (Cont.)

5. Self-knowledge	8	18	12	8	11	10
6. Catharsis	7	12	1	5	6	2
7. Challenge	22	11	9	22	13	12
8. Awareness	19	13	19	18	17	15
9. Relocation	20	20	16	18	22	19
10. Relationships	18	15	19	18	15	20
11. Maneuvering weight	15	19	18	15	19	18
12. Object projection	9	10	21	10	14	22
13. Object reception	14	17	21	17	16	20
14. Expression	15	15	17	12	11	15
15. Clarification	17	21	14	16	21	14
16. Simulation	20	21	15	21	19	15
17. Teamwork	10	2	1	9	1	10
18. Competition	11	7	9	12	18	13
19. Leadership	11	9	4	11	6	8
20. Participation	3	5	11	2	5	6
21. Movement appreciation	6	4	7	6	4	4
22. Cultural understanding	11	13	13	12	9	7

Note. From *A Cross-cultural Comparison of Purposes for Moving* (p. 63) by M.A. Speakman, 1985, unpublished doctoral dissertation, University of Georgia, Athens.

responded to a focus Delphi questionnaire in which they were asked to evaluate purposes as reasons for participating in movement activities in the next 20 years. She developed the Future Purposes Inventory (FPI) and administered it to three samples, American physical education curriculum specialists, U.S. members of the World Future Society, and adult Georgians randomly selected from telephone directories. The analysis demonstrated no significant difference in responses of the three groups. Among the 10 purposes of the FPI that can be compared to those validated by LaPlante (1973), the four ranked highest were circulo-respiratory efficiency, mechanical efficiency, catharsis, and joy of movement.

- *Health-related fitness and joy of movement are common purposes for participation in sport, dance, and exercise programs.*

Health-related fitness appears to be a growing and continuing concern throughout the world. There is substantial agreement among professional educators that circulorespiratory efficiency is a key purpose for engaging regularly in physical activity (LaPlante, 1973; Speakman, 1985). In all the curriculum research cited using the PPCF purposes, fitness emerges as the primary purpose of physical education. Studies of middle-school programs, of secondary school youth, of college students, and of older adults have all contributed to this conclusion (Chapman, 1974; James, 1984; Mangham, 1979; Neikirk, 1985; Pasternak, 1981).

Most of these same studies identified joy of movement as a top priority as well (Chapman, 1974; James, 1984; LaPlante, 1973; Mangham, 1979; Norton, 1982; Pasternak, 1981; Speakman, 1985). This may reflect increasing concern for individual development and the supporting commitment to personalization of the physical education curriculum. It may also be indicative of increasing sophistication concerning the nature of fitness behavior. Although much confusion still exists as to how we can influence individuals to commit themselves voluntarily to a healthy, physically active life-style, there is no longer much doubt that personal adherence to a sound exercise program depends more on psychological factors than on knowledge about exercise physiology or skill in particular physical activities. This suggests that participation in fitness classes does indeed need to be enjoyable.

• *Interest is increasing in individual development and in the psychological benefits of active participation; interest appears to be decreasing in competition as a motivator for long-term participation in physical activity and in educational environments emphasizing organized team activities.*

Professional literature and local physical education curriculum guides provide ample evidence of consensus that development of the individual as a fully integrated person is the central educational objective. The concept of holistic development implies integration of both physiological and psychological components. As already reported, health-related fitness and joy of movement are generally recognized as high priorities among purposes for engaging in physical activity.

The physiological purpose of circulorespiratory efficiency has been consistently identified as a top purpose both for present participation and for future participation. In addition to its three "physiological" purposes, the PPCF includes four "psychological" purposes. Even in the initial validation study (LaPlante, 1973), physical educators recognized that three of these four would be more important in the future than at the time of their rating (see Table 4). More recent researchers have acknowledged the need for construct validation that would more satisfactorily establish the psychological components (James, 1984; Neikirk, 1985; Norton, 1982; Pasternak, 1981). The present version of the PPMMI includes the following among its 22 purposes: aliveness, catharsis, joy of movement, attractiveness, self-integration, self-knowledge, self-transcendence, and challenge. Current research indicates that, however they are labeled or defined, purposes identifying psychological benefits also receive high ratings. Constructs of the individual development purposes as identified in the PPCF (Jewett & Mullan, 1977) and the PPMMI (Neikirk, 1985) are shown in Figure 2.

Increasing concern for holistic individual development during the past decade has been accompanied in this country by de-emphasis on competition as a meaningful purpose for activity participation and on organized team games as physical education curriculum content. American educators are likely becoming more concerned about the opportunity of the average student to be a fully active participant than

PPCF	PPMMI
Physiological	Physiological
Circulorespiratory efficiency	Circulorespiratory efficiency
Mechanical efficiency	Mechanical efficiency
Neuromuscular efficiency	Musculoskeletal efficiency
	Movement efficiency
	Weight
Psychological	Psychological
Joy of movement	Joy of movement
Self-knowledge	Self-knowledge
Catharsis	Catharsis
Challenge	Challenge
	Aliveness
	Self-integration
	Self-transcendence
	Attractiveness

Figure 2   Individual development purposes.

about the importance of vying for recognition. A growing number of physical education professionals also possibly view cooperative behavior as a more highly desired outcome than competitive skill.

- *Cultural understanding is not perceived as an important purpose for engaging in physical activity either by most professional physical educators or by program participants.*

It is asserted frequently that familiarity with and participation in the sport and dance activities of other cultures is a channel for intercultural understanding. Understanding, respect, and preservation of the movement activities of all ethnic groups can be a means for maintaining cultural plurality and strengthening both national and international heritages. Yet there is little evidence that cultural understanding is given any serious attention in planning or conducting physical education programs. Cultural understanding is ranked lowest or very nearly lowest in all of the research cited except the Speakman (1985) study, in which it was ranked 13 among the 22 as a present purpose of physical education. In this same investigation, although the American educators ranked cultural understanding similarly as a future purpose, the English ranked it 9 and the Japanese ranked it 7. If participation in physical activity is to make any genuine contribution to international understanding, some positive action is clearly needed.

In summary, a great deal has been learned about participant purposes for engaging in physical activity. A set of 22 valid purposes for curricular decision making and for asking more specific research questions has been established. Substantial information on common participant perspectives and on differences in priorities among various categories of participants has been gained.

Areas of Future Research

What are the next steps in this area of research? What questions should be asked during the 5 years immediately ahead? Four exceedingly challenging questions are proposed.

- *How can the existing purpose data base be strengthened?*
  A large-scale cooperative research program should be initiated to provide large masses of data appropriate for comparative studies of different categories of participants. These studies should also contribute toward modifying and increasing the reliability of the PPMMI. In addition to identifying more definitively purpose priorities by age group, gender, geographic location, and professional role, it is important to study ethnic and national differences and commonalities. Consensus on definitions of key terms and on a taxonomy is needed, as well as alternate language forms of the PPCF Purposes Rating Scale, the MPAI, and the PPMMI.
- *What are the significant elements of each purpose to be addressed in curriculum planning?*
  Much effort needs to be directed toward the development and testing of theoretical constructs. Some excellent research has been completed in validation of theoretical constructs of relocation (Jones, 1972), physiological efficiency (Tiburzi, 1979), teamwork (McGinn, 1979; Segall, 1984), competition (McGinn, 1979), and spatial relationships (Rady, 1981). It is particularly important to address construct validation studies of psychodynamic efficiency and cultural understanding soon. Successful construct validation will open up new channels for effective curriculum development.
- *How can completed research findings be implemented to improve curriculum practice?*
  Improvement of practice will require both quantitative and qualitative analyses. Solid progress will require more naturalistic inquiry. It will be necessary to gain much more accurate descriptions of particu-

lar educational environments in order to target innovation. Given better ethnographic analyses, it will be possible to design intervention research in "natural" educational environments. Ennis (1984) has completed a study of purposes for middle-school physical education that provides an excellent model for in-depth research of a selected educational environment. Her investigation was directed toward purposes identified in the approved physical education curriculum, perceived by the teachers, experienced by the students, and witnessed by an independent observer. Intervention studies that are directed toward helping teachers identify and satisfy participant purposes also have strong potential for effecting improvements in practice.

- *How can the degree to which participants achieve their purposes for engaging in physical activity be measured more satisfactorily?*

Most physical educators accept as an overall program goal the facilitation of a self-directing, personally active life-style. Commitment to an active life-style results from our programs only if participants achieve valued outcomes through their experiences. Thus, participant purposes should guide curriculum development as well as instructional practice. In a sense we "create the future" by acknowledging individual participant purposes. Better methods of program evaluation based on participant purposes are essential for continued progress.

References

Chapman, P.A. (1974). *Evaluation of affective responses of students to a selected list of purposes for human movement.* Unpublished doctoral dissertation, University of Wisconsin, Madison.

Ennis, C.D. (1984). *Purpose concepts in physical education curriculum development.* Unpublished doctoral dissertation, University of Wisconsin, Madison.

James, G.M. (1984). *Older adult perspectives on purposes for engaging in movement activities.* Unpublished doctoral dissertation, University of Georgia, Athens.

Jewett, A.E., & Bain, L.L. (1985). *The curriculum process in physical education.* Dubuque, IA: W.C. Brown.

Jewett, A.E., & Mullan, M.R. (1977). *Curriculum design: Purposes and processes in physical education teaching-learning.* Washington, DC: American Alliance for Health, Physical Education, Recreation and Dance.

Jones, L.S. (1972). *The construct of body awareness in space as reflected through children's ability to discriminate directions, levels, and pathways in movement.* Unpublished doctoral dissertation, University of Wisconsin, Madison.

LaPlante, M.J. (1973). *Evaluation of a selected list of purposes for physical education using a modified Delphi technique.* Unpublished doctoral dissertation, University of Wisconsin, Madison.

Mangham, P.N. (1979). *Attitudes of selected secondary school students toward purposes of human movement.* Unpublished master's thesis, University of Georgia, Athens.

McGinn, A.F. (1979). *Conceptual model for games teaching with focus on personal integration.* Unpublished doctoral dissertation, University of Georgia, Athens.

Neikirk, M.M. (1985). *Characteristics of reentry women students and their purposes for participating in movement activities.* Unpublished doctoral dissertation, University of Georgia, Athens.

Norton, C. (1982). *Student purposes for engaging in fitness activities.* Unpublished doctoral dissertation, University of Georgia, Athens.

Pasternak, M. (1981). *Adult perspectives on purposes for moving 1980–2000.* Unpublished doctoral dissertation, University of Georgia, Athens.

Rady, A.L.M. (1981). *A construct validation of spatial relationships.* Unpublished doctoral dissertation, University of Georgia, Athens.

Segall, B. (1984). *Development and validation of a teamwork construct.* Unpublished doctoral dissertation, University of Georgia, Athens.

Speakman, M.A. (1985). *A cross-cultural comparison of purposes for moving.* Unpublished doctoral dissertation, University of Georgia, Athens.

Tiburzi, A. (1979). *Validation of the construct of physiological fitness.* Unpublished doctoral dissertation, University of Georgia, Athens.

A Model for Teaching:
A Model of Learning

Ree K. Arnold

This conference and the program content provide evidence of the continuing interest of large numbers of professionals in the analysis of teaching physical education. Clearly, research on teaching has become a prominent area of investigation in physical education. I would like to comment briefly on three of the general research strategies that have produced impressive amounts of data concerning the teaching of physical education. The selection of studies for illustration is not intended as either a complete review or as an evaluation of the entire body of research on teaching physical education. The selection simply reflects the extent to which the studies illustrate a particular point of view of interest to me.

The three research strategies are all characterized by sequential investigation of a general problem area, replication of findings, and the development and use of objective, reliable instruments. The three strategies differ, however, in the general purpose or focus of the research effort.

The Process-Oriented Research Strategy

The first strategy is illustrated by the series of descriptive-analytic studies of teaching physical education conducted by Anderson, his students, and colleagues (Anderson & Barrette, 1978). In general, this research has focused on objective descriptions of student activity patterns, teacher functions and behaviors, student functions and behaviors, teacher-student interaction, and the like. According to Anderson (1978), findings from descriptive-analytic research are intended (a) to enable teachers to evaluate the appropriateness of what they and others are doing and to make the changes called for, and (b) to serve as an informative base for teacher educators in determining what to train teachers to do in the future. Clearly, the descriptive-analytic data on teaching provide a wealth of detailed, objective information on a variety of behaviors that are potentially useful for both of these broad purposes. However, a clear problem arises for me in attempting to use the data in these ways.

Data concerning exactly what teachers or students do, or do not do, may indeed as Anderson (1978) says, ''make physical educators more acutely aware of who we are and what we are doing" (p. 9). However, such data in no way indicate what teachers or students could, should, or ought to do. What is missing is a criterion for evaluating teacher and student behaviors.

For example, is it appropriate, or even logical, to design teacher-education programs based on analyses of what teachers currently do? In discussing their findings concerning patterns of teacher-student interaction in physical education, Cheffers and Mancini (1978) noted that teachers overwhelmingly adopted direct, traditional teaching behaviors, despite the continuing humanistic emphasis in education and despite strong evidence that supports the desirability of variety in teaching methods. The conclusion by Cheffers and Mancini (1978) that "immediate shifts in college, school, professional and local emphasis are probably warranted" clearly argues against using data concerning what teachers do as the basis for preparing future teachers (p. 49). What is missing in this descriptive-analytic approach to research on teaching is a criterion reference of what teachers ought to do.

A second purpose of descriptive-analytic research on teaching is to enable individual teachers to evaluate the appropriateness of their teaching after coding and analyzing their own teaching behavior. However, on what basis are teachers to make decisions about how to improve their teaching and their classes? Suppose that a teacher analyzes several of his or her classes relative to one or more selected aspects of teacher behavior such as percentage of time spent planning, observing student performance, and guiding student behavior. How is the teacher to evaluate the results of the analysis of teaching? Are the normative data in the literature to be considered the standard or the minimum? If, for example, the percentage of time spent by the teacher in guiding motor activities is higher than the figures reported in the literature, should the teacher conclude that he or she is using class time more appropriately than the teachers in the sample? How should the teacher evaluate the amount of time spent observing students? Is a large percentage of observation time judged "good" because it implies self-analysis by students, or is it judged "poor" because it implies no directive activity by the teacher? What is missing is a criterion against which to evaluate teacher behavior; that criterion is student learning.

Teaching is the facilitation of learning. If learning does not result, teaching has not occurred. Teaching behaviors may have been evidenced, but they were not successful. The most relevant criterion for measuring, assessing, and/or evaluating teacher behavior is its effectiveness in facilitating learning. Facilitation of learning means that students learn more, learn more quickly, or improve to a greater degree with the assistance of a teacher than without a teacher. It may be argued that many variables influence learning other than teacher behavior, most of which have to do with the prior experience and present state of the learner; therefore, the basis for evaluating teacher behavior cannot be limited to evidence of learning. However, this argument fails to recognize the essential nature of teaching. Teaching is a product-oriented activity and therefore cannot be evaluated relative to the process alone. One cannot determine the effectiveness of teacher behavior without applying a product criterion to the descriptive-analytic data. It is essential to be able to measure the process, but it is equally important to evaluate the product to which the process is directed.

The Product-Oriented Research Strategy

The product of teaching is the focus of the second general strategy for research on teaching, illustrated by the series of studies conducted by Silverman, Dodds, Placek, Shute, and Rife (1984). This research focuses on academic learning time, a type of time-on-task index, as an indirect measure of student achievement. One of the purposes of the research sequence is to evaluate the effect of different teaching strategies on measures of academic learning time (ALT). ALT would appear to be related to the concept of substantive activity time measured by Costello and Laubach (1978) in their descriptive-analytic study of student behavior in physical education. However, Costello and Laubach made no formal attempt to correlate student activity patterns with teacher behavior. In contrast, Silverman et al. (1984) used ALT as a dependent variable to evaluate different strategies of teaching, different activity units, and different types of students. However, the research design still fails to address the issue of student learning directly.

Of course, students cannot learn if they are not engaged in activity related to the objectives of the lesson. But can it simply be assumed when students are engaged in lesson-related activity that learning is occurring? Isn't the quality of time spent in substantive activity at least equal in importance to the quantity of time? Although the research strategy does focus on an evaluation of teaching in terms of student activity, it fails to apply a criterion of learning to evaluate student behavior. Learning could be evaluated by measuring, for example, changes in speed, accuracy, or duration of performance; consistency, timing, or efficiency of movement; and transfer or retention of skill. Learning, like teaching, is a complex phenomenon, involving many components of behavior.

Learning, as applied to motor skills, may be described as a series of information-processing tasks. The learner is an active, problem-solving, decision-making processor of information. In attempting a particular motor task, the learner must evaluate the environmental situation; plan an appropriate response; organize, execute, and control the movement; evaluate the effectiveness of the response; and store the relevant information about performance in memory for use in similar situations in the future. This is what is involved in learning a motor skill. Therefore, teacher behavior must facilitate this series of processes. And it is against this criterion of facilitating learning that teacher effectiveness must be judged.

It is not enough to provide opportunities for students to socialize, analyze, adjust, release energy, and/or play. It is not enough to reduce student waiting time, decrease teacher talking time, improve organizational and management skills, provide more augmented feedback, and increase academic learning time. Nor is it enough simply to teach students to move in new and/or more efficient ways. Students must be taught to select, recognize, discriminate, and compare information; to plan, adapt, organize, control, and modulate movement; and to interpret, evaluate, and remember information and motor responses. If students improve their ability to accomplish these tasks successfully, then teaching will have facilitated learning.

The Process-Product Research Strategy

Research on teaching should focus on variations in teacher behavior and on an evaluation of the relative effectiveness of these variations in facilitating the learning process for different skills, learners, and stages of learning. In 1977, Locke argued against this type of process/product experimental study, designed to evaluate alternative teacher behavior. Locke (1977) based his argument on the belief that it was first necessary to generate an adequate descriptive base regarding teaching of physical education. I maintain that the current descriptive data base on teaching physical education, developed over the past 8 years, is clearly adequate to support an experimental analysis of teaching. Indeed, an experimental paradigm has been used by Siedentop (1982) and illustrates the third general strategy of research on teaching physical education.

The research sequence directed by Siedentop (1982) involves an evaluation of changes in teacher behavior as a result of specific intervention programs. That is, the dependent variables are selected aspects of teacher behavior; the independent variable is the specific teacher training or supervision package. Siedentop (1982) has clearly demonstrated that the tools and data base of descriptive research on teaching can be applied within a general experimental framework. Teacher behavior has been clearly demonstrated to change through application of specific intervention strategies. However, there remains a need for more studies such as the research by Phillips and Carlisle (1983) in which teacher behavior is defined as the independent variable in the research design; that is, aspects of teacher behavior are systematically varied as the independent variable so that the effect on measures of learning, the dependent variable, can be evaluated. The basis for the selected variations in teaching should be a model of the learning process.

Fishman and Tobey (1978) spoke to this issue in discussing their data concerning frequency, type, and timing of teacher feedback to students. They concluded that many of the differences in the way feedback was administered by teachers in their sample were due to practical limitations and to what appeared to be a less difficult approach for the teacher; that is, "There was very little theoretical basis for variations in approach" (p. 61). Fishman and Tobey (1978) suggested that "it would appear possible to use a theoretical framework . . . to illustrate different ways to give augmented feedback for different situations" (p. 62). I submit that it is not only possible, but absolutely essential, to employ a model of learning as the basis, not only for decisions regarding feedback, but also for many decisions regarding the appropriate role, function, and behavior of the teacher.

The specific nature of the processes involved in performance and learning of motor skills clearly differs for different types of learners, skills, and stages of learning. Therefore, the nature of effective teaching must also differ for different learners, skills, and stages of learning. Teaching cannot and must not be viewed as an autonomous activity. Teacher behavior is dependent on, and must be regulated by, the process of learning it assists.

A Multidimensional Research Strategy

In reviewing descriptive-analytic research on teaching, Hurwitz (1978) noted that the data would serve as a starting point for the development of a model of teaching in physical education. I believe that the appropriate starting point for developing a model of teaching is a consideration of the learning process. In order to support such a model of teaching with findings from research, a multidimensional strategy for research is required.

The past 15 to 20 years of descriptive-analytic research, particularly the last 10 years, have produced many valid, reliable instruments for objectively describing and analyzing teaching. During the same time period, research findings related to the process of learning motor skills have been used to formulate several composite models of learning. What remains is to join the two fields of inquiry logically—to employ results, techniques, and instruments from both areas of research. The field of motor learning has examined the product, learning, but has given only minor attention to the process in terms of teaching. Teacher educators have analyzed the process of teaching with very little consideration of the product. To study learning without consideration of facilitation by a teacher is self-limiting; to study teaching without a learning referent is a contradiction in terms.

We need to measure, describe, analyze, and evaluate three factors: teacher behavior, student behavior, and student learning. First, systematic differences in selected aspects of teaching can be produced, verified, and applied using the techniques and findings from both descriptive-analytic research and intervention research on teaching. Second, subsequent differences in patterns of student behavior can be analyzed, compared, and evaluated using the techniques and data base of descriptive research on student activity and ALT. Third, specific, resultant differences in student performance and learning can be identified using the techniques and findings from research on motor learning. The research question must not be simply, What did the teacher do? or What did the students do? The question must be, What did they both do, and did it work in terms of improved student performance? The basis for determining teaching effectiveness must be an evaluation of student learning, and the development of a model of teaching must be guided by a model of learning.

References

Anderson, W.G. (1978). Introduction. In W.G. Anderson & G.T. Barrette (Eds.), *Motor skills: Theory into practice: Monograph 1. What's going on in gym* (pp. 1-9). Newton, CT: A.L. Rothstein.

Anderson, W.G., & Barrette, G.T. (1978). Teacher behavior. In W.G. Anderson & G.T. Barrette (Eds.), *Motor skills: Theory into practice: Monograph 1. What's going on in gym* (pp. 11-24). Newton, CT: A.L. Rothstein.

Cheffers, J.T.F., & Mancini, V.H. (1978). Teacher-student interaction. In W.G. Anderson & G.T. Barrette (Eds.), *Motor skills: Theory into practice: Monograph 1. What's going on in gym* (pp. 39-50). Newton, CT: A.L. Rothstein.

Costello, J., & Laubach, S.A. (1978). Student behavior. In W.G. Anderson & G.T. Barrette (Eds.), *Motor skills: Theory into practice: Monograph 1. What's going on in gym* (pp. 11-24). Newton, CT: A.L. Rothstein.

Fishman, S., & Tobey, C. (1978). Augmented feedback. In W.G. Anderson & G.T. Barrette (Eds.), *Motor skills: Theory into practice: Monograph 1. What's going on in gym* (pp. 51-62). Newton, CT: A.L. Rothstein.

Hurwitz, R. (1978). Review. In W.G. Anderson & G.T. Barrette (Eds.), *Motor skills: Theory into practice: Monograph 1. What's going on in gym* (pp. 75-81). Newton, CT: A.L. Rothstein.

Locke, L. (1977). Research on teaching physical education: New hope for a dismal science. *Quest* (Monograph 28), 2-16.

Phillips, D.A., & Carlisle, C. (1983). A comparison of physical education teachers categorized as most and least effective. *Journal of Teaching Physical Education, 2*(3), 55-67.

Siedentop, D. (1982). *Recent advances in pedagogical research in physical education.* Unpublished manuscript, Ohio State University.

Silverman, S., Dodds, P., Placek, J., Shute, S., & Rife, F. (1984). Academic learning time in elementary school physical education (ALT-PE) for student subgroups and instructional activity units. *Research Quarterly for Exercise and Sport, 55*(4), 365-370.

Visual and Kinesthetic Imagery Ability in Children: Implications for Teaching Motor Skills

Graham J. Fishburne
Craig R. Hall

It appears to be well accepted by researchers that imagery plays an important role in learning, memory, and performance of movements. However, numerous questions still remain about the nature of this role. Paivio (1985), in summarizing the literature on the effects of mental rehearsal on motor performance, suggests there is sufficient evidence to be confident that mental rehearsal, and more significantly imagery rehearsal, can improve motor performance. Paivio goes on to suggest further that there is also enough positive evidence to encourage researchers to pursue imagery and to look for ways of maximizing the benefits of imagery training.

The first question to be addressed is, What is an image? The fairly straightforward definition stating that imagery is a psychological activity that evokes the physical characteristics of an absent object will suffice for the purpose of this discussion. This definition does not limit the form of imagery to merely the visual, because evidence exists that other forms of imagery, such as kinesthetic, do occur.

Imagery and Children

Very few studies involving imagery and children's motor performance have been reported. However, a wealth of evidence from the wider population suggests imagery and psychomotor performance are linked. For example, imagery has been shown to act as a device for enhancing the memorability of kinesthetic information (Hall & Buckolz, 1981). Further, high imagers have also been found to reproduce movement locations more accurately compared to low imagers (Housner & Hoffman, 1981). Ryan and Simons (1982) studied the strength and type of imagery with reference to learning to balance on a stabilometer. They concluded that participants reporting strong visual images showed more improvement than those with weak visual images, and those reporting strong kinesthetic images were superior to those with weak kinesthetic images. In addition, people most prone to imaging spontaneously, or people instructed to image, have been shown to produce the greatest gains in the learning of a motor task

(Epstein, 1980; Hale, 1982). Such findings provide ample evidence of a relationship between imagery and psychomotor performance.

With regard to the question of age and imagery, two studies are worthy of report. In 1973, Rapp and Schoder reported 5- and 6-year-old children who mentally rehearsed rope skipping and, as a result, produced significant gains in actual performance. Further, Helson (1933) cites a 3-year-old child who reported afterimages and dreams and when just a little older reported eidetic images. Young children therefore seem to be capable of experiencing, utilizing, and reporting images. With these thoughts in mind, two research studies that considered individual differences in children's visual and kinesthetic imagery of movement will be discussed. In the interests of space, only a brief description of the research, together with findings, will be presented.

External Versus Internal Imagery Formation

Mahoney and Avener (1977) had 13 Olympic standard gymnasts respond to a questionnaire designed to inquire about strategies employed in training and competition. On the topic of imagery, Mahoney and Avener reported that all 13 gymnasts used imagery extensively, but the better athletes reported using *internal* rather than *external* images. This distinction refers to the perspective of the imagery. External imagery is to view oneself from the perspective of an external observer, much like seeing oneself on film. Internal imagery, on the other hand, requires the person to imagine actually being inside their body and experiencing those sensations that might be expected in the actual situation. Paivio (1985), commenting on imagery rehearsal and memory, has suggested that for imagery purposes the richness of the memory base is one of the crucial factors. The only way of increasing this memory base, however, is through direct practice or through the vicarious experience of observing the performance of experts. Paivio suggests film experience will increase the perceptual knowledge base for imagery rehearsal. He does acknowledge, however, that film experiences will only develop a knowledge base for external imagery. Because Mahoney and Avener state that successful athletes tend to use internal imagery, then the efficacy of Paivio's suggested procedure is questionable. It is, however, difficult to generalize from the limited study of Mahoney and Avener, and in this respect we present some data collected from a group of young children.

The effects of mental rehearsal, physical practice, a combination of mental rehearsal and physical practice, and no practice were studied in relation to improvement in the athletic skill of shotputting. The skill of shotputting is a closed skill and is similar in many instances to most gymnastic skills (i.e., the performer must execute a complex and precise motor skill that does not require reaction to a specific target). Sixty-four 12-year-old boys were initially tested on the skill of shotputting and then randomly assigned to one of four treatment groups. After seven daily practice sessions in each treatment condition, all four groups were retested in shotputting. The experiment followed the basic paradigm employed in most mental practice studies and observed the usual methodological requirements for conducting such research. The physical-practice group made the greatest mean gain (34 cm per subject), closely followed by the combined mental-rehearsal and physical-practice group (28 cm per subject). Both of these groups made significant gains ($p < .01$ and $p < .05$ level, respectively). The mental-rehearsal-only group improved their mean performance (9 cm per subject), and there was a slight improvement for the control group (3 cm per subject), which was probably due to the effects of motivation.

These results support similar findings from many other studies demonstrating the usefulness of mental imagery for improving motor skill performance. Further, this study demonstrates that school-aged children can benefit from imagery rehearsal. The most interesting part of the shotputting study, however, was revealed by a set of self-report questionnaires designed to elicit information on visual and kinesthetic imagery. Of those subjects who utilized mental rehearsal several findings are noteworthy. First, those students who experienced difficulty in visualizing a clear image tended to deteriorate in performance or stay at approximately the same level. Second, those boys who changed their rehearsal strategies during each practice session deteriorated in performance. These changes frequently involved the number of rehearsals and the form of the image (i.e., changing from an external to internal imagery perspective). Third, several subjects reported a change in visual or kinesthetic imagery over the 7-day experimental period. These boys claimed the clarity of their images improved. However, no trends in performance changes were evident for this select group. Finally, 16% of the subjects visualized some other person than themselves shotputting. Over 50% of the subjects imagined they were shotputting in front of a crowded audience; the remainder imagined performing alone. No real trends in performance, however, were correlated with these findings. Responses to the question regarding the subject imaging shotputting in the circle (internal imager) as opposed to viewing from outside the circle (external imager) elicited the most interesting result. A 50% response for each type of image was reported. However, when performance was considered, external imagers produced significantly better ($p < .05$) performance than the internal imagers. The internal imagers produced negligible improvement.

This finding is the exact opposite of that cited by Mahoney and Avener for Olympic gymnasts. Here, internal imagery was reported as most beneficial. There could be several reasons to account for this difference. First, the Olympic athletes were probably very close to the autonomous stage of learning for their gymnastic skills, having practiced them many times. Each practice elicits a knowledge of performance (kinesthetic feedback) in addition to a knowledge of results. The elite Olympic athletes more than likely had well-established, rich internal kinesthetic images formed. The young schoolboys were far from this autonomous stage and more than likely had poorly developed internal images formulated in their memory base. Rehearsing a poorly formed image or even an incorrectly formed image will no doubt have corresponding effects on performance. This could account for the poor performances of the internal imagers in the shotputting study. The use of external imagery, however, was very beneficial for the young boys, and so Paivio's suggestion for the use of film to enhance the perceptual knowledge base would seem very appropriate for performers still striving for the autonomous stage of learning. Further, not all the elite Olympic gymnasts utilized internal imagery in Mahoney and Avener's study. Obviously, using external imagery is still good enough to get to the Olympics!

Physically Adept and Physically Awkward Children

The second study to be reviewed is part of a 1985 study by Fishburne (in press) involving elementary-aged school children. Basically, the study attempted to test for any relationship between physically adept and physically awkward children and imagery. Elementary schools were chosen at random and children were administered motor development tests to assess their respective levels of psychomotor proficiency. The children were observed, filmed, and photographed while performing basic motor skills such as running, jumping, and throwing. Their performances were then compared with Wickstrom's (1983) developmental analysis of fundamental motor patterns. Those children classified as physically adept (gifted) and those judged to be physically awkward in psychomotor development were then administered a modified version (for children) of Hall and Pongrac's (1983) movement imagery questionnaire (MIQ) to acquire information on visual and kinesthetic imagery of movement. Only grade 6 data will be presented in an effort to make a comparison with a similar study by Hall (1983). He administered the same modified MIQ test to a random selection of 58 Grade 6 and Grade 8 students. Compari-

Table 1 Comparison of Children's Visual and Kinesthetic Imagery Scores

Study	Sample	Visual imagery	Kinesthetic imagery
Hall (1983) N = 58	Elementary school students Grades 6 & 8 (ages 11–15) Normal population	20.87 ∓ 8.51	23.10 ∓ 7.80
Fishburne (in press) N = 25	Elementary school students Grade 6 (ages 11–12) Gifted in psychomotor development	19.72 ∓ 6.84	20.23 ∓ 8.1
Fishburne (in press) N = 25	Elementary school students Grade 6 (ages 11–12) Physically awkward	26.15 ∓ 9.71	28.95 ∓ 9.77

son of results from these two studies are presented in Table 1, with mean and standard deviation scores being presented. Note that the lower the score, the more vivid and clear the image. Although Hall's study also included children in Grade 8, comparison of visual and kinesthetic imagery trends are interesting. The physically adept group of children experienced much clearer visual and kinesthetic images compared to the physically awkward children. This gifted group also experienced superior imagery when compared to Hall's normal population. In constrast, the physically awkward children were poor in both visual and kinesthetic imagery. Basically, it would appear the better the image the better the performance. Causal inferences are, however, difficult to make, since performance may also be dictating imagery. Nevertheless, there does appear to be a high correlation between imagery and children's motor performance.

Implications for Teaching Motor Skills

The studies cited, together with other published research, suggest imagery is intricately linked with motor behavior. Certainly children are capable of experiencing and utilizing both visual and kinesthetic forms of imagery in movement. Due to a scarcity of coherent and systematic research in this field, it is difficult to offer generalizations. However, certain points may be drawn. Whether imagery abilities (e.g., vividness, control, etc.) can be developed in children is unknown at the present time and obviously awaits future research. On the other hand, imagery skills (i.e., the effective use of imagery to benefit performance) can be developed in children. Galyean (1983), writing on guided imagery in the education curriculum, cites research evidence to suggest psychomotor skills can be improved by teaching children how to utilize their imagery abilities. Improvement in imagery (skill) appears to improve motor performance. Certainly, physically awkward children who possess such poor visual and kinesthetic imagery for movement may be one population to gain from the imagery improvement methods suggested by Galyean. Developing imagery techniques in children would appear to be sound educational practice. External imaging may also assist children in the acquisition of perceptual motor skills. The success noted by the external imagers in the shotput study attests to the potency of this form of imagery technique. Also, Paivio's suggestions on how to improve a child's perceptual memory base through practice and film viewing will help children to establish effective external images. Such information is vital to physical education teachers, who must be cognizant of the potential benefits to be accrued through the improvement of children's imagery skills.

References

Epstein, M.L. (1980). The relationship of mental imagery and mental rehearsal to performance of a motor task. *Journal of Sport Psychology*, **2**, 211-220.

Fishburne, G.J. (in press). *The relationship between imagery ability and children gifted in the motor domain.* Manuscript submitted for publication.

Galyean, B.C. (1983). Guided imagery in the curriculum. *Educational Leadership,* **40**(6), 54–57.

Hale, B.D. (1982). The effects of internal and external imagery on muscular and ocular concomitants. *Journal of Sport Psychology,* **4**, 379–387.

Hall, C.R. (1983). *Individual differences in grade 6 and grade 8 students' visual and kinesthetic imagery of movements.* Research report submitted to The Board of Education for the City of London, Ontario from the Department of Physical Education, University of Western Ontario, London.

Hall, C.R., & Buckolz, E. (1981). Recognition memory for movement patterns and their corresponding pictures. *Journal of Mental Imagery,* **5**, 97–104.

Hall, C.R., & Pongrac, J. (1983). *Movement imagery questionnaire.* London, Ontario, Canada: University of Western Ontario, Department of Physcial Education.

Helson, H. (1933). A child's spontaneous reports of imagery. *American Journal of Psychology,* **45**, 360–361.

Housner, L., & Hoffman, S.J. (1981). Imagery ability in recall of distance and location information. *Journal of Motor Behavior,* **13**, 207–223.

Mahoney, M.J., & Avener, M. (1977). Psychology of the elite athlete: An exploratory study. *Cognitive Therapy and Research,* **1**, 135–141.

Paivio, A. (1985). Cognitive and motivational functions of imagery in human performance. *Canadian Journal of Applied Sport Sciences,* **10**(4), 225–285.

Rapp, G., & Schoder, G. (1973). Bewegungsvorstellung und Bewegungslernen bei Kindern [Movement performance and the acquisition of movement in children]. *Psychologie in Erziehung und Unterricht,* **20**, 279–288.

Ryan, E.D., & Simons, J. (1982). Efficacy of mental imagery in enhancing rehearsal of motor skills. *Journal of Sport Psychology,* **4**, 41–51.

Wickstrom, R.L. (1983). *Fundamental motor patterns.* Philadelphia: Lea and Febiger.

Beyond the Development of a Utilitarian Teaching Perspective: An Australian Case Study of Action Research in Teacher Preparation

Richard I. Tinning

Victoria, one of the six states in Australia, is about the size of England and has a population of 5 million people. Teachers for primary schools are typically trained in colleges of advanced education (3 years in duration for the Diploma of Teaching), which are separate institutions from universities. Within the current 3-year program students typically complete about 100 days for school experience.

Physical Education in Victorian Primary Schools

Within the Victorian State Education Department, physical education is one of the curriculum areas within primary schools. Although the responsibility for teaching physical education rests with the individual classroom teachers, who are trained as generalists, there is a growing trend for schools to designate one of their teachers as the physical education specialist or coordinator. This teacher will also be a generalist, rather than a trained specialist, although some have majored in physical education in college.

In some schools these "specialist" teachers will take all the physical education for the entire school. Where this happens, class teachers use physical education time as time release, and children usually only get one timetabled session with the specialist each week. In some other schools, the specialist coordinates the physical education for the entire school, but class teachers are expected to do some of the teaching (usually in a facet or platoon system). Many of the schools that use this model for their program are implementing physical education on a daily basis for all children. In fact, daily physical education as an innovation may be judged by some to be a success simply in terms of the number of schools that have adopted the idea. Many of the schools have actually had to bring about significant changes in their timetables to accomplish the introduction of daily physical education. Increasingly, however, there has been some disquiet about the quality of physical education as it is being implemented in Victorian primary schools (see Tinning, 1982). It is my belief that, in general, the quality of physical education teaching is poor. But I don't just mean poor in a technical sense, that is, in terms of *how* it is implemented. I also mean poor in terms of its social, moral, and political underpinnings.

The Utilitarian Teaching Perspective

Why do I claim that the teaching of physical education generally leaves much to be desired? At one level I could claim that the actual academic learning time (ALT) in most classes is less than optimal, although I only have limited data collected by my own students from which to make this claim. Australia does not possess the extensive information that, for example, the Teachers College Data Bank gives U.S. physical education teaching analysts.

However, at another level I would claim that teachers seldom ask questions related to the implications of what they teach in physical education or the way they teach it. Many physical education classes are characterized by poor choice of activity, little attempt to develop appropriate social behavior, inequitable distribution of teacher attention to pupils, sexism, and inappropriate expectations with respect to pupil performance. The problem is that teachers don't necessarily ignore these issues, but most likely they never even think of them *as* issues. Their teaching in physical education is characterized more by filling in available time with some form of activity that is defined as physical education, which gives the children a break from classroom activities and which doesn't create too many hassles in the area of class preparation, management, and control. In summary, the general approach to physical education could be characterized by a mentality of "enjoy the fresh air, keep the kids cooperating (not necessarily active), and spend a minimal amount of time planning and reflecting." By and large, little or no attention is given to what kids learn either from the explicit or implicit curriculum. Perhaps it's the antipodean equivalent of Placek's (1983) "busy, happy, and good" physical education classes.

At this point it must be stressed that this criticism of what counts for primary school physical education in Australia is not meant to lay blame at the feet of the teachers. Those of us who spend a good deal of time in primary schools recognize the often unrealistic demands placed on generalist teachers. It is my view that we need to look to teacher education programs as *one way* to begin to address the issue of what counts for quality physical education teaching in primary schools.

Teacher education programs need to lay the foundations for the development of educational practice that is reflective, collaborative, sensitive to contradictions, just, and purposeful. What we see in our schools is physical education that operates from a utilitarian teaching perspective, and we find the beginnings of this perspective developed and reinforced in our teacher education programs (Zeichner, 1980).

Zeichner (1981) claims that teaching is often separated from its moral, ethical, and political dimensions. If a particular procedure or activity works to solve the immediate problem at hand, it is considered as good for that reason alone. In teacher education, the issue of "*why* something is taught and the possible long-term effects of a particular classroom action are typically not addressed by student teachers" (p. 3). Furthermore, "student teaching as it presently exists seems to further utilitarian thinking and a search for recipe knowledge to guide classroom practice" (p. 8). The apparently universal tendency of teacher education programs to graduate teachers with utilitarian teaching perspectives is revealed in the studies of Gibson (1976) in the U.K., Tabachnick, Popkewitz, and Zeichner (1980) in the U.S.A., and Turney et al. (1982) in Australia. Nothing I have seen in the U.S.A. or Australia suggests that the situation is in any way different within the physical education context.

Granted, changes to teacher education programs will do nothing to alter the accountability mechanisms that operate in schools with respect to quality physical education, but I believe that it is in teacher education that we must begin to prepare teachers for accountability in the gymnasium. This notion of preparing for accountability is described by Elliott (1982) in his paper "Preparing Teachers for Classroom Accountability." In essence, Elliott claims that fair accountability "can exist only when an outsider's judgement is open to defeat by the agent" (p. 314). Elliott contends that teachers need to be prepared to defend their action on the basis of their practical and their moral and ethical considerations. The ability to defend one's actions will depend on acquiring self-monitoring skills and a reflective attitude to one's practice. For Elliott it "will demand a radically different sort of teacher education curriculum from the one that has been established over the last fifteen years" (p. 321). It would need to be a program that has the potential to take student teachers beyond the development of a utilitarian teaching perspective.

Teacher as Researcher:
Student Teacher as Learner Teacher-Researcher

How can we establish a form of teacher education that has the potential to move teachers beyond the utilitarian and toward a critical reflective perspective that enables them to take greater control over their teaching in ways that are just, rational, and moral?

Pickle (1984) calls for a "teacher preparation model that might lend continuity across both pre- and inservice development" (p. 13). It seems to me to be essential that notions of professional development thought worthwhile for practicing teachers should also be the basis for professional development during teacher preparation programs. There should be a consistent epistemology of practice in both preservice and inservice programs. An appropriate notion that has potential for professional development across both pre- and inservice teacher education is Stenhouse's (1975) "teacher as researcher." According to Stenhouse, teacher-researchers have a "capacity for autonomous professional development through *systematic self study*, through the study of the work of other teachers and through the testing of ideas by *classroom research procedures*" (p. 144). These teachers do not uncritically accept curriculum packages as given, nor do they regard pedagogy as nonproblematic. They do not embrace research findings simply because they are written in some learned journal by some learned expert. They are critical consumers and developers of knowledge, and their own practice is a continual source of inquiry and of professional renewal.

Certainly in Australian primary schools the idea of teachers systematically studying their own physical education teaching and actively considering the problematic nature of their theories-of-action (Sanders & McCutcheon, 1984) is far from commonplace. Physical education inservice still consists mainly of "one-off" curriculum days in which an expert presents ideas for curriculum practice that teachers are then presumed to implement in their own settings. That this form of inservice has been shown to be a consistent failure in the education literature seems to have been totally ignored by the Australian physical education profession. Henry (1984) claims that typical inservice programs and conventional teacher education programs embody asymmetrical power relations between expert and the learner and that this is incompatible with the idea of developing teacher-researchers. As Beyer (1984) claims, "experiences which promote uncritical replication of observed practice are antithetical to the purposes of education itself. Promoting activities for student teachers and others which generate such perspectives is, thus, contradictory to some fundamental purposes of education . . ." (p. 37). In 1982 McTaggart wrote that "Australian teachers are thinking more reflectively and critically about their work than ever before. This is evident in a growing literature of teachers' accounts of their attempts to implement improvement and change in classrooms and schools" (p. 101). In 1985 there was still little evidence that this process has ever begun with respect to physical education teaching in primary schools.

It is important to understand that the notion of systematic self-study suggested by Stenhouse is different to behavioristic-oriented approaches to teacher education not just at the level of technique but at the more fundamental level of supporting epistemology. Unlike behavioristic approaches to teacher education, which are informed by a positivist epistemology, advocates of the teacher-as-researcher notion recognize professional knowledge as that which is embedded within action itself. Observable behavior is seen as a necessary, but not sufficient, reference point from which to bring about changes in the professional practice of teachers. Research into one's practice will involve more than counting the number of positive reinforcement statements or determining the amount of academic learning time. Whereas these data may indeed be important with respect to certain issues of concern for teachers, in and of themselves they are technical questions that represent part of the current problem in trying to improve schooling in general and physical education specifically (see Schön, 1982; Tinning, 1985). These questions only become useful when the dialectic nature of the relationship between means and ends is fully understood. A question like, How much time does the class spend in activity? is too often left in an instrumental form whereby it is assumed that more ALT will produce more learning. Increasing ALT becomes an end in itself, and the concern is to find the most efficient means to achieve that end.

In some sense I think that the physical education profession has been lead to believe that all we need to do to improve physical education in schools is to increase ALT. The profession by and large has embraced the technical rationality model of science, in which solutions to complex problems are sought by simplistic "objective" measurements. As Schön (1982) has argued, the current crisis in confidence in the professions in general (including teaching) is that the model of technical rationality that they embrace has been unable to "fit" societal problems that are embedded in phenomena like "complexity, uncertainty, instability, uniqueness and value conflict" (p. 39). Within the teacher profession we need to begin to reshape our teacher education programs such that the limits of technical rationality are understood by our future teachers and that practices that embody a different epistemology are considered. The concept of teacher-as-researcher has potential to reshape teacher education in this way.

Action Research as a Process for Teacher-Researchers

For teachers-as-researchers, a process that has the potential to employ an alternative epistemology of practice to that of positivism and that fosters a "reflective orientation which informs and influences practice" is *action research* (Henry, 1982, p. 3). Although action research has had a long and somewhat tortured history in education (see Kemmis & McTaggart, 1982), according to Grundy and Kemmis (1981)

> there are two essential aims of all action research activity: to *improve* and *involve*. Action research aims at improvement in three areas:
> - The improvement of practice
> - The improvement of the understanding of the practice by its practitioners, and
> - The improvement of the situation in which the practice takes place (p. 84)

In essence, educational action research involves practitioners (teachers or student teachers) in cycles of planning, action, observation, and reflection with respect to their educational practice. The steps in the cycle are seen as a dynamic process that aims to bring together discourse and action. Improvements in understanding and practice can be made systematically, responsively, and reflectively. It is claimed that a rationale for practice can be both articulated and tested through the process. "In the long term, these propositions [being tested] will develop into a perspective on education itself, becoming a critical theory . . ." (Kemmis & McTaggart, 1982, p. 10). This cycle of planning, acting, observing, and reflecting is deceptively simple, but it can represent a radical shift in terms of a view of professional development. It has the potential to help teachers move beyond that which is taken for granted in their everyday practice.

Using Action Research with Student Teachers

In 1981 a small pilot program in school-based teacher education (SBTE) began at Deakin University. The staff who began the program believed that the traditional teacher education program did little to assist learner teachers to become active shapers of their own professional development. Moreover, the very nature of the traditional program actually maintained the theory-practice gap that is said to characterize most teacher education and most teaching (see Carr, 1980).

The SBTE program, as it became known, was an attempt to operationalize a different epistemology in teacher education. Knowledge about teaching was considered to be more than that conceived by experts and then dutifully implemented by practitioners. Rather, teachers are believed to hold their own "practical theories of teaching" (Elliott & Adelman, 1982), and the program holds that teacher education should be about learning to develop one's own practical theories that are informed both by one's practice and the educational literature. Such theories should also be the continual focus for validation with respect to one's moral judgments about teaching in general (and all teaching involves constant moral judgment) and one's own teaching practice in particular.

The jargon used for the program was *research-based teacher education*, but this phrase has also been used to describe very traditional programs in which worthwhile knowledge is contained in learned journals and the lecture notes of professors. In the Deakin SBTE program it means teacher education based on research into *one's own practice*. This is a very different notion from basing a teacher education program on the research of experts into the practice of teachers. It is not to say, however, that such research findings are not important or useful. Rather, it is assuming that such research is only meaningful to student teachers (and teachers) when the need to try out the ideas of research has originated in their own practical concerns. An essential feature of the SBTE program is its attempt to raise the consciousness of student teachers to issues of concern that might be outside the limited history of each individual. In the words of Henry and Charles (1985),

Our intention was to change the material, interpersonal and evaluative conditions of school-based experiences for student teachers in the program. The direction of change was intended to promote open attitudes of inquiry into teaching and learning, to promote an independence of thinking, and to promote a reflective orientation towards one's teaching.

In practice this has meant students spending extended periods of time in schools in which their actual teaching forms the testing ground for ideas that may or may not be conventionally taught as curriculum and teaching studies. In the SBTE program there is no preplanned course of theory in curriculum or teaching. Students attempt to improve and understand their educational practice by using the process of action research. A key feature of the program is working through the action research cycles where other student teachers, cooperating teachers, and university supervisors act as critical friends with whom to share insights, data, and reflections.

The Action Research Focus and Its Results in Physical Education

As a requirement for teacher registration in the state of Victoria, all teachers must have completed curriculum studies in all curriculum areas. In physical education, students in the conventional program do a rather traditional unit (of approximately two credit hours' value) that includes lectures, practical sessions, and peer teaching sessions. Students in the SBTE program received no such course but instead were required to teach a series of physical education lessons and to use these lessons as the venue to improve their educational practice in physical education. Students were also required to identify an issue of concern in their physical education teaching (all students had taught at least three physical education lessons on previous school experience) and to work through action research cycles with other students, cooperating teachers, and myself as the critical friends. My role was that of facilitator, and I organized the action research tutorials in which students were required to present data that were collected on an aspect of their teaching by a peer of by the cooperating teacher. The data were to serve as the focus for tutorial sessions in which discussion would be concerned with interpretation of the data and with suggesting strategies for change, including relevant research literature that might be useful in helping to understand current practice and to suggest alternative practices worthy of testing.

At the outset it needs to be understood that the success or failure of this project was not something that could be measured in any absolute way. The aim was to move students toward an alternative consciousness with respect to their own professional development. By giving student teachers more control over their own professional development and by encouraging collaborative ways of working with peers and significant others, it was hoped to *begin* a process rather than to produce a product.

That said, it would be misleading to suggest that this small project was a resounding success, given its lofty ideals. But then again, we are not ignorant to the difficulties of working with student teachers in nonconventional ways. Zeichner and Liston's (1985) account for the University of Wisconsin's student teaching program makes chilling reading in this regard. However it would also be misleading to overlook some of the useful understandings that were born out of this project.

To be sure, the idea of students working with their peers to collect data on each others' teaching was more difficult to organize than was anticipated. But students did manage to get data collected in numerous lessons that were relevant to their particular action research focus. Within the length of this paper it is not possible to present case report data with respect to how two student teachers worked through action research into their own teaching. Readers interested in these two case reports should contact that author directly.

Repeatedly it was found that it is difficult for cooperating teachers to readily change their form of note taking during lessons, and equally difficult to get student teachers to define precisely a particular data collection focus for a given lesson. I am certain that, given the development of observation and recording skills and explicit expectations relating to collaborative learning based on data collected from actual lessons, these problems will become less significant.

Another issue that affected the success of the project was the difficulty students had in taking a more long-term view of changing their own practice. To be sure, the actual school experience round was short, but typically students identified an issue of concern in one lesson and dealt with it in the next lesson. There was, it seemed, a view that an issue must be solved in one lesson and that it was then time to move on to another concern. Certainly a more extended view of change is necessary as well as an emphasis on the fact that in any given lesson it is not possible to focus on more than one issue and collect useful data with respect to that issue.

I feel reasonable comfortable with the claim that at least two of the aims of action research (Grundy & Kemmis, 1981) were partially fulfilled within this project. Students did actually improve some aspects of their practice (aspects that *they* considered important), and they did improve their understandings of the issues involved in their own physical education teaching.

Finally, and most importantly, these student teachers began a process of professional development that is consistent with inservice processes that recognize teachers' practical knowledge and that allow teachers to shape and control their own professional development through collaborative endeavors. It was an important beginning.

References

Beyer, L. (1984). Field experience, ideology, and the development of critical reflectivity. *Journal of Teacher Education, 25*(3), 36–41.

Carr, W. (1980). The gap between theory and practice. *Journal of Further and Higher Education, 4*, 60–69.

Carr, W., & Kemmis, S. (1983). *Becoming critical: Knowing through action research.* Geelong, Victoria: Deakin University Press.

Dodd, G. (1984, January). *Daily physical education in Australia.* Paper presented at the 15th National Australian Council for Health, Physical Education, and Recreation Biennial conference, University of New South Wales, Sydney.

Elliott, J. (1982). Preparing teachers for classroom accountability. In S. Kemmis & R. McTaggart (Eds.), *The action research reader.* Geelong, Victoria: Deakin University Press.

Elliott, J., & Aledman, C. (1982). Reflecting where the action is: The design of the Ford Teaching Project. In S. Kemmis & R. McTaggart (Eds.), *The action research reader.* Geelong, Victoria: Deakin University Press.

Gibson, R. (1976). The effects of school practice: The development of student perspectives. *British Journal of Teacher Education, 2*, 241–250.

Grundy, S., & Kemmis, S. (1981, November). *Educational action research in Australia: The state of the art (an overview).* Paper presented at the annual meeting of the Australia Association for Research in Education, Adelaide.

Henry, J. (1982).*Teachers as researchers: An action research model applied to inquiry teaching.* Unpublished paper, Deakin University.

Henry, J. (1984, July). *Action research for teacher reflectiveness.* Paper presented at the 6th "Drive In" Curriculum Conference, Western Australian College of Advanced Education, Perth.

Henry, J., & Charles, R. (1985). Collaborative relationships within school-based experiences. *The South Pacific Journal of Teacher Education, 13*(1), 53–63.

Kemmis, S., & McTaggart, R. (1982). *The action research planner.* Geelong, Victoria: Deakin University Press.

McTaggart, R. (1982). Introduction. In S. Kemmis & R. McTaggart, *The action research reader.* Geelong, Victoria: Deakin University Press.

Pickle, J. (1984). Relationships between knowledge and learning environment in teacher education. *Journal of Teacher Education, 35*(5), 13–17.

Placek, J. (1983). Conceptions of success in teaching: Busy, happy and good? In T. Templin & J. Olson (Eds.), *Teaching in physical education* (pp. 46–56). Champaign, IL: Human Kinetics.

Sanders, D., & McCutcheon, G. (1984, April). *On the evolution of teachers' theories of action through action research.* Paper presented at the Annual Conference of the American Educational Research Association, New Orleans.

Schön, D. (1982). *The reflective practitioner.* New York: Basic Books.

Stenhouse, L. (1975). *An introduction to curriculum research and development.* London: Heinemann Educational Books.

Tabachnick, R., Popkewitz, T., & Zeichner, K. (1980). Teacher education and the professional perspectives of student teachers. *Interchange, 10,* 12–29.

Tinning, R. (1982). Teacher reaction to the trial materials: A Victorian case study. *Australian Journal for Health, Physical Education, & Recreation, 95,* 11–14.

Tinning, R. (1985, August). *Student teaching and the pedagogy of necessity.* Paper presented at the International Association for Physical Education in Higher Education World Conference, Adelphi University, Garden City, NY.

Turney, C., Cairns, L., Eltis, K., Hatton, N., Thew, D., Towler, J., & Wright, R. (1982). *The practicum and teacher education. Research, practice & supervision.* Sydney: Sydney University Press.

Zeichner, K. (1980). Myths and realities: Field based experiences in preservice teacher education. *Journal of Teacher Education, 31*(6), 45–55.

Zeichner, K. (1981). Reflective teaching and field-based experiences in teacher education. *Interchange, 12,* 1–12.

Zeichner, K., & Liston, D. (1985, April). *Theory and practice in the evolution of an inquiry-oriented student teaching program.* Paper presented at the annual meeting of the American Educational Research Association, Chicago, IL.

Five Years of Program Development: A Retrospective

William G. Anderson

Five years ago, we established the Physical Education Program Development Center. It was a collaborative venture involving Teachers College, Columbia University, and several school districts. Our purpose was to help the districts develop and maintain effective physical education programs. At the time there was a need for program and staff development; physical education was under pressure and the teaching staffs were aging and in need of revitalization. We believed that a college teacher education program, in partnership with the schools, could provide the outside stimulation and resources needed to initiate and sustain improvement.

From the outset, we were interested in sustained improvement—not a transitory project of some kind that would make a big splash and then fade. So we realized that an extended commitment would be necessary. The center would have to be an ongoing operation. For how long we were not sure—perhaps for as long as the need persisted and we were able to provide useful services.

Five years later we are still in operation. The need persists; indeed, the teaching staffs are even older and the pressure on physical education has never been greater. The school districts have just voted unanimously to continue support for the center, which indicates that we are continuing to provide some useful services. And so we are planning for year 6. Although we still don't know how long the center will persist, I must confess that it is gratifying to realize that it has come this far.

I've reported elsewhere on the work of the center during its earlier stages. The 5-year mark seems to be an appropriate time to issue a follow-up report. Our 5 years of experience have given us a somewhat different perspective; I would like to think that we are older and wiser now, but perhaps we are just older.

The principal motivation for making these reports is that we firmly believe that this kind of work with inservice teachers and ongoing programs is extremely important to the future of physical education. We recognize that our approach is only one of many possible ways to stimulate program development. Nevertheless, we do hope that by sharing our experiences others will be prompted to take up the cause and start their own centers or similar undertakings.

Organization of the Center

Organizationally, we have tried to create a stable institution somewhere in the space between the schools and the university. To do so you need physical space, staff, funding, programs, and, especially, people who maintain a major commitment to the operation over time. This is not easy to do, particularly when the people involved have primary commitments to other institutions (i.e., school people to their schools and college people to their colleges). We knew this from the beginning, and so our efforts to create a workable institution have always been tempered by the knowledge that we would be partially suspended in space. We simply had to make certain that we were sufficiently well tethered to the ground to keep from floating away.

First of all we needed a place—literally a physical space to occupy. Fortunately, the Tarrytown school district has donated unused offices in their administration building for our office and resource room. This place has been pivotal in sustaining our sense of identity as an institution.

The center staff consists of two codirectors (myself and Jack McCleery, director of physical education for the Tarrytown schools), normally at least two doctoral students who serve as assistant director and center associates, and other consultants from Teachers College.

The executive council (formerly called the advisory council) is made up of the directors of physical education from each affiliated district and the center's codirectors and assistant director. The council sets policy, plans and approves programs, and monitors progress. One noticeable change in the governance of the center in recent years is that the executive council has assumed more direct responsibility for the work of the center; thus, the local directors of physical education exercise more control over operations. This we regard as a healthy trend—local district administrators should accept as much responsibility for program development as possible. It helps to enhance their vested interest in the program and thereby ensures follow-through on projects.

Funding for the center is provided by (a) the Horace Mann-Lincoln Institute and the Division of Instruction of Teachers College, which pays for release time for me; (b) the Department of Movement Sciences and Education, Teachers College, which pays a partial stipend to a student-staff member; and (c) annual dues from each affiliated school district, which cover stipends and miscellaneous costs. Our funding sources have remained stable through the years. We have never been threatened by withdrawal of support, perhaps because we have not asked for much (e.g., $600 dues per district) and we have stayed with local sources. On the other hand, we have not been successful in locating promising sources of sizable contributions. (We received only one small grant for an adaptive physical education project.) But then, from the beginning we never counted on major funding from outside agencies. Frankly, I am thankful that we have not been subjected to the vicissitudes of grant applications and renewals, and furthermore that we have not had to shape our programs to suit the demands of a granting agency. I don't think we could have survived under those conditions.

We now have six affiliated school districts; we started with five, but one dropped out and two were added. We have had numerous requests from other districts to join the center, but we have had to turn them down because we are operating at absolute capacity. Also, schools from other areas have asked that we start another center in their region, which of course is well beyond our capabilities. I have suggested that they contact other universities to work with them, but I don't know what the outcome has been. So, our operation remains relatively small. Perhaps that is for the better. Maybe a center with a larger number of affiliated districts would be unwieldy and impersonal. In any event, who's to say what is "small"? Perhaps six districts is as much as anyone should hope to influence in his or her professional career.

Operating Features

We have used a substantial range of operating procedures over the years. In fact, this kind of program development work is much like teaching in the sense that you have to be responsive to constantly changing realities. We have continuously experimented with new approaches to meet new situations. Furthermore, we have different districts, different schools, and different teachers to contend with—all of which demand some degree of individualized attention. The result is that the cumulative array of operating procedures used has been quite extensive.

Administrative Support

In each district we start by obtaining the cooperation and interest of the director of physical education. The director in turn gets the support of other key administrators, usually superintendents and principals. If the director of physical education is not interested and, in fact, not enthusiastic, then the program in that district is doomed.

Self-Assessment

A district joining the center is obligated to have the physical education staff complete an assessment of its current program. This assessment is repeated each year and sets the basis for their program development priorities. This procedure helps to assure that whatever major directions are set come from the grass roots (i.e., the teachers who eventually are going to have to carry out any proposed changes).

District Staff Meetings on Program

Early on we discovered that districts did not devote a meaningful amount of staff meeting time to issues of program development. We all (i.e., center staff, administrators, and teachers) thought this simply had to be corrected, so regular staff meetings devoted to program discussions and planning were encouraged. Center staff members attended these meetings whenever possible to act as facilitators. Directors reported at center executive council meetings on the results of their district staff meetings. Thus it became an understanding that such meetings and consequent program planning were an obligation of center membership.

Regular Workshops

Unquestionably the key feature of our program has been to bring teachers together from across districts to participate in center workshops. These full-day workshops are structured to have teachers share ideas, plan program improvements, and report back to the group at a subsequent workshop on the implementation of the plan. Whereas center staff members and outside resource persons often contributed to the workshops, the teachers themselves were the main source of ideas. Normally we held three workshops per year for elementary teachers, three for middle school, and three for high school; we supplemented these with special-purpose workshops and miniworkshops for administrators. These workshops were the touchstones for program change. Commitments to change were forged at the workshops, and teachers were subsequently held accountable for what they had done.

Teacher Ownership

From the beginning we have done all that we can to promote teacher ownership. They chose to participate and they chose what they wanted to do (as individuals or as groups). While they were doing the job and when it was completed it was theirs! They owned it. In our judgment, this is an enormously important feature of the center's work. Teacher ownership sustained teacher effort and commitment. Besides, I seriously doubt that we would have made it through 1 year had we tried to foist our priorities on them.

Visitations to Classes

Center staff members visited teachers a lot. As you know, teaching can be an isolated job. Teachers appreciate a show of interest and support, and that is what we tried to provide. Teachers do not appreciate being spied on and judged; that is what we tried to avoid. Overall, these visitations seem to have been crucial; they helped to create a sense of the "presence" of the center and of the concern for curriculum improvement. When we did not show up for extended periods of time in a particular district, they let us know that something was missing or that we were delinquent.

Teacher Rewards

We started by arranging for in-service credit for all teachers who participated in workshops or projects. For many, there had to be a tangible reward for getting involved in the first place. Now, 5 years later, those who participate do so for whatever intrinsic rewards accrue to them. We are fond of inferring that the need for extrinsic rewards has been replaced by the intrinsic joys of working to improve one's program. There may be other explanations, and in any case the motivation varies by individual.

Publicity/Reports

We do all sorts of reporting on our activities. In fact, in one sense, the center is a continuing network of communications. Directors report to other directors in executive council meetings; directors report to their staffs; teachers report to other teachers in their district (at staff meetings) and to teachers in other districts (at workshops); the center staff prepares written reports on all meetings and circulates them; written and oral reports are also made to district administrators, to school boards, and to the public. All of this reporting has several virtues, not the least of which are that a climate of activity is created, people know what other people are doing, and ideas used in one place are constantly showing up elsewhere.

Let me make a few overall comments about our mode of operation. First, this operational model we use is a particular way of approaching the task of program development. Whereas some of its characteristics were based on suggestions of researchers and others were borrowed from other centers, much of what we do has evolved to fit the situation—some of it rationally, some of it not so rationally. I must confess that many of these procedures reflect my own prejudices and preferences. For example, I don't especially like to tell other people what they should do, so this model is designed virtually to coerce people to do what *they* want to do. In many other ways this is an idiosyncratic approach to program development. It may well not work elsewhere. I would invite others who venture into this sort of center work to have fun evolving their own set of idiosyncrasies. It's a necessary part of the game.

Second, operating procedures have to change over time. Some of the procedures I just told you about are not working as well as they used to. For example, self-assessment procedures are not being taken as seriously as they once were. There is nothing quite as sinful in program development work as to allow routine to take over. Change agents cannot allow themselves to stagnate. After 5 years many of our procedures are becoming too routine. One of our main procedures for the 6th year will be to change procedures. The tricky part will come in deciding which ones to change and how much.

Projects and Programs

The center has been responsible for an enormous number and variety of projects during the past 5 years. Most of these have been directly initiated through our workshops and visits to schools. Many others, however, have been indirect outgrowths of our work. Teachers initiate a center-sponsored project in their school, and if it works they share it with others in neighboring schools, who in turn adopt the innovation or some variation of it. Or perhaps a director of physical education sees an effective project in operation at one school and proceeds to make sure that it is tried out at other schools. In fact, in a whole variety of ways, projects initiated by the center are extended and diffused throughout the districts, and in many cases are transformed to suit the special characteristics of the particular school.

Of course, this is precisely the kind of "spread of effect" we had hoped to facilitate. Indeed, the center would have been a comparative failure if its programs had been limited to a restricted set of neatly planned projects with beginnings, middles, ends, and final reports.

This diffusion, however, makes it difficult to monitor the progress of all center projects carefully. For example, it is not unusual for us to be surprised to find a fitness program we initiated in an elementary school show up 2 years later in a middle school in another district.

So, when it comes to reporting on the projects undertaken by the center over the past 5 years (see Figure 1) we try to confine it to those efforts that we have had a very direct role in initiating or extending. In so doing we recognize that the distinction between program features we have initiated and indirect outgrowths of those features are not easily made. In our more optimistic moments we like to think that our "reportable projects" are only the tip of the iceberg, and that the center's influence extends below the surface to countless unobserved and unreported aspects of the daily lives of teachers and students. Of course, in our moments of despair we feel that all the ice is melting.

Figure 1 Overview of Center Programs (1980–85)

The following list contains a sample of the types of projects carried on over 5 years. In most cases, each listed activity occurred on multiple occasions in various forms—that is, in different schools, in different school districts, and in successive years. A rough estimate of the total number of projects introduced would be 300 (not counting direct repetitions, which were cumulative for each teacher).

Fitness Programming and Projects (primarily middle and upper elementary school)
Fitness testing: pre-, mid- and posttests; diagnostic use; maintain records; motivational awards for achievement/improvement; communicate results to parents.

Figure 1 (Cont.)

Regular program features: fitness warm-ups; combined sports/fitness circuits; special fitness units (e.g., weight training, rope jumping, jogging, etc.). Study fitness concepts; modify sports activities to increase aerobic component; maximize pupil participation; special classes for deficiencies; exercise homework.

Special events/programs (examples): jump rope for heart; run for your life; fitness Fridays; swim to Bermuda; 10–20-mile running clubs; fitness contests (various types); run to Albany; fitness trail/outdoor course.

Elective Programming and Projects (high school)

Introduced, revised or revived elective units (emphasis on lifetime activities): tennis; racquetball; orienteering; concepts in exercise and health; Frisbee; golf; aerobics; new games; handball; lacrosse; square dancing; paddleball; Swedish gymnastics; circuit training; juggling; table tennis; advanced classes in tennis, badminton, golf, basketball, and so forth; slimnastics; team handball, speedball; floor hockey; indoor soccer; fencing and others.

Improved program management: improved scheduling to allow greater choice by students; counseling students on choices; use of outside facilities; more selective staff assignments; more efficient use of school facilities; assigning staff responsibilities for program areas.

Competency-Based Program Segments (elementary school)

Used competency-based framework to develop instructional units. Framework emphasized establishing goals/objectives, selecting appropriate activities, formulating written plans, assessing pupil achievement, using assessment data to assist in design of subsequent units. The focus of the segments ranged considerably. A few examples include: throw for accuracy; rope jumping; basketball skills; nutrition concepts; balance skills; upper-body strength; swimming skills; gymnastic routines; and volleyball skills.

Adaptive Programs (all levels)

Programs varied by district. Some typical components included: screening and diagnostic testing; individualized programming; modification of activities; new approaches to mainstreaming; individualized instruction.

Administrative arrangements: coordination with school administrators; liaison with COH, special educators and parents; specialized training/updating of staff.

Movement Education and Cooperative Games (elementary school)

Several teachers revised their programs to provide more movement education activities and cooperative games—especially for the lower elementary grades. Emphasis on: exploration, developmental activities and non-competitive settings.

Special Events and Intramurals (all levels)

An enormous variety of special events were held to highlight program features and enhance motivation. A few of many possible examples are: gymnastics night; parent-child volleyball night; special track meets (interschool); all-school color war (sports and academics); two-on-two basketball tournament; new games night; obstacle course contest.

Intramurals were revived and revised in several secondary schools. Scheduled before and after school, and during recess they focused on a variety of activities, most commonly volleyball, basketball, floor hockey, and soccer.

Figure 1 (Cont.)

Record Keeping and Assessment (all levels)
As a separate project, all districts reexamine their procedures for assessment, record keeping, and grading. Emphasis is placed on: clarifying objectives; knowledge, skill, and fitness testing; systematic performance rating; and maintenance of permanent records.
Improved assessment and record keeping have also been linked to other projects, for example, the competency-based segments, fitness programs, and adaptive programs.

Class and Behavior Management Practices (primarily elementary and middle school)
These practices were normally integral parts or outgrowths of more formal projects. They included: establishing behavioral goals (e.g., sportsmanship, cooperation, etc.); posting and enforcing rules; teaching self-management skills; using contingency reward systems; organizing classes to increase on-task time; optimizing practice conditions; providing maximal participation; using task cards/posters and other written materials; and related methods.

Developing Statements of Goals and Written Curriculum Plans
Resource lists of goals have been developed and are being used to reexamine and revise existing statements of goals—to be used in curriculum revision.
Selected schools have revised entire written curricula; others have developed detailed written unit plans.

Public Relations/Public Information
Efforts carried on at the district level (by directors) and at the school level (by teachers) include: letters explaining program features to parents; demonstration nights; presentations at parents' night; presentations to boards of education; articles on programs in school/district/town newspapers; presentations at faculty meetings; special sports participation programs for parents and non-physical-education faculty.
Center staff communications/reports are sent regularly to superintendents, principals, and, when appropriate, to school board members.

Figure 1 (Cont.)

The projects and practices outlined in Figure 1 vary in scope and longevity. Some involved staffs from all six districts; others involved a single teacher working with selected classes. Some projects started years ago and continued; others expanded noticeably over the years; others were abandoned after a semester; and still others were abandoned and revived. I've estimated that about 300 projects were undertaken during the 5 years, or about 60 per year, not counting replications by the same teacher(s).

First, understand that this array of projects is a reflection of the physical education teachers' and administrators' agenda. They set the priorities. Surely, we had some influence when it came to suggesting new possibilities and providing resources, but in the final analysis they set the directions and made the final decisions. For example, in the early years we thought that extensive curriculum writing would surely emerge as a focal point for our activity. It was vetoed in all but a few instances. The teachers preferred action. In another instance, the high school elective program has received a disproportionate amount of attention, not because of any a priori importance we attached to it, but because it was in desperate need of repair in most districts. So, as a consequence, the configuration of programs, projects, and practices we have fostered follows no refined theoretical structure, resembles no textbook plan, and certainly does not reflect a college professor's academic view of the world. Instead it reflects the interests, concerns, perceived needs, attitudes, and capacities of practicing teachers and administrators in six school districts. In my opinion, although it may not be a perfect agenda, it is a very good one.

Physical fitness programming has been a major thrust for all 5 years. Why? Because teachers and administrators truly believe it is a most important aspect of physical education and at the same time they acknowledged that they were not doing an adequate job in the area. Of course, one of the main reasons for this deficiency was that teachers (and students) didn't particularly like fitness training and testing—they viewed it as an intrusion on their sports program and as a threat to the enjoyable climate in their classes. Nevertheless, recognizing what they perceived to be their obligation for the health and fitness of young people, they reluctantly began to bolster their fitness programs, and to do so in some ingenious ways that were fun for students and for them. Now, many of the teachers (not all of them) are doing a lot of fitness programming and, surprisingly, they like it. No doubt this is all being helped along by the currency of fitness and the good public relations that flow from a sound fitness program.

I've already mentioned the extensive attention we have given to the high school elective program. It's been a constant struggle to enrich, and then to reenrich, these programs. Our principal modes of development have been adding new activities and increasing the students' legitimate elective options. Although several teachers have introduced successful electives and upgraded past offerings, progress has been spotty overall. Our high schools have been plagued by many of the problems commonly cited in the current literature, not the least of which is that 10th, 11th, and 12th graders can be a recalcitrant bunch to deal with in the gym or any other class. Our response to these obstacles has been not to be satisfied by the less-than-perfect world we see, to keep plugging away, to keep trying to make things a little better than they were last time, and *not* to despair and abandon ship.

Our elementary school projects, including competency-based segments, cooperative games, movement education, and fitness activities, have been particularly successful. The teachers have control over their own programs (there is a resident specialist in each school). Despite arduous schedules they seem to have the energy to pursue innovations. The students, of course, are not only cooperative, but they are enthusiastic—they energize the teachers. As a consequence so many new program ideas seem to work, whether it be mastering rope jumping, learning a cooperative game, exploring an obstacle course, or studying nutritional concepts. A program development center that is working with elementary school physical education programs is positioned well to take credit for a lot of improvements. All you have to do is get the teachers together, give them some support, and ask, What would you like to do next?

We have worked with adaptive physical education programming, but it is a very tricky business to be involved in. Teachers need thorough training. Most districts cannot afford to hire a trained specialist. Coordination is required with the district committee on the handicapped (COH), the director of special education, and other administrators. Our solution has been to work through the district directors of physical education who design their own programs to suit the needs and personnel in their districts. Even though we secured a small grant to support our work in this area, the best we could do was to provide resource persons, resource materials, and some meeting times for teachers.

Other major aspects of our programs include special events like "all-school color war" or "parent-child volleyball night," which are worth the extraordinary effort they require. They bring excitement to the program and sometimes to the whole school.

Record keeping and assessment are an anathema to most physical educators. We are persistent in our efforts to encourage teachers to fulfill their responsibilities in this area.

Finally, of course we do our part to facilitate improved class management. We could hardly overlook promoting higher levels of motor engagement time or ALT-PE. I must confess we've done relatively little in the way of developing teaching skills in general. Most of the teachers that we meet with 15 to 30 years of experience don't take kindly to being told how to teach.

Conclusion

One of the inescapable realities of public-school teaching is the relentless demands of the daily routine. Teaching five or six classes a day, 5 days a week, can sap the enthusiasm of the most energetic teachers. We have worked with some wonderful teachers during the past years, but not one of them is impervious to the perpetual regularities of the gym. In a very real sense the center's mission is to struggle continually against these realities by introducing novelty, sparking enthusiasm, and purposefully disrupting routine. Clearly, we've had several successes in this struggle. Some of the successes have lasted for years. Yet in a larger sense the routine persists and it limits our effectiveness. Even our most innovative teachers have to face the third-period class waiting at the door as they line up the second-period class for dismissal. It's not easy to be innovative under these conditions. We have had to learn to live with these realities, and after several years we are much more empathetic to the plight of the teacher. So we adjust our expectations accordingly. We expect what is reasonable under the conditions—not ideal, but reasonable.

On a related matter, getting teachers to change behavior or to institute a new program feature is not easy, but it's considerably more difficult to maintain that new approach over extended periods of time. In our experience, the changes that produced intrinsically satisfying rewards for teachers (e.g., fitness circuits that worked efficiently and made classroom management easier) usually persisted from year to year. On the other hand, projects that did not yield some discernable benefit for the teachers were often discarded (e.g., curriculum writing or knowledge testing). As I look back over the past 5 years I'm heartened by the number of changes that have persisted and grown. But I'm also cognizant of the many changes that turned out to be transitory.

A 5-year perspective also forces you to regard each teacher as a very special, individual human being. Of course, from the beginning you recognize that some teachers are stars, others are average, and a few don't measure up. But, over time, you also see how teachers can change from year to year. One of our most productive teachers announced 2 years ago that due to some personal problems she would not participate in anything new that year, then last year she made a comeback. Furthermore, as you come to know the teachers as people, you learn about important things in their lives: births, deaths, divorce, illnesses, children, parents, and so forth. Indeed, in many instances you are forced to see the work you are doing with the teacher in the larger context of the teacher's personal life. Knowing teachers as individuals makes you deal with them as individuals in program development work. You have to adjust your plans to their capabilities, interests, temperament, limitations, values, and particularly to the fluctuations in their personal lives. If you don't adjust, much of your effort will be misdirected.

A final word about this program development work from my own personal perspective as a teacher educator is in order. Working with teachers and administrators in schools is an enlightening experience. It certainly has deepened my understanding of teaching and of physical education. Without question it has profoundly influenced my actions as a teacher educator. I am much more of a realist than I ever was before. My suggestions to teachers are more likely to be grounded in reality. I am much less likely to come up with the easy solution (which should work in theory). I am much more reluctant to criticize teachers and programs. In fact, I respect them more—they have tough jobs, more difficult than mine.

Cognitive Aspects of Interaction in Physical Education

Udo Hanke

This chapter is a report on the results of a research project that was supported by the German Federal Institute of Sport Science and conducted jointly at the Department of Physical Education and the Teacher Training College of the University of Heidelberg. These results are compiled in our final report and have not been reported elsewhere before (Treutlein, Hanke, Janalik, & Sprenger, 1984).

In order to facilitate the understanding of the methods applied and the interpretation of the results I will make some introductory remarks on our theoretical framework, our position in cognitive psychology, and our focus on the physical education student and then report on our methods and results and give some conclusions.

Theory

We are all aware that teaching is a difficult task and that theoretical instruction alone does not make the "ideal" PE teacher. My experience in over 10 years of teacher training has shown that concentrating on the observable aspects of interaction alone allows us only a partial insight into the origin or causes of action.

Following the behavioristic paradigm, it is presumed that interaction is mainly guided by what the teachers or students hear or see. If we switch to the cognitive domain, however, we believe that it is not only the observable behavior alone that guides our actions, but that we also react to what we expect, fear, or hope for from the interacting partner. This approach is generally referred to as the epistemological paradigm, which considers the teacher and the students as active, information-gathering, and information-processing individuals, not only reacting in an everyday, routine manner but also acting as conscious decision makers, viewing their action as part of a meaningful framework of interaction (Groeben & Scheele, 1977).

Switching to the cognitive aspects of interaction also has far-reaching effects on research methodology. Rather than analyze students' and teachers' verbal or motor behavior by correlating frequencies or ratios in order to infer which learning outcomes are produced by which kind of interaction pattern, we have to develop methods that allow us to take a look into the "black box."

This brings me to my second point, our position in cognitive psychology. For the analysis of cognitions it is necessary to use a model of action, the elements of which reflect the main aspects of teacher-pupil interaction. For this purpose we designed a model similar in some structural aspects to one by Hofer and Dobrick (1978) (see Figure 1). This model, which is too elaborate to describe in detail here, is based on the theories and empirical results by Mischel (1973), Miller, Galanter, and Pribram (1973), Rotter, Chance, and Phares (1972), and Thibaut and Kelley (1959).

The model serves as a guideline for the development of our research methodology, especially for the design of our questionnaire. The fact that the model is very detailed in nature does not mean that we presume that teachers or their students will report cognitions equally differentiated. In order to be able to implement the results, however, the model should be wide enough to integrate all reported cognitions. So far, after more than 200 interviews, the model is still serving this purpose.

An analysis of the past research in teacher-pupil interaction has shown that to a great extent research has been "teacher centered," with students being considered mostly only the passive, recipient element of teacher behavior. Their perceptions, intentions, and evaluations have only seldom been the focus of analysis.

From previous studies, and as the result of more than 25 teacher-training clinics that we have conducted, it seemed to us that many of the problems occurring in PE classes result from mutual misunderstanding of the interacting partners. By talking of misunderstanding we do not mean acoustic problems, but misunderstanding

- as the result of inadequate verbal utterances or motor behavior (something that can be analyzed by using the conventional methods of interaction analysis); and
- as something that we found even more important and therefore more interesting to probe—misunderstanding as the result of uni- or bilateral *inadequate implications*.

From the point of view of social psychology the consideration of the possible perceptions, thoughts, views, aims, and emotions of the interacting partner must be considered equally important. Only by taking into consideration these aspects is a mutually fulfilling and meaningful interaction possible.

Method

The methodological problems in connection with the use of "verbal reports as data" (to use the title of the basic publication by Ericsson & Simon, 1980) were described at the 1982 International Association for

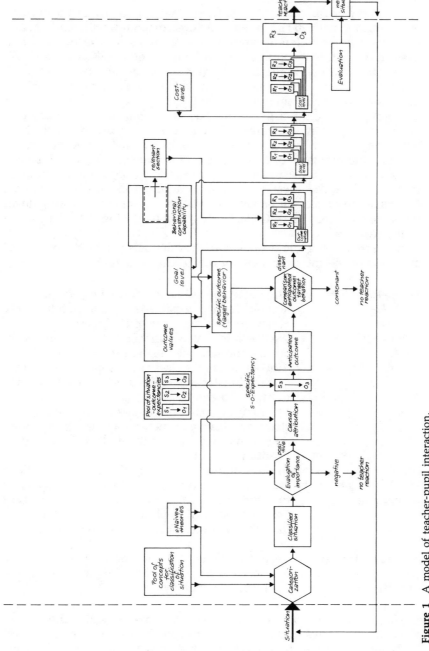

Figure 1   A model of teacher-pupil interaction.

Physical Education in Higher Education (AIESEP) conference in Finland (Hanke & Treutlein, 1983).

To investigate PE teachers' and PE students' cognitions, in a pilot study we conducted over 200 so-called structured dialogues with teachers and students of three different types of schools and with coaches and athletes of five different sport games (basketball, volleyball, field-handball, soccer, and hockey). In this 2-year phase we developed, tested, revised, and retested our questionnaire, with which the main elements of our model of action are being investigated.

In order to avoid the criticism that has been published concerning narrative techniques, in which the subjects were simply asked to talk about what they thought in certain situations, our method concentrates on avoiding the problems of memory, inference, justification and defense, verbalization, and the use of a cognitive model by using certain techniques such as *Störfragen* (questions pointing at contradictions in the verbal reports of the subject) and *Eingrenzungsfragen* (questions narrowing down the subjective reports to the actual cognitions during the event being analyzed).

Rather than going into the details of the interview I will give you a short overview of the different steps of our testing situation.

Before the interview:	We contact the teachers, inform them about our intention, reduce possible fears, and point out the nonevaluative character of the interview.
Before PE class:	We give informal information to the students without mentioning the ensuing interview.
During PE class:	Videotaping of the class and selection of situations that might later be identified as "critical incidents" by the teacher.
	We concentrated on remarkable elements of instruction because in such situations cognitions are more conscious and can be recalled better than in "routine" situations.
Student interview: (20–25 minutes with audiotaping)	In the student interview the student's cognitions are reconstructed using the "structured dialogue for students." The two interviewers encourage "don't remember" replies and encode the answers into the analysis sheet, using scientific terminology.
Teacher interview: (20–25 minutes with audiotaping)	Reconstructions of the teacher's cognitions. The teacher's consent is necessary for the encoding into scientific terminology.

After both interviews the audiotapes are analyzed again, and the entries into the analysis sheets are reexamined. In case of problems, a second consent phase with the teacher or student is necessary. The videotape is used for the analysis and identification of observable behavior but is not shown to the teacher or student prior to the interview. We purposely did not use "stimulated recall" so that subjective situation-perceptions were not modified by viewing the "objective" outside view of the videocamera.

In our main study, using the final version of our "structured dialogues," 28 interviews with male and female PE teachers of Grades 6 to 8 were conducted in the manner described above. One student interview could not be conducted because the critical incident meant the breaking of the student's elbow (as the obvious result of the teacher's poor organization).

Results

Some selected major findings concerning the 18 cognitive elements that we investigated can be divided into two groups:

- Description of frequencies of the reported cognitions
- Comparison of teacher and student cognitions (relating to the identical situation)

Frequencies

The "critical incidents" were characterized as "unexpected" by half of the 28 teachers. On a scale of 1 to 6 relating to the "importance of the situation," 24 considered the situation as "important" to "very important," with the emotional involvement being rather negative in nature in 18 of the teachers. The majority were able to give reasons for their emotional commitment.

Quite important are the results concerning the causal attributions mentioned by the teachers: 17 did not think of any reasons why the situation occurred, 13 saw the origins in the student, and only 3 mentioned that they were aware that they themselves had caused the incident. Because probing for reasons is a decisive element for the selection of reactions, thinking of causal attributions seems to be underdeveloped in our sample.

With regard to the choice of possible reactions to the incident, 27 teachers reported that they reacted immediately without trying to gain additional information about the incident, and only 6 of the 28 were thinking of alternatives to the first possible reaction that came to their minds.

In the second part of the interview the teachers were asked if they had thought about possible cognitions of the student. Eighteen teachers did not think about the student's perception of the situation, 20 teachers did not spend any time on thinking about the student's evaluation of the "importance" of the situation, and 17 did not think about the student's feelings.

The students were asked about two phases of the interaction. The first phase dealt with their cognitions up to the point of the observable behavior, that later on was to be selected as the "critical incident." The second phase referred to their cognitions after the teacher's intervention. Of the 27 students, 23 described their behavior as being "spontaneous," and 18 considered their behavior as being "negative" with regard to the teacher or the instruction. Asked about the perspective of their action, 26 said they acted without taking the teacher into consideration (which seems to be the reason why the teacher considered their behavior as being "disruptive"). The following teacher reaction was clearly identified as a reaction to their own behavior by 26 students.

Another important question was whether the students were aware of the teacher's intention (i.e., if the students could detect any aims in the intervention of the teacher). Only 2 mentioned that their teacher had given a reason for his or her intervention.

Looking at the students' considerations of the teacher's cognitions, it can be remarked that they thought even less frequently about the teacher's thoughts than the teachers had thought about their students' thoughts.

Comparison of Cognitions

In the second group of analysis, a one-by-one comparison of teacher and pupil cognitions was analyzed. Because of the missing student who was injured, only 27 comparisons could be made.

In the first set of comparisons we compared the reported cognitions of the teacher with those of the student, matching the corresponding cognitive elements. In 21 cases teacher and student agreed on the description of the situation. As far as the importance of the incident is concerned, the ratio was 19 to 8 in favor of disagreement. Only in 12 cases were the reported emotional involvement of teacher and student identical.

Looking at the causal attribution, however, there was a disagreement in 19 cases with regard to the origin of the critical incident. When comparing the expressed aims of the teacher with the aims perceived by the student, there was disagreement in 18 cases.

In the second set of comparisons we compared the actual reported cognitions with the alleged or implied cognitions of the other interacting partner. Without going into detail, the picture is very clear here: Only very few actually thought of the other person, and of those only a fraction were correct in their implications.

Conclusion

Satisfactory interactions and meaningful learning situations require an atmosphere of mutual understanding. When planning classes, and during actual instruction, the consideration of the cognitions of the interacting partner concerning his or her perception of the situation, the emotional involvement, the causal attribution, and the aims and evaluations must be seen as important prerequisites for the improvement of instruction. Although additional research is necessary, we believe that our results, which are in agreement with the findings of our 200-interview pilot study, show that the teachers' abilities to consider the cognitions of the students have to be developed more than has been the case in the past. In addition to that, the modification of behavior should not only focus on observable behavior but should also include cognitive intervention methods in order to develop a more differentiated cognitive repertoire. These methods should concentrate on the expansion of perceptive abilities, the development of flexible attribution patterns, and the development of techniques that enable the teacher to gather additional information and to give him or her time for information processing and selection of alternative reactions. In a follow-up project such training materials are being developed and tested.

References

Ericsson, K.A., & Simon, H.A. (1980). Verbal reports as data. *Psychological Review, 87*(3), 215–251.

Groeben, N., & Scheele, B. (1977). *Argumente für eine Psychologie des reflexiven Subjekts* [Arguments for a psychology of reflective subjects]. Darmstadt: Steinkopff.

Hanke, U., & Treutlein, G. (1983). What P.E. teachers think: Methods for the investigation of P.E. teacher cognitions in teaching process. In R. Telama et al. (Eds.), *Research in school physical education* (pp. 31–37). Jyväskylä: Foundation for Promotion of Physical Culture and Health.

Hofer, M., & Dobrick, M. (1978). Die Rolle der Fremdattribution von Ursachen bei der Handlungssteuerung des Lehrers [The role of external causal attribution in teachers' decision making]. In D. Görlitz, W.U. Meyer, & B. Weiner (Eds.), *Bielefelder Symposium über Attribution* (pp. 51–63). Stuttgart: Klett.

Miller, G.A., Galanter, E., & Pribram, K.W. (1973). *Strategien des Handelns: Pläne und Strukturen des Verhaltens* [Strategies of action: Plans and the structure of behavior]. Stuttgart: Klett.

Mischel, W. (1973). Toward a cognitive social learning reconceptualization of personality. *Psychological Review, 80*(4), 252–283.

Rotter, J.B., Chance, J.E., & Phares, E. (1972). *Applications of a social learning theory of personality*. New York: Holt, Rinehart and Winston.

Thibaut, J.W., & Kelley, H.H. (1959). *The social psychology of groups*. New York: Wiley.

Treutlein, G., Hanke, U., Janalik, H., & Sprenger, J. (1984). *Abschlußbericht über das Forschungsprojekt "Methoden zur Erfassung Handlungssteuernder Kognitionen bei Lehr- und Lernprozessen im Sport"* [Final report on the research project "Methods for the investigation of teacher and student cognitions in physical education"]. Unpublished manuscript.

Professional Profiles of Physical Education Teachers and Students' Learning

Bart J. Crum

After an era of superficial control of educational effectiveness in the 1970s, the school system is faced with educational accountability. However, a major problem in the evaluation of the effectiveness of Dutch physical education is that there is no consensus in regard to the evaluation criteria.

Only a few years ago a proposal was made (Crum, 1982) to conceive physical education as a school subject with well-defined learning outcomes. Physical education should focus on the students' mastery of those skills that facilitate a lifetime participation in movement outside the school. The repertoire of competencies or skills may be classified as (a) technomotor (solve technical and tactical movement problems), (b) sociomotor (solve interpersonal problems), (c) cognitive-reflective (knowledge about training and health or relationships between sport and business), and (d) affective (enjoy participation). The proposal met with increasing support from the Dutch physical education profession, therefore there is some basis for the assessment of effectiveness.

The view that physical education teachers are professionals who base judgments and decisions in their practice on professional knowledge and convictions is of importance (Clark & Yinger, 1979; Schön, 1983; Shavelson & Stern, 1981). According to Lawson (1985), concepts held by the teacher are developed during the process of occupational socialization. Therefore, it is hypothesized that the variability of effectiveness can partly be explained by differences in work practice, that differences in work practice can partly be explained by differences in the professional concept of physical education, and that conceptual differences can partly be explained by differences in occupational socialization.

A pilot study explored whether the effectiveness of physical education could be assessed in a reliable and valid way by using a learner report questionnaire composed of items representing the domains of learning mentioned previously (technomotor, sociomotor, cognitive-reflective, and affective). Moreover, a first attempt was made in order to collect some evidence for the existence of relationships between learning outcomes and students' perception of the concept of physical education held by their teachers. Students were asked whether their teachers perceived physical education predominately as fitness training, recreation, or a teaching-learning activity. These alternatives were chosen because of earlier interview experiences with physical education teachers. They were asked which quality criteria they used in the evaluation of their classes. It was interesting to note how often "whether my students sweat" and "whether my students participated with pleasure" were mentioned as criteria for good classes (Crum, 1983; Placek, 1983).

The learner report method was found to be a suitable procedure for global assessment of learning outcomes in physical education. Moreover, the results indicated that learning outcomes may differ strongly by school and by the individual physical education teacher as a consequence of the differences in the concept of physical education held by the teachers (Crum, 1985).

A subsequent investigation, which is the focus of this report, was carried out in the spring of 1985. The purpose of the study was to increase the understanding of the relationship between variability of learning outcomes and the differences in the professional concept held by the physical education teacher.

Method

As in the pilot study, an indirect approach was chosen because of considerations of time and expense (i.e., all data were obtained from students using questionnaires). Thirty physical education teachers volunteered to participate with their students in the study. Each teacher provided three class groups (from Grades 9, 10, or 11) of about 25 students each. The total sample included 2,052 students. All class groups were randomly divided into three subsamples, and each subsample responded to one of the three different questionnaires to be described.

Questionnaire 1 contained 27 items and was aimed at the assessment of learning outcomes. Each item was prefaced by a standard opening sentence: "The PE classes in the current schoolyear have contributed to my learning. . ." The technomotor, the sociomotor, and the cognitive-reflective domain of learning were each represented by seven items, and the affective domain was represented by six items. Item examples are presented in Table 1. Responses were required on a 5-point scale (a score of 5 indicating a very positive outcome and 1 indicating no learning at all).

Two other questionnaires were constructed for an indirect assessment of the professional work style of PE teachers. Questionnaire 2, labeled as the "outline ranking questionnaire," consisted of three prototypical outlines of PE classes. Outline A gave a prototypical description of PE classes, which are organized according to the "PE as entertainment" concept; outline B did the same for the "PE as training" concept, as did outline C for the "PE as teaching" concept. The respondents were asked to rank the three outlines with respect to the criterion "similarity with the classes of my PE teacher."

Table 1   Examples of Items in the Learner Report and the Profile Questionnaire

Learner report questionnaire:	"The PE classes in the current school-year have contributed to my learning . . .
Technomotor domain:	— . . . to play well-known ball games." — . . . to apply right movement techniques."
Sociomotor domain:	— . . . to adapt my way of playing and moving to the level of others." — . . . how to play and engage in sports with members of the opposite sex."
Cognitive-reflective domain:	— . . . to be able to apply the basic principles of endurance training." — . . . how sport relates to commerce and politics."
Affective domain:	— . . . to enjoy exercising my body." — . . . to obtain pleasure from sport participation."
Profile questionnaire:	"My PE teacher . . .
Physical educator as a teacher:	— . . . is satisfied with a class if we learned in it." — . . . considers learning goals when making groups."
Physical educator as a trainer:	— . . . chooses activities that make us really tired." — . . . assesses regularly our physical fitness."
Physical educator as an entertainer:	— . . . is satisfied with a class if we were happy." — . . . gives us above all opportunity for free play in ball-games."

Questionnaire 3, labeled as the "profile questionnaire," included 22 items. Each item began with the standard sentence "My PE teacher. . . ." Nine items were considered to be operationalizations of the "physical educator as a teacher" idea; six items represented the "physical educator as a trainer" idea; and seven items represented the "physical educator as an entertainer" prototype. Item examples are presented in Table 1.

Responses were required on a 5-point scale (a score of 5 indicating the answer "certainly true" or "always" and a score of 1 indicating the answer "certainly not true" or "never"). Factor analysis was utilized to determine the extent to which the 27 learner report items as well as the 22 profile questionnaire items could be clustered. The results supported our a priori models. On the basis of these results, scales for learning outcomes and for profile scores were developed. Tests for internal consistency with respect to the learning outcome scales provided satisfactory results. Cronbach's alpha for the scale for technomotor learning was 0.65; for the sociomotor learning scale, 0.72; for the cognitive-reflective learning scale, 0.77; and for the affective learning scale, 0.76.

Tests for internal consistency with respect to the profile-score scales resulted after deletion of three items in scales that were also considered as sufficiently reliable. Cronbach's alpha for the teacher-profile scale was 0.80; for the trainer-profile scale, 0.65; and for the entertainer-profile scale, 0.64. Spearman's rho correlations between the rank scores of the three outlines (Instrument 2) and the profile-scale scores were all in the predicted direction. This was considered as a positive indication for the validity of the profile-score scales.

Results

Table 2 presents information with regard to the variability in teacher effectiveness. The data revealed that the 30 teachers differed significantly in effectiveness with regard to all four domains of learning. Moreover, it should be noted that with respect to the cognitive-reflective domain low learning was reported in general. In order to examine relationships between the professional style of the teachers and the learning outcomes, the teachers were grouped based on their profile-score patterns. Therefore, each teacher was classified as a high, low, or medium scorer on each of the scales. With respect to the teacher-profile scale (mean = 3.35) the chosen classification limits were low < 3.2 < medium < 3.5 < high; for the trainer profile scale (mean = 3.13) the limits were low < 3.0 < medium < 3.3 < high; and for the entertainer scale (mean = 3.25) the limits were low < 3.1 < medium < 3.4 < high. Considering the profile-score patterns, the following four groups were distinguished: (a) the group "high teach," composed of all teachers who scored high on the teacher-profile scale, independent of their scores on the two other scales ($n = 11$); (b) the group "high trai," composed of all teachers who scored high only on the trainer profile scale ($n = 5$); (c) the group "high ent," composed of all teachers who scored high only on the entertainer profile scale ($n = 6$); and (d)

Table 2   Means, Standard Deviations, and Ranges of Learning Outcome Scores for all Subgroups (30)

Domain of learning	M	SD	Range	Significance of univariate F
Technomotor	3.8	0.62	3.4–4.1	$p < .01$
Sociomotor	3.6	0.66	2.9–4.2	$p < .01$
Cognitive-reflective	2.6	0.75	2.0–3.2	$p < .01$
Affective	3.8	0.66	3.2–4.5	$p < .01$

the group "flat," composed of all teachers who scored either medium or low on all three scales ($n = 8$). Multivariate analysis of variance indicated significant differences in learning outcomes (the four domains considered in connection) between the groups (Wilks' F [12,1090] = 2.52, $p < .01$).

Subsequently, univariate analysis of variance was used in order to explore the differences between the groups for each of the four scales in some detail. Table 3 shows that profile groups differed especially with respect to the technomotor and the sociomotor domain. On both scales the group with a high teacher-profile score showed the highest results, and the group with only a high trainer-profile score showed the lowest results. For the cognitive-reflective domain a similar tendency appeared. The differences on the scale for affective learning were not significant; however, also in this case the score of the high trainer-profile group was the lowest.

The relatively large group with a high score on the teacher-profile scale was split up into subgroups for further analysis: (a) the subgroup "teach," composed of the teachers with only a high score on the teacher-profile scale ($n = 3$); (b) the subgroup "teach-trai," composed of the teachers with a high score on the teacher- and trainer-profile scales ($n = 3$); (c) the subgroup "teach-ent," composed of the teachers with a high score on the teacher- and the entertainer-profile scales ($n = 2$); and (d) the subgroup "teach-trai-ent," composed of the teachers with a high score on all three profile scales.

Multivariate analyses of variance indicated significant differences in learning outcomes between the subgroups (Wilks' F [12,400] = 4.17, $p <$

Table 3 Means, Standard Deviations, and Levels of Significance for the Learning Outcome Scales: First Division of Profile Groups

Learning outcome scale	"high teach" M SD (n=229)		"high trai" M SD (n=84)		Profile groups "high ent" M SD (n=113)		"flat" M SD (n=163)		Significance of univariate F
Technomotor	3.9[a]	0.61	3.6	0.64	3.8	0.64	3.8	0.66	$p < .05$
Sociomotor	3.7	0.70	3.2[b]	0.66	3.6	0.80	3.7	0.68	$p < .01$
Cognitive-reflective	2.7	0.78	2.5	0.74	2.6	0.84	2.5	0.79	$p < .10$
Affective	3.8	0.85	3.6	0.82	3.9	0.80	3.8	0.67	n.s.

[a]Scheffe's test indicated that this mean differs significantly from the mean of the "high trai" group. [b]Scheffe's test indicated that this mean differs significantly from the three other means.

Table 4   Means, Standard Deviations, and Levels of Significance for the Learning Outcome Scales: Subgroups Within the High-Teach Profile Group

Learning outcome scale	"teach" M SD ($n=66$)	"teach-trai" M SD ($n=66$)	"teach-ent" M SD ($n=45$)	"teach-trai-ent" M SD ($n=52$)	Significance of univariate F
Technomotor	3.8 0.64	4.0 0.58	3.8 0.61	3.9 0.57	$p < .10$
Sociomotor	3.7 0.73	3.7 0.73	3.9[a] 0.58	3.4 0.67	$p < .05$
Cognitive-reflective	2.6 0.70	3.0[b] 0.74	2.5 0.80	2.5 0.79	$p < .01$
Affective	3.8 0.78	3.9 0.95	4.1 0.63	3.6 0.91	$p < .05$

[a]Scheffe's test indicated that this mean differs significantly from the mean of the "teach-trai-ent" group. [b]Scheffe's test indicated that this mean differs significantly from the three other means.

.01). Univariate analysis of variance was used in order to explore differences between the subgroups in more detail. Table 4 shows that the group with a combination of a high teacher- and a high trainer-profile score had the highest outcomes with respect to the technomotor as well as the cognitive-reflective domain. On the other hand, the group with a combination of a high teacher- and a high entertainer-profile score was shown to produce the highest outcomes in the sociomotor and affective domains.

Discussion

The results of this study support the assumption that the distinction of teacher, trainer, and entertainer features in the working style of physical educators is relevant for the explanation of variability in the learning of students. On the one hand, the data suggest that a high teacher profile of the physical educator is a favorable condition for student learning. On the other hand, physical educators with only a high trainer profile arrange learning conditions that are not the most favorable. An interesting feature is that for all domains a combination of either a teacher-trainer profile or a teacher-entertainer profile appears to be the most favorable condition for the production of learning outcomes. The effectiveness of the teacher-trainer with respect to technomotor learning could be interpreted by considering that it is relevant for this domain to combine teaching with care for a high level of motor activity. The effectiveness of the teacher-trainer with respect to cognitive-reflective learning could be interpreted by the consideration that the scale for cognitive-reflective learning consisted half of items directly related to training and health. For an interpretation of the effectiveness of the teacher-entertainer with respect to sociomotor and affective learning, it appears to be a relevant consideration that in this case the features of a teacher (planning, accountability, etc.) are completed with more student-oriented features. A provisional conclusion is that receipts for the working style of a physical educator should be related to the domain of learning that is planned to be in the forefront in a certain class activity. The distinction between teacher, trainer, and entertainer features appears to be relevant for the tracing of such receipts. In order to obtain more detailed knowledge about effective and ineffective working styles of physical educators, subsequent research data will be obtained by systematic observation of classes of PE teachers whose students reported both high and low learning outcomes.

Acknowledgment

I am indebted to my students Wil Koch, Han Rutten, and Harry van Verendaal for their help in data collection and data analysis.

References

Clark, C.M., & Yinger, R.J. (1979). Teachers' thinking. In P.L. Peterson & H.J. Walberg (Eds.), *Research on teaching* (pp. 231–263). Berkeley: McCutchan.

Crum, B.J. (1982). Over de gebruikswaarde van bewegingsonderwijs [Concerning the usefulness of physical education] NKS-cahier 14, *Bewegen op school en wat daarna?* (pp. 16–24). Den Bosch: Nederlandse Katholieke Sportfederatie.

Crum, B.J. (1983). Auswerten als Aufgabe des Sportlehrers. [Evaluation as a task of the physical education teacher]. *Sportpädagogik, 5,* 12–19.

Crum, B.J. (1985). The use of learner reports for exploring teaching effectiveness in physical education. In M. Piéron & G. Graham (Eds.), *The 1984 Olympic Scientific Congress proceedings: Vol. 6. Sport Pedagogy* (pp. 97–102). Champaign, IL: Human Kinetics.

Lawson, H.A. (1985). *Occupational socialization and curriculum studies: The case of physical education.* Unpublished manuscript.

Placek, J.H. (1983). Conceptions of success in teaching: Busy, happy and good? In T.J. Templin & J.K. Olson (Eds.), *Teaching in physical education* (pp. 46–56). Champaign, IL: Human Kinetics.

Schön, D.A. (1983). *The reflective practitioner.* New York: Basic Books.

Shavelson, R.J., & Stern, P. (1981). Research on teachers' pedagogical thoughts, judgments, decisions and behavior. *Review of Educational Research, 4,* 455–498.

Preinteractive Cognitions of Physical Education Teachers with Varying Levels of Expertise

Michael A. Sherman
Warren D. Sipp
Mohammad A. Taheri

This paper presents some of the planning data from two studies of pedagogical expertise in physical education. According to Chi and Glaser (1980), expertise refers to the possession of superior knowledge and skill in a particular domain. It results from long and repeated periods of domain-specific experience, often under the guidance of a master practitioner. The scientific analysis of expertise in teaching is a logical prerequisite to curriculum design in teacher education, for without knowing how experts do their work it is quite difficult to convert novices into experts.

The analysis of expertise paradigm assumes that teachers are active information processors who gather cues from a dynamic environment and use them to select, prepare, and evaluate their teaching routines (Hanke & Treutlein, 1983). Studies of master clinicians in education, medicine, and other professions suggest that experts not only know more than novices, but are more adept at rendering rational judgments, making intelligent decisions, and solving complex problems (Shavelson & Stern, 1981).

The general intent of our research was to describe how physical education teachers solve rather messy instructional planning problems. To do this, we confronted them with situations in which they knew nothing about the conditions under which they would plan and conduct an instructional episode. The specific objective of the two studies was to discover expert/novice differences in the information gathering and decision-making phases of instructional planning. We also attempted to identify teachers' strategies for making planning decisions and assessed their affective reactions and temporal requirements to confirm prevalent theories about the differential planning behavior of experts and novices.

Our interest in how teachers with varying levels of expertise plan for instruction was motivated by the assumed importance of preinteractive decision making. Recent research in physical education indicates that teachers, though they do not always follow prescriptive models of planning, do make preinteractive decisions and that different approaches to planning seem to account for variations in teachers' classroom behavior (Housner & Griffey, 1985; Imwold et al., 1984; Placek, 1984).

The conceptual basis of our work reflects an information processing orientation to the study of preinteractive cognitions. This orientation suggests that planning begins with the acquisition of environmental cues and ends with the development of a plan of action. The cues are first used to make judgments about the state of the environment and then to make decisions about ways of coping with the environmental demands. In the jargon of information science, judgment (stimulus identification) is associated with problem finding, and decision making (response selection) is associated with problem solving. Teachers' planning, then, involves both the identification of instructional problems and the selection of appropriate solutions. Once prepared, instructional plans are verified and, if necessary, revised during interactive teaching.

Method

Table 1 describes the main features of our research on teachers' preinteractive cognitions. Taheri (1982) compared five exercise physiologists

Table 1   Description of Research on Teachers' Preinteractive Cognitions

Main features of research	Health-related fitness study	Adapted physical education study
Investigator	Taheri, 1982	Sipp, 1983
Teachers	Experts were 5 exercise physiology professors and advanced doctoral students; novices were 5 college PE majors	Specialists were 3 adapted PE teachers; generalists were 3 elementary PE teachers
Learners	6 middle-school students, aged 11 to 13 years	3 trainable, mentally retarded students, aged 10 to 20 years
Problem	Teachers had 90 min to plan a 30-min lesson on body composition	Teachers had 90 min to plan a 25-min lesson on the standing long jump
Cues provided	No cues given in advance; single cues given per request during planning	No cues given in advance; multiple cues given per request during planning
Data source	Think-aloud protocols	Think-aloud protocols
Data analysis	Frequency counts of cue requests and decisions, with categories known in advance	Frequency counts of cue requests and decisions, with categories derived from protocols

and five undergraduate physical education majors who had 90 minutes to plan a 30-minute health-fitness lesson on body composition for six students, aged 11 to 13 years. Prior to planning, teachers were told they would teach a physical education class but were unaware of the content, context, or students for the lesson. During planning, teachers received single bits of information, but only in response to questions asked of the investigator. The information came from a prepared cue list available only to the investigator.

Sipp (1983) studied 10 adapted physical education specialists and 10 elementary physical education generalists (note that data are only presented for three teachers in each group). In general, Sipp followed Taheri's method of conducting the planning session. He allocated 90 minutes to plan a 25-minute lesson on the standing long jump that would be taught to three trainable mentally retarded (TMR) students, aged 10 to 20 years. However, unlike Taheri, Sipp gave multiple bits of information in response to teachers' cue requests, partly to minimize the stress he thought generalists might have if suddenly confronted with TMR students. Another feature of Sipp's study was the attempt to control for general teaching experience. His teachers had comparable years of total experience, but generalists had no previous exposure to TMRs.

The think-aloud procedure was employed to capture teachers' preinteractive cognitions. Teachers were asked to report their inner thoughts as they planned for instruction. Although the validity of introspective verbalizations is often suspect (Hanke & Treutlein, 1983), think-aloud methods have been used in other studies of pedagogical decision making (Housner & Griffey, 1985; Peterson & Clark, 1978; Peterson, Marx, & Clark, 1978).

Teachers' reported cognitions were audiotaped, then transcribed into verbatim protocols. Cue requests and decisions in the protocols were identified and coded with category-type instruments. Operationally defined, cue requests were questions seeking information about the upcoming lesson; decisions were choices of intended actions in the lesson. Taheri's instrument, adapted from Peterson, Marx, and Clark (1978), had intercoder agreements of 95% for cue requests and 82% for decisions. Sipp's instrument was created by inductive analysis, in which cue requests and decisions in the protocols were first recorded on index cards and then sorted into categories.

Results

Table 2 presents the descriptive data for selected planning variables. The high-experience teachers in both studies requested more information than the low-experience teachers. Teachers' questions usually sought information about the nature of the students, the time and space for instruction, and the availability of equipment. The mean difference in cue requests was statistically significant in the health-fitness study. The

Table 2   Mean Values for Selected Planning Variables

Planning variables	Health-fitness		Adapted physical education	
	Experts ($n = 5$)	Novices ($n = 5$)	Specialists ($n = 3$)	Generalists ($n = 3$)
Cues requests	14	1	10	8
Adjustment cues	—	—	21	4
Planning decisions	72	26	69	15
Planning time (min)	34	64	—	—
Self-rated anxiety	5	4	5	3

Note. All table values are rounded to the nearest whole number. On a 6-point scale, high anxiety ratings indicate "very relaxed," and low ratings indicate "very nervous" about teaching the planned lesson.

between-group difference in the adapted physical education study was less pronounced, perhaps because generalists and specialists had comparable teaching experience and/or because we gave the teachers more information than they asked for. One interesting finding in the adapted physical education study was that specialists requested much more information about the health and medical status of TMRs. For example, they asked whether students had cardiac problems, cerebral palsy, seizures, or other physical handicaps. No such inquiries were made by the generalists.

The occurrence data for planning decisions clearly indicated that experts and specialists were much more prolific than novices and generalists. Both studies revealed that most preinteractive decisions focused on the content and process of instruction. The generalists and specialists in the adapted physical education study also made several decisions about objectives, equipment, and evaluation procedures.

An earlier study of teachers' planning (Sherman, 1979) suggested that experts consider advance information about students somewhat unreliable and prefer to do their own intelligence gathering during the actual lesson. The cues that experts gather during interactive teaching help them decide whether to continue or adjust their planned teaching routines. In fact, the experts in the 1979 study entered the classroom with more than one plan, a main routine, and one or more backup routines that might be called upon if things did not go as expected.

Table 3 shows large differences in the number and type of cues specialists and generalists said they would attend to during the standing long jump lesson. Specialists indicated that their adjustment decisions would be mostly contingent upon students' general motor ability and jumping skill. They also planned to monitor students' cognitive, personal, and social behavior. The generalists, on the other hand, had little idea

Table 3 Adjustment Cues Sought by Adapted Physical Education Teachers

Adjustment cues	Specialists (n = 3)	Generalists (n = 3)
Performance cues	31 (49%)	6 (54%)
Ability	12	0
Fatigue	1	0
Physique	1	0
Skill	17	6
Personal/social cues	17 (27%)	2 (18%)
Moods and feelings	10	1
Work habits	5	1
Safety	2	0
Cognitive cues	10 (16%)	2 (18%)
Attention span	1	0
Comprehension	8	2
Creativity	1	0
Miscellaneous	5 (8%)	1 (10%)
Total adjustment cues	63 (100%)	11 (100%)

what to expect during the lesson although they, too, planned to check students' jumping skill.

Psychological research on human problem solving suggests that experts plan differently from novices (Anderson, 1980). When experts solve familiar problems, they simply retrieve solutions from memory. When they solve novel problems, they try to transform them into familiar problems for which solutions are already known. In contrast, novices are less skilled at problem identification and problem solving and, because their knowledge is sparse, are forced to produce new solutions from scratch. The complexity of novices' productive planning causes them to work slower and with more psychic stress than experts.

The experts and specialists in our research were definitely using retrieval strategies for planning. The temporal data (see Table 2) from the health-fitness study revealed that experts averaged about 34 minutes for planning, whereas novices averaged 64 minutes. Although planning time was not assessed in the adapted study, both generalists and specialists said they were using old plans to teach the standing long jump. However, the generalists had little idea whether the routines they used in elementary physical education would work in a TMR setting. Furthermore, they were quite reluctant to finalize their plans without first seeing and interacting with the TMRs.

As noted above, planning is not only complex and time-consuming for novices but stressful as well. The responses (see Table 2) to a postplanning question about whether teachers felt nervous or relaxed about teaching the lesson indicated that experts and specialists had lower levels of anxiety than either novices or generalists. Similar trends were also found on self-reported measures of confidence and satisfaction.

Conclusions and Recommendations

Based on two studies of teachers' preinteractive cognitions, it was concluded that teachers with more domain-specific experience plan differently than teachers with less domain-specific experience. High-experience teachers request more information, make more decisions, and retrieve previously used plans from memory. They plan faster, with less anxiety, and know what cues to gather in class for the purpose of making interactive adjustment decisions. Finally, high-experience teachers are more keenly aware of critical moments that might arise during interactive teaching and are ready to call up contingency plans at such moments.

These conclusions are compatible with those reported some time ago by Sherman (1979) and more recently by Housner and Griffey (1985). We suspect that expert/novice differences in planning are due to variations in knowledge of specific pedagogical situations. If this is true, then it behooves teacher educators to provide preservice teachers with early, continuous, and lengthy periods of clinical practice in various instructional settings so they can build the kind of knowledge base that facilitates reproductive planning.

Still unanswered by our research is the question of whether expert/novice differences in planning translate into differential patterns of interactive teaching behavior. From stimulated recall data (Sherman, 1983) we know that experts think differently in the classroom. They attend to different cues, perceive fewer problems, don't panic at critical moments, and make quick, fine-tuning adjustments. Although some recent research by Imwold et al. (1984) suggests that planners and nonplanners act differently as well, the issue is far from settled.

References

Anderson, R. (1980). *Cognitive psychology and implications.* San Francisco, CA: W.H. Freeman.

Chi, M.T.H., & Glaser, R. (1980). The measurement of expertise: Analysis of the development of knowledge and skill as a basis for assessing achievement. In E.L. Baker & E.S. Quellmaz (Eds.), *Educational testing and evaluation: Design, analysis, and policy* (pp. 37–48). Beverly Hills, CA: Sage Publications.

Hanke, U., & Treutlein, G. (1983). What P.E. teachers think: Methods for the investigation of P.E. teacher cognitions in teaching process. In R. Telama (Ed.), *Research in school physical education* (pp. 31–37). Jyväskylä, Finland: Foundations for Promotion of Physical Culture and Health.

Housner, L.D., & Griffey, D.C. (1985). Teacher cognition: Differences in planning and interactive decision making between experienced and inexperienced teachers. *Research Quarterly for Exercise and Sport,* **56**(1), 45-53.

Imwold, C.H., Rider, R.A., Twardy, B.M., Oliver, P.S., Griffin, M., & Arsenault, D.N. (1984). The effect of planning on the teaching behavior of preservice physical education teachers. *Journal of Teaching in Physical Education,* **4**, 50-56.

Peterson, P.L., & Clark, C.M. (1978). Teachers' reports on their cognitive processes during teaching. *American Educational Research Journal,* **15**(4), 555-565.

Peterson, P.L., Marx, R.W., & Clark, C.M. (1978). Teacher planning, teacher behavior, and student achievement. *American Educational Research Journal,* **15**, 417-432.

Placek, J.H. (1984). A multi-case study of teacher planning in physical education. *Journal of Teaching in Physical Education,* **4**, 39-49.

Shavelson, R.J., & Stern, P. (1981). Research on teachers' pedagogical thoughts, judgments, decisions, and behavior. *Review of Educational Research,* **51**(4), 455-498.

Sherman, M.A. (1979, December). *Teacher planning: A study of expert and novice gymnastics teachers.* Paper presented at the Pennsylvania State Association for Health, Physical Education, and Recreation Annual Convention, Philadelphia.

Sherman, M.A. (1983). Pedagogical cognitions in physical education: Differences between expert and novice teachers. In T.J. Templin & J.K. Olson (Eds.), *Teaching in physical education* (pp. 19-34). Champaign, IL: Human Kinetics.

Sipp, W.D. (1983). A comparison of specialist and generalist physical education teachers on selected elements of augmented feedback. *Dissertation Abstracts International,* **45**, 453-A. (University Microfilms No. 8411798)

Taheri, M.A. (1982). *Analysis of expertise in planning and interactive decision making among health related physical fitness teachers.* Unpublished doctoral dissertation, University of Pittsburgh.

Perceived Skill Level: A Critical Factor in the Strength of Valuing Movement Purposes

Kathryn L. Kisabeth

Lifelong participation has been identified as a goal of curriculum designers and the focus of research by sport psychologists and sociologists. Physical education curriculum designers approach this goal from many perspectives in curricular planning. Jewett and Bain (1985) identified three major perspectives on curriculum design: (a) movement skill development, (b) health-related fitness, and (c) socialization or "play." Whereas all three perspectives are considered essential as aims for a well-balanced physical education program, the weight or emphasis placed on each viewpoint varies greatly. Curriculum designers can agree on lifelong participation as a goal, but they do not agree on the processes by which this goal can be achieved. Sport psychologists and sociologists have approached the participation phenomena from a different perspective. The factors that influence participation have been the focus of numerous research studies that examine sociological, psychological, and physical factors as either antecedents to, or consequences of, participation (Dishman, 1981, 1982; Greendorfer, 1977, 1978; Kenyon, 1968; McPherson, 1980, 1984; Snyder & Spreitzer, 1973, 1976, 1979, 1984; Sonstroem, 1978, 1982). The findings of such studies are of importance to curriculum researchers and designers as well. The connection relates to the formulation of physical education programs that facilitate lifelong participation habits. In particular, curriculum workers need to attend to those factors that can be most affected by schooling experiences.

Perceived ability or estimation is one factor that can be affected by physical education school experiences and that has been identified by researchers as having a critical influence on participation. Bain and Steinhardt (1985) have defined perceived ability as an individual's self-perception of his or her ability to exercise and to perform sport skills. Self-efficacy (Bandura, 1977) provides the foundation for understanding perceived ability. The four expectation sources of personal efficacy as noted by Bandura are:

- performance accomplishments,
- vicarious experiences,
- verbal persuasion, and
- physiological state.

The first three of these expectation sources can be affected by systematic school experiences, and this effect can be either positive or negative. The research evidence to date indicates that perceptions of personal abilities are more powerful influences on participation than are actual abilities. Sonstroem (1978) indicates that perceived ability might be a mediating variable between physical ability and self-esteem. Perception has also been linked to initial recruitment into exercise programs.

The predictive power of perceived ability has been identified by other researchers as well (Snyder & Spreitzer, 1976; Spreitzer & Snyder, 1976, 1983). Spreitzer and Snyder (1976) have suggested that perceived ability is influenced by parental encouragement, actual childhood and adolescent participation, and evaluation of ability by self and others. In addition, Spreitzer and Snyder (1976) found that perceived ability was the strongest causal model for adult involvement in sport. The results of these studies lend support for the idea that perceived ability has a more direct influence on participation than does actual ability.

Other authors have suggested that the development of positive personal perception of abilities is of equal, if not greater, importance than actual physical ability. Bain (1985) collected ethnographic data on participants enrolled in an exercise class. The results of this study indicated that, whereas course content and procedures focused on information giving and increased knowledge, student reactions were more personal and related to feeling. The conclusion reached was that in order for participation habits to be most positively affected, personal meanings need to be made part of the instructional focus. Corbin, Laurie, Gruger, and Smiley (1984) found evidence to support this contention in a study that examined the effect of vicarious success experiences in adult women. Movement confidence, as identified by Griffin and Keogh (1982), also relies on self-perception as a major component. Bressan and Weiss (1982) and Griffin and Keogh (1981) have also indicated that the development of self-perception is critical to continued participation. The process utilized to develop self-perception and self-confidence in movers involves attention to personal meanings and motivations for movement. Movement activities must be perceived as meaningful or meaning fulfilling by participants if such activities are expected to facilitate continued participation.

The focus of this study was to examine the effect that perceived skill ability had on the strength of valuing for movement purposes. For purposes of the study perceived skill ability was self-reported on a 9-point Likert scale, and the responses were grouped into high, medium, and low perception groups.

Method

The Personal Purposes and Meanings for Movement Inventory (PPMMI-83) consists of 30 items. The 22 positive movement purpose statements were randomly ordered on the inventory. Each purpose item was rated on a 9-point Likert scale. The ends of the continuum were defined as not meaningful (1) and very meaningful (9). The points between were not labeled. The stem of each movement statement was "I move to. . . ." Four demographic items appeared at the beginning of the inventory. These items were (a) human consent, (b) sex, (c) age, and (d) ethnic origin. Three additional descriptive items related to enrollment in physical education classes were included at the end of the inventory. The final question on the inventory required subjects to rate their level of skillfulness on a 9-point Likert scale. The ends of the continuum were defined as not skillful (1) and highly skillful (9), with the between points unlabeled.

The subjects for this study (N = 409) included college-aged students enrolled in activity classes (n = 251), college athletes (n = 74), and wheelchair athletes (n = 84). There were 247 males and 160 females in the sample. Two individuals did not respond to the sex item. The age range was from 18 and under to 40 plus, with a mean age of 22 to 24 years. Five ethnic groups were represented in the sample; the majority, however (79%), were white. Perceived skill level ranged from not skillful to highly skillful in both the general college group and the athlete group.

The data were analyzed using t tests, means, and standard deviations for each perceived skill group. The t tests were performed on the means of each movement purpose by perceived skill level. High and low means were identified for each movement purpose for each perceived skill level group. The perceived skill level groups (high, medium, low) were established by dividing the 9-point Likert scale into three equal parts.

Results

The t tests for perceived skill level among athletes indicated 12 significantly different items when subjects were grouped into high, medium and low skill response categories (Table 1). Individuals who perceived themselves as highly skilled differed from the medium group on 7 items and from the low group on 4 items. The medium and low groups differed on only 1 item.

The high group differed from the medium group on items related to competition, musculoskeletal efficiency, aliveness, movement appreciation, self-transcendence, movement efficiency, and mechanical efficiency. The high group valued each of these items more highly than the medium group. The 4 items that were significantly different between the high and low groups were object manipulation, competition, musculoskeletal efficiency, and movement appreciation. These items were valued more highly by those individuals who perceived themselves as highly skilled. The medium and low perceived-skill groups were found to differ on only 1 item. Medium-skilled individuals valued object manipulation more highly than low-skilled individuals.

The t tests for perceived-skill-ability groups within college students indicated 14 significantly different movement purpose items. The high-perception and low-perception groups differed significantly on 12 movement purposes. Four items were found to be significantly different for

Table 1   Athletes' Skill Level (Means and *SD*)

Item	Low M	Low SD	Medium M	Medium SD	High M	High SD
Catharsis	6.44	2.35	6.65	2.13	6.66	2.11
Attractiveness	6.00	2.73	6.75	1.96	6.58	2.11
Self-knowledge	6.44	2.40	6.33	2.25	6.62	2.13
Leadership	6.88	2.61	5.91	2.55	6.38	2.08
Self-transcendence	7.11	2.57	5.84	2.63	6.92	2.08[c]
Participation	7.55	1.33	7.38	1.93	7.34	1.99
Object manipulation	4.00	2.64[a]	6.17	2.22[b]	6.80	2.12[c]
Teamwork	5.55	3.08	6.87	1.86	6.87	2.17
Spatial orientation	6.55	2.65	6.45	2.03	6.71	2.22
Cultural understanding	5.88	3.48	5.69	2.48	5.62	2.57
Joy of movement	6.66	2.87	6.47	1.97	6.99	1.99
Weight control	6.50	2.72	6.76	2.01	7.06	2.07
Competition	6.50	3.02[a]	6.90	2.25	7.75	1.05[c]
Movement efficiency	8.11	1.05	7.29	1.86	7.88	1.32[c]
Challenge	6.11	3.25	6.81	1.82	7.35	1.88
Circulorespiratory efficiency	6.33	2.90	7.26	1.76	7.18	2.08
Expression	5.66	2.78	6.73	1.92	6.50	2.13
Self-integration	6.22	2.58	6.44	1.98	6.57	2.18
Musculoskeletal efficiency	6.33	3.00[a]	7.02	2.26	7.88	1.63[c]
Aliveness	6.11	2.66	7.35	1.43	7.90	1.29[c]
Movement appreciation	5.55	3.16[a]	6.61	1.97	7.44	1.78[c]
Mechanical efficiency	7.22	2.58	6.61	1.78	7.67	1.58[c]

[a]Significant t ($p \leqslant .05$) for High versus Low group comparison. [b]Significant t ($p \leqslant .05$) for Medium versus Low group comparison. [c]Significant t ($p \leqslant .05$) for Medium versus High group comparison.

the medium- and high-perception groups, and the medium group differed significantly on 5 items when compared to the low-perception group. Seven of these significant items were found to be unique to particular pairings. Most of the unique items were between the high- and low-perception groups. The data for these findings are presented in Table 2.

Five movement purpose items were found to be uniquely significant between the high- and low-perception groups. Seven other items were significantly different for these groups but were also significant between other pairings. The 5 unique items were spatial orientation, movement efficiency, challenge, expression, and musculoskeletal efficiency. All of these purposes were valued more highly by the high-perception group. The high-perception and medium-perception groups were found to be significantly different on 4 items. The high-perception group valued participation, competition, circulorespiratory efficiency, and movement appreciation more highly than did the medium group. Five items were found to be significantly different for the medium- and low-perception groups.

Table 2 College Students' Perceived Skill Level (Means and *SD*)

Item	Low M	Low SD	Medium M	Medium SD	High M	High SD
Catharsis	5.28	2.55[b]	6.66	2.12	6.80	2.15
Attractiveness	6.63	2.46	6.96	2.30	7.10	2.14
Self-knowledge	5.00	2.56	5.65	2.41	5.90	2.50
Leadership	3.58	2.71	4.28	2.49	4.96	2.43
Self-transcendence	3.45	1.86[b]	5.54	2.71	6.13	2.30[a]
Participation	5.38	2.53	6.27	2.47[c]	6.98	1.98[a]
Object manipulation	4.37	2.20[b]	6.28	2.34	6.70	2.25[a]
Teamwork	4.83	3.09	5.17	2.55	5.47	2.31[a]
Spatial orientation	4.00	2.95	5.55	2.54	5.97	2.50[a]
Cultural understanding	4.25	2.98	3.44	2.46	3.59	2.36
Joy of movement	6.15	2.47	7.08	2.08	7.23	1.92
Weight control	7.40	1.83	7.06	2.35	7.46	1.90
Competition	4.78	2.60[b]	6.21	2.28[c]	7.19	1.96[a]
Movement efficiency	6.16	2.48	7.27	2.06	7.50	1.77[a]
Challenge	4.14	2.64	5.60	2.49	6.25	2.33[a]
Circulorespiratory efficiency	5.81	2.85	6.67	2.44[c]	7.30	2.00[a]
Expression	2.91	2.42	4.13	2.55	4.55	2.47
Self-integration	5.09	3.08	5.38	2.86	5.96	2.62
Musculoskeletal efficiency	6.81	2.60	7.72	1.70	8.06	1.27[a]
Aliveness	6.80	2.30	7.24	2.06[c]	7.43	1.65
Movement appreciation	5.00	2.51	6.12	2.24	6.77	1.98[a]
Mechanical efficiency	5.92	2.32[b]	7.45	1.76	7.82	1.23[a]

[a]Significant t ($p \leqslant .05$) for High versus Low group comparison. [b]Significant t ($p \leqslant .05$) for Medium versus Low group comparison. [c]Significant t ($p \leqslant .05$) for Medium versus High group comparison.

groups. All of these items—catharsis, self-transcendence, object manipulation, competition, and mechanical efficiency—were valued more by the medium group.

An examination of the means for college students revealed that the low group had only one movement purpose that was valued highly (7.0 or better). This item related to weight control. In addition, three means were within the low range. The medium group had six movement purposes in the high range and only one movement purpose in the low range. The high-skill group ranked nine movement purposes in the high range and only one in the low range.

The specific movement purposes that were valued highly by the high-perception group were weight control (7.46), attractiveness (7.10), competition (7.19), movement efficiency (7.50), joy of movement (7.23), circulorespiratory efficiency (7.30), musculoskeletal efficiency (8.06), aliveness (7.43), and mechanical efficiency (7.82). The six highly valued movement purposes for the medium group were joy of movement (7.08), weight control (7.06), movement efficiency (7.27), musculoskeletal efficiency (7.72), aliveness (7.24), and mechanical efficiency (7.45). The low-valued movement purpose for the high and medium groups was cultural understanding. The low-perception group rated leadership (3.58), self-transcendence (3.45), and expression (2.91) in the low-valued range. Weight control (7.40) was the only item in the high range for the low-perception group.

Means for the athletes group are reported separately for the high-, medium-, and low-skill groups. Ten means were rated high by the high-skill group. Five and 4 items were highly valued by medium and low groups, respectively. No items were valued in the low range for any of the athlete groups. The 10 items rated high by the high skill group were aliveness (7.90), movement efficiency (7.88), musculoskeletal efficiency (7.88), competition (7.75), mechanical efficiency (7.16), movement appreciation (7.44), challenge (7.35), participation (7.34), circulorespiratory efficiency (7.18), and weight control (7.06).

The medium group highly valued participation (7.38), aliveness (7.35), movement efficiency (7.29), circulorespiratory efficiency (7.18), and musculoskeletal efficiency (7.02). The 4 items with high means for the low group were movement efficiency (8.11), participation (7.55), mechanical efficiency (7.22) and self-transcendence (7.11).

Discussion and Implications

The subjects for this study represent two different populations. Therefore, the results are discussed separately and then compared. The *t* tests for the athlete group indicated greater differences between the high- and medium- and the high- and low-perception groups than between the medium and low groups. The medium and low groups are therefore more similar in their valuing patterns than they are similar to the high group. The *t* test for college students demonstrated a similar trend to the athlete group. There were greater differences between the high to medium and low groups than between the medium and low groups. There were, however, fewer differences between the high to medium low groups than between the medium and low groups. There were, also, greater differences overall among college student groups than among the athlete groups. These findings would indicate that similar motivation techniques might be applicable for medium- and low-perception groups, whereas different techniques would be necessary for high groups. The two sample groups demonstrated great similarities in *t*-test results. The two samples shared all but three significantly different purposes.

The highly valued movement purposes for high-perception athletes were participation, weight control, competition, movement efficiency, challenge, circulorespiratory efficiency, musculoskeletal efficiency, aliveness, movement appreciation, and mechanical efficiency. The high-perception college group ranked competition, weight control, movement efficiency, circulorespiratory efficiency, attractiveness, joy of movement, musculoskeletal efficiency, aliveness, and mechanical efficiency as highly valued. The two samples differed on four purposes: participation, challenge, joy of movement, and attractiveness.

The medium-perception athletes rated participation, movement efficiency, circulorespiratory efficiency, musculoskeletal efficiency, and aliveness as highly valued. The medium college group highly valued musculoskeletal efficiency, aliveness, joy of movement, weight control, and mechanical efficiency. These samples varied on five purposes. The low-perception athlete group highly valued four purposes: self-transcendence, participation, movement efficiency, and mechanical efficiency. The low-perception college group rated only weight control in the highly valued category.

The implications that these findings have for curriculum workers relate to the instructional phase of the program. The instructor could use the movement purposes as a foundation for phrasing teaching cues and developing motivation techniques for the various skill perception groups. The matching of cues with personal meaning could provide a more effective feedback system. A second implication lends support for the Bain and Steinhardt and Sonstroem, Snyder, and Spreitzer findings. The high-perception groups, college students and athletes, ranked more movement purposes in the high category than did the medium and low groups. This finding indicates that high-perception groups find more meaning in movement activity than individuals who report medium- or low-skill perceptions. In addition, athletes in general ranked more purposes in the high range than did college students. The apparent conclusion is that the more skilled in actuality and perception an individual is, the more varied meanings that an individual identifies with activity. This might in turn facilitate participation habits. The other implication is that curriculum workers and instructors need to concentrate effort on the development of stronger and more varied personal meanings for medium- and low-skill perception individuals. As indicated by Sonstroem (1978) and Bain and Steinhardt (1985), the development of self-confidence is just as crucial, if not more so, as the development of competence in movement programs. As physical educators, if we are to achieve our goal of lifelong participation we must design success-oriented programs for our students. Success must be more than fun; it also must contain a skill component that allows the individual to formulate a realistic image of self as a mover.

References

Bain, L. (1985, April). *Ethnographic study of an exercise class.* Paper presented to the Annual Convention of the American Alliance for Health, Physical Education, Recreation and Dance, Atlanta, GA.

Bain, L., & Steinhardt, M. (1985). Factors influencing participation in physical activity: Implications for curriculum theory. In *Proceedings of the*

Fourth Conference on Curriculum Theory in Physical Education. Athens, GA: University of Georgia.

Bandura, A. (1977). Self-efficacy: Toward a unifying theory of behavioral change. *Psychological Review,* **84,** 191–215.

Bressan, E., & Weiss, M. (1982). A theory of instruction for developing competence, self-confidence and persistence in physical activity. *Journal of Teaching in Physical Education,* **2**(1), 38–47.

Corbin, C.B., Laurie, D.R., Gruger, C., & Smiley, B. (1984). Vicarious success experiences as a factor influencing self-confidence, attitudes and physical activity of adult women. *Journal of Teaching in Physical Education,* **4**(1), 17–23.

Dishman, R.K. (1981). Biologic influences on exercise adherence. *The Research Quarterly,* **52,** 143–159.

Dishman, R.K. (1982). Compliance/adherence in health-related exercise. *Health Psychology,* **1,** 237–267.

Greendorfer, S.L. (1977). Role of socializing agents in female sport involvement. *The Research Quarterly,* **48,** 304–310.

Greendorfer, S.L. (1978). Social class influence on female sport involvement. *Sex Roles,* **4,** 619–625.

Griffin, N.S., & Keogh, J.F. (1981). Movement confidence and effective movement behavior in adapted physical education. *Motor Skills: Theory into Practice,* **5**(1), 23–35.

Griffin, N.S., & Keogh, J.F. (1982). A model for movement confidence. In J.A.S. Kelso & J.E. Clark (Eds.), *The development of movement control and coordination* (p. 198). New York: Wiley.

Jewett, A., & Bain, L. (1985). *The curriculum process in physical education.* Dubuque, IA: W.C. Brown.

Kenyon, G.S. (1968). Six scales for assessing attitude toward physical activity. *The Research Quarterly,* **39,** 566–574.

McPherson, B.D. (1980). *Social factors to consider in fitness programming and motivation: Different strokes for different groups.* Paper presented at the Ontario Task Force on Sport and Physical Recreation Research Workshop on Fitness Motivation, Geneva Park, Ontario.

McPherson, B.D. (1984). Sport participation across the life cycle: A review of the literature and suggestions for future research. *Sociology and Sport Journal,* **1,** 213–230.

Snyder, E.E., & Spreitzer, E.A. (1973). Family influence and involvement in sports. *The Research Quarterly,* **44,** 249–255.

Snyder, E.E., & Spreitzer, E.A. (1976). Correlates of sport participation among adolescent girls. *The Research Quarterly,* **47,** 804–809.

Snyder, E.E., & Spreitzer, E.A. (1979). Lifelong involvement in sport as a leisure pursuit: Aspects of role construction. *Quest, 31,* 57–70.

Snyder, E.E., & Spreitzer, E.A. (1984). Patterns of adherence to a physical conditioning program. *Sociology of Sport Journal, 1,* 103–116.

Sonstroem, R.J. (1978). Physical estimation and attraction scales: Rationale and research. *Medicine and Science in Sports, 10,* 97–102.

Sonstroem, R.J. (1982). Attitudes and beliefs in the prediction of exercise participation. In R.C. Canter & W.J. Gillespie (Eds.), *Sports medicine, sport science: Bridging the gap* (pp. 3–16). Lexington: D.C. Heath.

Spreitzer, E.A., & Snyder, E.E. (1976). Socialization into sport: An exploratory path analysis. *The Research Quarterly, 47,* 238–245.

Spreitzer, E.A., & Snyder, E.E. (1983). Correlates of participation in adult recreational sports. *Journal of Leisure Research, 15,* 27–38.

Social Motives as Determinants of Physical Recreation at Various Life Stages

Pauli Vuolle

It is the purpose of the present study to determine the significance of and fluctuations in social motives associated with physical recreation in a person's life cycle. Defined generally, life cycle means the sum total of an individual's life stages. Life cycle denotes the unique life of an individual, consisting of various kinds of events, life episodes, crises, and life changes. Linked with the life cycle and its particular events is the temporal orientation of humans, in other words the structuring of time into days, weeks, or longer periods. Usually, life is structured into working days and weekend days, as well as into the annual working and vacationing times.

Social life imposes certain expectations, requirements, and duties on individuals as well as endowing them with certain rights. Consequently, the life cycle of people living according to the rules of social life can be structured in very much the same way as far as numerous central life events and their temporal orientation is concerned. Common stages in the life cycle include attending school, studying at a university, assuming an occupational role and simultaneously starting a family plus the life stages associated with it—the birth of one's children, their growth, and their leaving the home—and, after this, withdrawal from occupational life into retirement (Vuolle, 1984, pp. 149–151).

In this chapter, Levinson's model is used to describe changes in the sports activity of Finns at various stages in the life cycle (see Figure 1). Levinson divided the life cycle into four broad stages. The first stage covers childhood and adolescence, and lasts until age 17. This is followed by about 5 years of what Levinson calls the early adult transition into the next stage, which is early adulthood and covers ages between 22 and 40. After the midlife transition, an individual enters middle adulthood. This stage covers the years 45 to 60. The late adult transition stage between ages 60 and 65 means a transition into late adulthood (Levinson, 1978, p. 168).

Implementation responsibility

Basic motive	Acquisition	Mastery			Integration
Life cycle	Childhood	Adolescence	Early adulthood	Middle adulthood	Late adulthood
Physical recreation motive	Skill learning and training		Maintaining ability to work and function		Maintaining and restoring ability to function
	Competitive activity		Fitness and recreational activity		Fitness and recreational activity, rehabilitative action
Organization	School system Sports organizations		Fitness organizations in cooperation with families, employers, housing communities, senior citizens' organizations and other reference groups		Rehabilitation units

Figure 1   Functions of physical recreation at various stages of the life cycle.

Method

The empirical data in this report are derived from studies on the physical recreation behavior of the Finnish population carried out in recent years. The sketching out of an overall picture of the physical recreation behavior of the Finnish population was begun in the late 1970s with extensive surveys that were completed and deepened with questionnaire and interview techniques in the beginning of the next decade. In this sense, the 1970s can appropriately be called the period of basic survey work in physical recreation behavior, and the 1980s can be called a period of attempting to obtain in-depth data about an individual's physical recreation behavior in relationship to his or her environment.

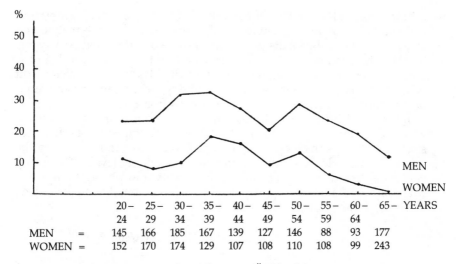

Figure 2 Membership in sport clubs (Reference: VÄLI Study).

Results and Discussion

In the description of social motives, Finns' participation in both organized and unorganized physical activity is described. The indicator of organized activity was participation in sports club activities and in mass physical recreation events. The indicator of unorganized social activity was physical recreation that takes place in various informal, small groups.

The question of the incidence of social motives in the motivational field of physically active people is approached in terms of a description of the motivational responses related to various events, as obtained in the interview study, both on a general level for each age group and separately for the most popular types of physical recreation.

Figure 2 shows fluctuations in sports club membership at the various stages of the life cycle. As is apparent from the figure, club activities are mainly the domain of youth. According to projects of Research on the Finnish Population's Sport Behavior (from here on referred to as the VÄLI Study), the Health Habit Study on Youth (NTTT Study), and the Seppänen (1983) study, some 40% of boys aged 7 to 14 are members of a sports club. Membership rates steadily decrease with increasing age such that, for instance, of women aged 60 or higher, only a few percent belong to a sports club.

In the project Research on the Finnish Population's Time Distribution, daily participation in different forms of sports and outdoor recreation was analyzed. Table 1 shows the proportional share of different activity types. Most of the leisure-time physical recreation of the population is in the nature of nonorganized, light outdoor activity. The share of what might be termed utilitarian physical activity (hunting, fishing, mushroom hunting) is considerable, allowing for seasonal variation.

In the VÄLI Study, the physical recreation motivation was measured with a questionnaire and focused interviews among subjects that consisted of 549 persons employed for a period of 10 or more years by the town of Jyväskylä and representing all occupational levels. The group was nonselected in terms of movement ability and physical interest.

The subjects' answers to the question, "With whom do you participate in your *favorite sport?*"[1] were as follows:

	Men %	Women %
Alone	34	39
With wife/husband	22	24
With friends	25	18
With children	10	14
With dog	3	2
In sports club	5	1
Some other way	1	2
%	100	100
N	239	258

Table 1   Daily Participation in Different Forms of Sports and Outdoor Recreation on Different Days (10- to 64-Year-Old Population)

Type of sport and outdoor recreation	Weekday		Saturday		Sunday	
	%	persons	%	persons	%	persons
Organized sport activity	3.4	119.000	1.9	67.000	1.5	53.000
Unorganized sport activity	11.9	417.000	12.5	438.000	17.1	600.000
Outdoor activity, walking	18.5	649.000	25.2	884.000	39.7	1392.000
Hunting, fishing, gathering mushrooms	2.3	81.000	6.8	238.000	8.2	288.000

Note.   From *The Finnish Population's Time Distribution* (Study 65) by I. Niemi, S. Kiiski, and M. Liikanen, 1981, Helsinki: Central Statistical Office.

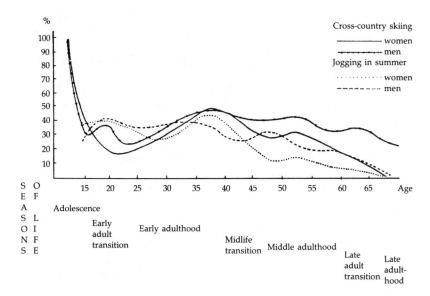

Figure 3 Commonness of activity in cross-country skiing and jogging (at least once a week) at various stages in life cycle.

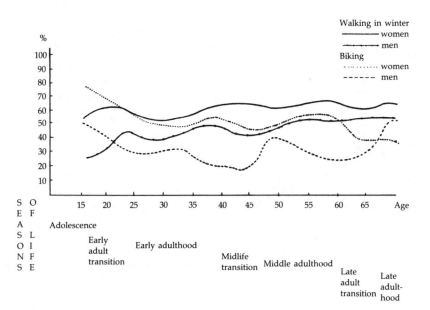

Figure 4 Commonness of activity in walking and biking (at least once a week) at various stages in life cycle.

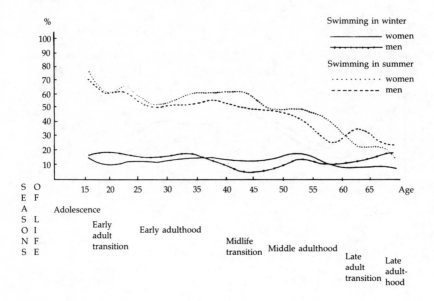

Figure 5 Commonness of activity in swimming (at least once a week) at various stages in life cycle.

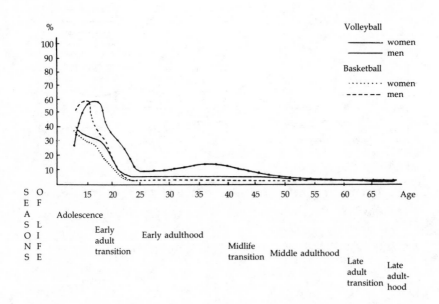

Figure 6 Commonness of activity in volleyball and basketball (at least once a week) at various stages in life cycle.

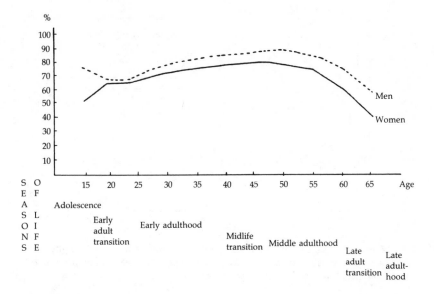

%

Figure 7 Commonness of utilitarian exercise (berry picking, mushroom hunting, game hunting, fishing) at various stages in life cycle.

With the exception of the first alternative, all other responses entail social participation. Thus, it can be said that some 60% of women and 65% of men do their preferred type of physical recreation under the influence of some social motive. Most commonly, people participate in physical recreation together with a spouse, friends, and children. In contrast, only a few percent of the respondents do their physical recreation in a sports club.

As was stated earlier, personal physical recreation motives vary greatly in complexity. According to research findings by Silvennoinen (1981), the sport activity motives of young people are diffuse. The most consistent motivational behavior, as measured in two successive repeat surveys, was recorded for motives describing an emphasis on performance and competitiveness. In addition, young people are fairly conscious of the social significance of sports (see Figure 8). Important factors contributing to participation in sports include meeting friends and getting new friends.

Among the workers of the town of Jyväskylä, recreation, relaxation, and mental health motives are strongly internalized throughout the individual's life (see Table 2). Very close to these are motives related to being outdoors and in nature. Motives related to general fitness and health, as well as those related to fitness of various parts of the body, become stronger with age. Social motives play an important role in early adulthood, yet their significance decreases in older age groups.

Most of the motives described above are connected with the experiences the population has received when engaging in the most popular individual

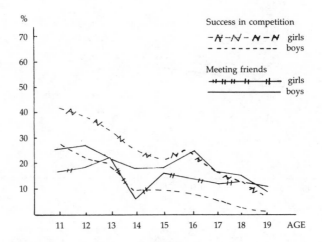

Figure 8 Meeting friends and success in competition as motives for sports activity in 11- to 19-year-olds (percentage of persons whose activity has been greatly influenced by this motive). (Reference: Silvennoinen 1981, pp. 53–55).

Table 2   Central Sports Motives in Different Age Groups

Group of motives	27–39 years		40–49 years		50–60 years	
	men %	women %	men %	women %	men %	women %
Recreation, relaxation, and mental health	79	90	81	89	83	83
Being out-of-doors and in nature	48	69	56	82	55	74
General fitness and good health	55	48	56	59	48	57
Fitness of different parts of the body	25	46	30	43	55	50
Social aspects	52	31	36	33	19	24
Habit	55	46	45	47	50	46
Features of given type of sports	77	63	53	70	48	59

Note.   From "The Status and Meaning of Sport for Finns in Different Stages of Life Cycle" by P. Vuolle, 1984, in *Contribution of Sociology to the Study of Sport: Studies in Sport, Physical Education and Health 18*, pp. 158–163, Jyväskylä: University of Jyväskylä.

types of sports. Of the motives of men doing game-type sports, those of recreation, relaxation, and mental health emerged as the primary ones. In addition, social motives, habitual activity in a given type of sport, and factors connected with being outdoors and in nature were emphasized in the oldest group (50 to 60 years).

In volleyball, the most popular of the team sports, the most typical individual answers related to motives included the following: "I've been playing volleyball all my life," "Volleyball is a good way of staying fit," "You can play volleyball even if you're no longer so young," and "A relaxed atmosphere and camaraderie make you keep on going." In the most popular individual sports, such as walking, jogging, skiing, and utilitarian exercise, a rather consistent emphasis was placed on the following motives: "You can do them with members of your family and friends," "You don't necessarily need anybody's company to do them," "They are easy types of exercise," "They make you feel physically and mentally refreshed and relaxed," and "They provide a change from sedentary work."

Apart from sports club activities, participation in mass physical recreation events organized by various communities has become a visible type of social physical recreation in Finland. According to a study conducted by the Finnish Recreational Sport Association (Kuntoliikuntakalenteri, 1985), 323 jogging events, 109 cycling events, and 317 skiing events were organized in the country in 1985.

The social background, health, physical recreation interest, and life-style of participants in mass physical recreation events have been described in the context of the Impivaara Run (Heikkinen, Lehtonen, & Pohjolainen, 1972, pp. 122–126), the 6th Aulanko Run (Vuolle, 1979, pp. 69–93), and the Finlandia Marathon (Kannas, Heikkinen, Rahkila, Suominen, & Laakso, 1983, pp. 164–173). The risks associated with skiing tours have been described by Vuori (1972). The Finlandia Marathon, held in the city of Jyväskylä in 1980, was participated in by 1,596 runners. A study carried out during the run showed that a large number of participants were people whose life-style can be characterized as methodical. A methodical life-style entails a certain ascetism and puritanism, an activeness both in sports and social life, and a well-planned organization of one's leisure time.

The 6th Aulanko Run in the city of Hameenlinna in 1978 had 1,830 participants. When asked about their reasons and motives in a questionnaire distributed immediately after the run, about one male respondent in four and more than 40% of the women's respondents indicated they had participated in the run as representatives of some team or community. (For a comparison of these results with the respondents' answers to the Kenyon [1971] Scale, see Vuolle, 1984.)

Physical recreation motives have been classed both theoretically and on the basis of empirical data. Kenyon's internationally known structured motive classification groups motives on the basis of their purpose into a six- or seven-class category (Kenyon, 1971, pp. 71–81). One of these is physical recreation as a social experience.

Comparing Kenyon's scale to one developed in a Finnish study, it can be seen that, in the physical recreation interests of Finns, motives associated with nature and outdoor life (what could be called *national activity motives*) were very strongly emphasized. These motives were apparent in Nordic skiing, walking, and jogging, as well as in backpacking and orienteering, and do not surface in a sufficiently independent way in the Kenyon scale.

Measurements intended to find out about the stability of motives during a period of 1 year showed that the top physical recreation motives, whether obtained with one or the other of the methods, as a whole proved rather stable, although attempts were made to influence them via information containing different motivational material (Vuolle, Laakso, Telama, & Saukkonen, 1980).

Conclusion

Social motives become apparent in physical recreation that is done within the framework of various organized reference groups or unorganized small groups. Participation in sports club activities, mass physical recreation events, or doing physical recreation with spouse, friends, or one's children are among the most common indicators of social motives. Social motives, like the individual's activity motives in general, are factors tied to the progress of the life cycle and undergo change at the various stages of the life cycle.

It is typical of young people's social activity motives that they are linked to training and skill mastery situations. Motives are not generally expressed through competitive activity in sports clubs.

The social motives of adults and people of working age are most readily apparent in activities in which people seek fitness and recreation as members of a reference group or some small group.

The social motives of elderly people are linked with physical recreation in small groups in which the goals of fitness and recreation are often joined by rehabilitatory goals. The types of physical recreation most popular with Finns (i.e., Nordic skiing, jogging, walking, biking, swimming, and utilitarian physical recreation such as berry picking, mushroom hunting, game hunting, or fishing) are types of physical recreation realized as activities incorporating social motives.

Thus, physical activity motives are logically related to basic human aspirations and can be seen in relation to Schaie's (1979, p. 108) model of the aspirations of various age groups in the life cycle.

Note

1. The most popular sports in Finland closely correspond to favorite types of sport. Figures 3 through 7 show the variation in interest during a

person's life cycle in the most popular types of physical activity (i.e., Nordic skiing, jogging, walking, biking, swimming, volleyball, basketball, and utilitarian types).

References

Heikkinen, E., Lehtonen, A., & Pohjolainen, P. (1972). Kilpa-ja kuntourheilijat Impivaaran juoksussa. *Stadion*, **4**, 122–128.

Kannas, L., Heikkinen, E., Rahkila, P., Suominen, H., & Laakso, L. (1983). Piirteita Finlandia Marathon-holkkatapahtumaan osallistuneiden elamantyylista. *Liikunta ja Tiede*, **4**, 122–128.

Kenyon, G. (1971). A conceptual model for characterizing physical activity. In J. Loy & G. Kenyon (Eds.), *Sport, culture and society: A reader on the sociology of sport* (3rd ed.). New York: Macmillan.

Kuntoliikuntakalenteri. (1985). Helsinki: Finnish Recreational Association.

Levinson, D. (1978). *The seasons of man's life.* New York: Alfred A. Knopp.

Niemi, I., Kiiski, S., & Liikanen, M. (1981). *The Finnish population's time distribution* (Study 65). Helsinki: Central Statistical Office of Finland.

Schaie, W. (1979). The primacy mental abilities in adulthood: An exploration in the development of psychometric intelligence. In P. Baltes & G. Brim (Eds.), *Life-span development and behavior.* New York: Academic Press.

Seppänen, P. (1983). *About Finnish sport organizations and their function.* (Research Rep. No. 28). Jyväskylä: University of Jyväskylä, Department of Sociology and Planning for Physical Culture.

Silvennoinen, M. (1981). *Physically active interests, motives for physical activity and the factors explaining them among 11- to 19-year-old pupils: Report of physical culture and health.* Jyväskylä: Research Institute of Physical Culture and Health.

Vuolle, P. (1979). *VI. Aulanko-juoksuun osallistuneiden sosiaalinen rakenne, liikuntaharrastus ja holkkaharrastuksen motiivit.* Seminar report, Hameenlinna.

Vuolle, P. (1984). The status and meaning of sport for Finns in different stages of life cycle. In K. Olin (Ed.), *Contribution of sociology to the study of sport: Studies in sport, physical education and health 18.* Jyväskylä: University of Jyväskylä.

Vuolle, P., Laakso, L., Telama, R., & Saukkonen, O. (1980, October). *A study of the stability of the motives for physical activity.* Paper presented at the World Scientific Congress, Tbilisi, USSR.

Vuori, I. (1972). *Sydameen kohdistuva kuormitus laturetkihiihdossa.* Turun yliopiston julkaisusarja, sarja C 12.

PART III

Methods

The papers presented in Part III focus on qualitative and quantitative methodological perspectives in physical education and sport pedagogy research. Together they represent a refreshingly broad spectrum of various lines of inquiry and types of methodological approaches and provide provocative suggestions and analyses.

Paul Godbout, Jean Brunelle, and Marielle Tousignant review their 3-year research program, comment on the impact and refinement of ALT-PE (academic learning time in physical education) research, and advocate a twofold research strategy focusing on quantitative aspects of motor and cognitive engagements and the study of process variables related to qualitative aspects of engagement time. Judith Rink and Peter Werner present a theoretical perspective on the inherent problems of using student responses to instructional tasks as a teacher effectiveness measure in achieving a psychomotor skill. They raise some important issues and question the validity of using ALT-PE alone as a predictor of teacher effectiveness. The study by Paul Paese focuses on the nature and specificity of feedback and picks up on some theoretical assumptions discussed by Rink and Werner.

Marielle Tousignant and Jean Brunelle's teacher education study is instructive with respect to both the findings and the qualitative methodological approach that was used. Wilma Harrington's paper, also an ethnographic study, demonstrates the broad range and various forms that characterize qualitative research.

Five quantitative studies focusing at least in part on academic learning time in physical education, sport, and dance comprise the balance of this section. Vincent Mancini and Deborah Wuest focus on coaches' interactions with high- and low-skilled athletes. Risto Telama and his coauthors present learning behavior findings on high- and low-skilled physical education students, whereas Maurice Piéron and Carlos Gonçalves report on study and athlete engagement time and teacher feedback profiles in the instructional and coaching contexts. Similarly, Claude Paré and his fellow authors report on student active learning times findings and comparisons at the elementary and secondary levels. The last paper, by

Madeline Lord and Bernard Petiot, provides us with one of the few descriptive analytic studies on the dance-teaching process. Using adapted observation systems focusing on teacher professional function and academic learning time, the authors have generated some interesting data that begin to shed some light on prevailing dance-teaching practices and related student behavior characterizations within the recreational dance context.

Who Benefits from Passing Through the Program?

Paul Godbout
Jean Brunelle
Marielle Tousignant

Nowadays, anybody involved in research on physical education teacher effectiveness will readily admit that in the first half of this decade the proposal of using ALT-PE as a major process variable has had a considerable impact. Whether this is due to an unusual and fortunate combination of events or can be explained partly by a cause and effect relationship remains for the historians of sport pedagogy to tackle some day; there has been, nevertheless, an interesting coincidence in time between the spreading out of the ALT-PE concept and the recognition of sport pedagogy as an emerging research area, or as some of us see it, as a new subdiscipline of the physical activity sciences.

After the initial launching of ALT-PE in 1979, a series of shock waves was registered by sport pedagogy monitors in late 1982 and in 1983 (Dodds & Rife, 1983; Piéron & Cheffers, 1982; Telama, Varstala, Tiainen, Laakso, & Haajanen, 1983; Templin & Olson, 1983). Since then, the incoming flow of data has been regular and, as could be expected, is progressively delineating various channels of inquiry. Of course, the now-classic triadic loop of the research process can still be found throughout the literature, although one might wish to read more about experimental studies.

The increasing reliance of researchers on more comprehensive theoretical models, such as the one proposed by Dunkin and Biddle (1974), has led many of them to examine the relationship between ALT-PE and various context, presage, process, and product variables. As could be expected, one important line of inquiry has been the verification of the initial hypothesis that a greater amount of ALT-PE would lead to a greater amount of learning. The fact that many failed to register such a relationship has drawn our attention to other variables that could be taken into account in teacher-effectiveness studies (among such variables, one finds the initial skill level of the learners, the quality of augmented feedback, the so-called criterion time-on-task, etc.).

Because a great number of studies have made use of the ALT-PE observational system, we have been able to make numerous comparisons across studies. Due to the importance of such comparisons on an international basis, we hope that as many researchers as possible will keep using this system instead of trying to put forward their own. At the same time, there should be some effort to refine ALT-PE data beyond what we are getting now. Such a refinement could be twofold. On the one hand, efforts should better characterize the type and the quality of motor or cognitive engagements registered in a given interval of time. Our lack of specificity in registering time-on-task units may explain why we often get inconsistent, if not conflicting, results when we try to relate ALT to achievement. On the other hand, the collection of ALT-PE data could be enriched by the simultaneous registering of other process variables that, for their part, might focus on the qualitative aspects of the engagement time.

The Conceptual Frame of Reference of the Research Program

During the fall of 1981, a research proposal was submitted to a Quebec research funding agency (FCAC) for a 3-year grant. The purpose of the proposed research program was to attempt to pin down some major learning conditions associated with various levels of motor achievement in youth sports. For the long run, our goal was, and still is, to develop supervision of teaching models that would focus on such conditions.

We were aware of Rosenshine and Berliner's (1978) conclusion to the effect that the trend in research on teaching efficiency had been focusing more on students' behaviors than on teachers'. The studies surveyed derived from the presage-context-process-product paradigm (Dunkin & Biddle, 1974) and were conducted in natural teaching settings. In 1980, after reviewing studies based on this approach, Stallings had concluded that the body of knowledge put together in the 1970s suggested two principles to teachers:

- Provide more time for the learning of the content
- Take into account the students' skill level so that they will spend more time working on appropriate tasks in light of specific criteria for success

In the same period of time, Cooper (1977) and Locke (1977) had indicated that few researchers of the field of pedagogy of physical activity had investigated the relationship between student learning and student behaviors. The same opinion was to be expressed a few years later by McEwen and Graham (1982) and by Piéron and Piron (1981) in connection with the various components of active learning time. This phenomenon could probably be explained in part by the problems associated with achieving valid and reliable measurement of motor achievement. For our part, we had devised systematic procedures to develop rating scales and to establish the various types of reliability involved with such instruments (Godbout & Schutz, 1983). We were familiar with the original ALT-PE system and with its 1982 revision (Siedentop, Tousignant, & Parker, 1982).

We were also aware of the underlying assumption of the positive relationship between active learning time and student learning.

This kind of background, combined with our wish to develop a comprehensive, integrated model for the supervision of professional practice in physical activity, led us to put together a research program that would attempt to take into account as many different types of variables as seemed feasible.

Method

Because the purpose of this first phase of our research program was to identify variables associated with learning or lack of learning, we chose to conduct correlational studies. Also, in an effort to limit the variety of the objectives pursued and content covered, we chose to investigate instructional programs offered by sport bodies instead of regular PE classes.

The Design of the Studies

Over a 3-year period, four studies were conducted within the framework of that project. Because the second study was a replication of the first one and yielded similar results, the data were combined and are presented as one single study dealing with the teaching of ice hockey skills. The two other studies dealt with Olympic handball and volleyball. Table 1 presents the main features of the three studies.

Table 1   Features of the Three Correlational Studies

Subject matter	Ice hockey	Olympic handball	Volleyball
Sponsorship	Fédération Québécoise de Hockey sur Glace	Fédération Québécoise de Handball Olympique	Fédération de Volleyball du Québec
Main characteristics of the proposed program	Series of 20 lessons containing specific activities	Repertoire of basic individual and collective skills grouped according to the players' levels: beginner, intermediate, advanced	Lists of basic individual and collective skills grouped under the three goals of the beginners program: acquisition, refinement, integration

(Cont.)

Table 1 (Cont.)

Duration of the program	20 lessons of 60 minutes spread across 10 weeks during fall '82 and fall '83	8 periods of 2 hours spread over 6 consecutive days during summer '84	11 periods of 2½ hours spread over 6 consecutive days during summer '84
Number of players in each group	8–12	15	14
Number of teachers observed	12	3	3
Number of players pretested and posttested	58	23	22
Number of players observed during the process	37	16	18
Players' age	8–10	12–17	14–16
Players' sex	Male	Male & female	Female

Note. The studies were supported by FCAC (EQ-2121), Province of Quebec.

As can be seen from the content of Table 1, we dealt with regular programs offered in a relatively short period of time and centered on the learning of specific sport skills. Once we had reached an agreement to include a pretest and a posttest session, we ended up with what might be qualified as "naturally occurring experimental teaching units." It should be clearly understood, however, that the inclusion of pretests and posttests was the only change made to the regular programs and that there was no other interference on our part during the offering of the programs.

The Variables Investigated

The basic theoretical model used in our research program was the one suggested by Dunkin and Biddle (1974) with a few modifications. The adapted model is presented in Figure 1; those already familiar with this paradigm will note three modifications to the original model:

Planning	Interaction	Summative evaluation
Presage variables - Teacher's professional preparation & teaching experience - Cognitive & learning styles - Learner's entry skill level *Context variables* - Material resources - Human resources (other than teacher) *Program variables* - Types of objectives - Nature of contents - Pedagogical directions - Directions for evaluation	*Process variables* - Teacher and learner behavior as they interact - Formative evaluation - Content covered - Hidden curriculum	*Product variables* - Learner's achievement with regard to specific goals of the program - Participant's level of satisfaction

Note. This model is an adaptation of Dunkin and Biddle's model (1974).

Figure 1   A comprehensive model that includes the variables associated with the three dimensions of the teaching-learning conditions.

- The learners' characteristics prior to the application of the program were considered as "presage variables" because we could not, in a study focusing on teacher-learner interactions, bring ourselves to consider the learners as part of the context.
- Program variables were added as a new category, for the characteristics of the program available to the teachers may have an impact on some process variables.
- The actual content covered was included as a process variable. The hidden curriculum was also included the first year but was deleted in the following two studies due to the fact that we were dealing with rather intensive types of programs that left little room for the subjects to engage in similar physical activities elsewhere.

The list of the variables investigated and the type of instruments used to do so are presented in Table 2. It should be noted, however, that this paper discusses only the results concerning skill learning as it relates to initial skill level and to instructors' and learners' behaviors.

Reliability coefficients were computed for the ALT-PE results and for the skill measurements. In the case of the ALT-PE data, percentages of agreement were regularly (16 times) computed for each one of the three main categories considered in our adapted coding system. Mean values of 95%, 87%, and 82% were obtained for the context, the learners' involvement, and the teacher's behavior categories, respectively. Several rating scales of the descriptive numeric type were developed to cover the various skills involved in each of the three programs. The interrater reliability of the ratings varied from 0.74 to 0.98 and the score reliability from 0.71 to 0.96 for the 13 rating scales involved. These various reliability coefficients were computed using the theory of generalizability and following procedures described by Godbout and Schutz (1983).

Results

Instructors' and Learners' Behaviors

Results yielded by the ALT-PE observational system are presented in Table 3. The time devoted by the groups to motor content was quite consistent between the three programs (from 60 to 64%). Motor engaged time (which in our case did not include the supporting category) varied from 24 to 32%, whereas the subjects spent a great percentage of the class periods waiting or in interim (31 to 40%).

Table 4 Mean Percentages (%) of Overall Class Period Attributed to Each Category of Instructor Behavior from Standpoint of Target Subjects

Instructors' behavior	Ice hockey			Volleyball			Olympic handball		
	M	SD	Range	M	SD	Range	M	SD	Range
1. Information									
Structures or directs	23	3.5	15–23	21	2.9	17–28	20	5.2	14–30
Explains as planned	5	4.8	0–33	3	1.1	0– 4	5	1.7	1– 7
2. Interaction									
Academic questions	0.2	1.0	0– 7	0.5	0.4	0– 1	0.7	0.5	0– 2
Explains as needed	1	.9	0– 4	1	0.6	0– 3	2	0.8	0– 3
Academic feedbacks	2	1.2	0– 6	4	1.3	2– 6	5	2	2– 9
Task engagement feedbacks	0.4	.5	0– 2	0.5	0.2	0– 1	0.8	0.7	0– 2
Stimulates	1	1	0– 5	1	0.7	0– 3	1	0.4	0– 2
Monitoring	6	3.4	0– 6	14	2.4	8–18	11.5	4	5–18
3. No intervention	61.4	7.3	27–74	55	4.6	49–63	52	4.6	45–63
4. Varia	—	—	—	—	—	—	1	0.7	0– 2
5. No coding possible	—	—	—	—	—	—	1	1.8	0– 5

Table 5 Pretest and Posttest Results for the Various Motor Skills Considered in Each Program

Motor skill and specific program	Pretest			Posttest		
	M	SD	Range	M	SD	Range
Ice hockey (N = 58)						
Skating agility (s)[a]	51	9.3	37–79	45 ***	5.4	37–61
Stopping (6)[b]	2.4	1.2	0– 4.8	2.9	1.2	0– 5.4
Turning (6)	1.4	1.1	0– 3.9	1.7	0.9	0– 4.4
Pivot backward (6)	3.2	0.8	1.2– 4.6	3.2	0.7	1.4– 4.7
Pivot forward (6)	3.0	0.7	1.4– 4.7	3.1	0.7	1.3– 4.6
Sum of ratings (24)	10.1	3.0	2.7–15.9	10.9**	2.7	5.0–17.3
Volleyball (N = 18)						
Setting (11)	8.2	0.9	6.8– 9.8	8.7	0.9	6.2–10.0
Positioning (5)	2.6	0.7	1.6– 4.0	3.2	0.8	1.7– 4.3
Sliding aside (5)	2.6	1.1	0.4– 4.2	3.3	0.8	1.1– 4.3
Bumping (6)	3.7	0.6	2.5– 5.0	3.9	0.3	3.4– 4.9
Spiking (9)	4.9	1.3	1.5– 7.0	5.5	1.3	1.7– 7.3
Sum of ratings (36)	21.9	3.3	13.5–26.6	24.5***	3.3	14.5–28.5

(Cont.)

Table 5 (Cont.)

Olympic handball (N = 16)

Passing (7)	3.5	1.4	0.7– 6.2	4.3	1.0	2.2– 6.0
Receiving (8)	5.4	1.5	2.7– 7.6	4.7	1.4	2.3– 7.2
Defensive movement (14)	7.2	1.7	4.8–11.4	10.2	1.0	8.2–11.9
Shooting (12)	6.3	1.8	2.6– 8.6	7.8	2.0	3.1–10.3
Sum of ratings (41)	22.4	3.9	14.0–32.1	27.0***	3.6	17.8–31.7

[a]A reduction in skating test results indicates a better performance. [b]Number in parentheses indicates the upper limit of the rating scale, the lower limit being 0 in each case.
**p < .01. ***p < .001

Table 6 Classification of Subjects on the Basis of Their Initial Skill Level and of That Obtained at the End of Each Program (Scores Based on Average of Ratings)

Program of activity	Level of gains	Initial skill level			Number of subjects
		Low	Average	High	
Ice hockey (N = 58)	No gain	4 (0)[a]	14 (5)	9 (13)	27
	Small gain	6 (4)	10 (13)	4 (9)	20
	Moderate gain and more	4 (10)	5 (4)	2 (0)	11
Volleyball (N = 18)	No gain	1	1	4	6
	Small gain	0	1	4	5
	Moderate gain and more	1	4	2	7
Olympic handball (N = 16)	No gain	1	0	2	3
	Small gain	1	6	0	7
	Moderate gain and more	2	4	0	6

[a]Numbers in parentheses are the results for the skating agility test.

skill to the other. The use of average values is, however, misleading, as can be seen in Table 6, in which changes in performance are examined on an individual basis for each program in light of the subject's initial skill level. Although one certainly cannot make it an absolute rule, there was nonetheless a tendency for the initially higher performers to stabilize or to improve less than the lower performers.

Relationships Between Presage, Process, and Product Variables

In an effort to better understand the trend illustrated in Table 6, we examined the relationship between five selected variables of interest: the initial skill level of the learners, their improvements, their motor engaged time, the amount of feedback received, and the proportion of time they had been monitored. The various correlation coefficients computed are presented in Table 7. In all three programs there was a negative relationship between the initial skill level and the improvement of the performers; this finding supports the trend mentioned earlier in connection with

Table 7 Correlation Between Selected Presage, Process, and Product Variables

Variable involved	Activity program		
	Ice hockey (N = 37)	Volleyball (N = 18)	Olympic handball (N = 16)
1. Initial skill level VS gain	−.55 (−.84)**	−.30	−.55*
2. Initial skill level VS terminal skill level	.76 (.44)**	.83**	.57*
3. Motor engaged VS initial skill level	−.15 (−.14)	.21	.35
4. Motor engaged VS gain	.004(.16)	.33	−.24
5. Feedback VS gain	−.01 (.29)	.08	.55*
6. Feedback VS initial skill level	−.09 (.15)	−.27	−.16
7. Monitoring VS gain	−.25 (−.12)	.08	−.01
8. Monitoring VS initial skill level	.09 (.16)	.15	−.17

$*p < .05.$ $**p < .01.$

Table 6. However, it must also be noted that there was a definite trend for the best initial performers to remain among the best at the end of the program.

The analysis of the results based on all subjects as a group in each program showed no significant correlation between either learning or initial skill level and motor engaged time. Likewise, on the whole, there was no significant correlation (with one exception for handball) between feedback and monitoring, on the one hand, and learning and the initial skill level, on the other hand.

Discussion

Considering that the three programs of activity investigated were offered to young players who registered on a free basis to take these courses during their vacation time or during the weekends, and considering the fact that most of the instructors involved in the study did not have a degree in the teaching of physical activities, it is interesting to note that the mean values recorded for motor engaged appropriate are higher than those recorded for PE classes and reported by Dodds, Rife, and Metzler (1982).

Contrary to what has been reported in mini-ETU studies in which the teaching-learning settings are purposely simplified, we were unable to establish a clear-cut relationship between engaged time and learning in any of the three studies. In a recent paper, Silverman (1985) reported that "when all students were analyzed together, no engagement variable was a significant predictor of residualized achievements" (p. 69). In order to find some relationship, he had to distinguish between highly, moderately, and less-skilled students and was faced with a significant *positive* relationship for the highly skilled and with significant *negative* relationships for the others. In his study, De Knop (1983) concluded that specific motor activity accounted for 22% of the variance in terminal skill performance but did not report any relationship between motor activity and technique performance improvement. However, our findings are contrary to what has been reported by Phillips and Carlisle (1983).

From our results one should not, however, conclude that learning occurred without motor engaged time. A close examination of individual data indicates that the players who did improve were among those whose level of ability matched the level of difficulty of the task and who did engage in practice. Unfortunately, others who engaged in practice as well did not improve. In other words, motor engaged time seems to be a necessary, but not sufficient, condition for learning. Whenever possible, efforts should be made in our research to consider both quantitative and qualitative aspects of ALT-PE.

In our three studies, the analysis of gains in motor performance in light of initial skill level suggests that, unless a program is geared to take individual needs into account, the subjects whose skill level matches the difficulty of the tasks are likely to profit more from that program than the others, whatever level of engagement they may display. The negative correlations we obtained between initial skill level and gains were also observed by De Knop (1983) and can be deducted from Silverman (1985), who reported an average gain of 1.36 for the initially highly skilled as opposed to an average gain of 3.98 for the less-skilled subjects. Considering the upper limit of the various rating scales used, one could hardly invoke a ceiling effect, or even the law of nonproportional results, to explain the relatively small gains on the part of the better skilled subjects. Likewise, there seems to be little chance that the phenomenon can be explained by a regression toward the mean. Because the three programs covered by our studies were content-oriented rather than objective-oriented, it may be that the players who started at a higher level were not offered appropriate learning experiences.

Coming to the matter of augmented feedback, we seem, as reported by others (Piéron, 1983; Yerg & Twardy, 1982), to be faced with conflicting results. We found a significant correlation of .55 between teacher's feedback and gain in the handball study, but we obtained small, nonsignificant ones in the two other studies. A further analysis of individual data showed that the players who did improve were among those who interacted with their instructor. Unfortunately, others who also interacted with their instructor did not improve.

The crux of the matter may very well lay in our methodology, or as expressed by Yerg (1983) in her paper on the reexamining of the process-product paradigm, in our ways of identifying instructional parameters. For instance, we need to consider not only the amount of augmented feedback but its content as well. The examination of the relationship between augmented feedback and learning in the gymnasium should also take into account the stage of learning of the subjects, the type of activity involved (closed or opened skills), the source of feedback (instructor, peer, video replay), and so forth. The theoretical importance of specific augmented feedback for learning has been repeatedly emphasized, but practical and efficient ways of making it an everyday reality in the gym are yet to be confirmed empirically.

Conclusion

In light of the theoretical model used as a frame of reference for our research program, the results of the three studies reported in this chapter suggest the following conclusions:

- Many instructional programs of the kind offered in youth sport organizations are still designed in terms of general goals and series of activities rather than in terms of specific objectives.
- The lack of specificity of physical activity program objectives makes it difficult for the instructors to consider individual needs, to diagnose learning problems, and to pursue appropriate learning tasks; this may

be amplified by a lack of basic teaching skills, including task analysis and discriminative monitoring.

- In teaching situations in which systematic and regular supervision is out of reach, self-supervision skills must be developed if we expect teachers or instructors to recognize inefficient learning conditions and engage appropriate courses of action to enhance learning for all.

References

Brunelle, J. Tousignant, M., & Godbout, P. (1983). Notion de temps d'apprentissage et son évaluation en situation d'enseignement [The concept of active learning time and its evaluation in teaching situations]. *Canadian Journal of Education, 8*(3), 232–244.

Cooper, S.H. (1977). Hope for the future: A view of research in teacher effectiveness. *Quest, 28*, 29–37.

De Knop, P. (1983). Effectiveness of tennis teaching. In R. Telama, V. Varstala, J. Tiainen, L. Laakso, & T. Haajanen, (Eds.), *Research in school physical education* (pp. 228–235). Jyväskylä, Finland: The Foundation for Promotion of Physical Culture and Health.

Dodds, P., & Rife, F. (Eds.). (1983). Time to learn in physical education: History, completed research, and potential future for academic learning time in physical education. *Journal of Teaching in Physical Education* (Monograph No. 1).

Dodds, P., Rife, F., & Metzler, M. (1982). Academic learning time in physical education: Data collection, completed research and future directions. In M. Piéron & J. Cheffers (Eds.), *Studying the teaching in physical education.* Liège, Belgium: University of Liège.

Drouin, D., & Talbot, S. (1984). Indice de conformité de l'application du gramme débutant III de la Fédération québécoise de hockey sur glace [Congruence index of the actual offering of the Beginners Program III of the Quebec Ice Hockey Federation]. *Revue de l'Association Canadienne pour la Santé, l'Éducation Physique et la Récréation, 51*(1), 18–22.

Dunkin, M.J., & Biddle, B.J. (1974). *The study of teaching.* New York: Holt, Rinehart and Winston.

Godbout, P., & Schutz, R.W. (1983). Generalizability of ratings of motor performances with reference to various observational designs. *Research Quarterly for Exercise and Sport, 54*(1), 20–27.

Karp, S.A., & Konstadt, N. (1971). *Children embedded figure tests.* Berkeley: CA.: Consulting Psychologists Press.

Locke, L. (1977). Research on teaching physical education: New hope for a dismal science. *Quest, 28*, 2–16.

McEwen, T., & Graham, G. (1982). Patterns of teaching behavior employed by physical education teachers and skill learning time. In M.

Piéron & J. Cheffers (Eds.), *Studying the teaching in physical education* (pp. 69–77). Liège, Belgium: University of Liège.

Phillips, D.A., & Carlisle, C. (1983). A comparison of physical education teachers categorized as most and least effective. *Journal of Teaching in Physical Education*, **2**(3), 55–67.

Piéron, M. (1983). Effectiveness of teaching a psychomotor task (gymnastic routine): A study in a class setting. In R. Telama, V. Varstala, J. Tiainen, L. Laakso, & T. Haajanen (Eds.), *Research in school physical education* (pp. 222–227). Jyväskylä, Finland: The Foundation for Promotion of Physical Culture and Health.

Piéron, M., & Cheffers, J. (Eds.). (1982). *Studying the teaching in physical education*. Liège, Belgium: University of Liège.

Piéron, M., & Piron, J. (1981). Recherche de critères d'efficacité de l'enseignement d'habiletés motrices [A search for efficacy criteria for the teaching of motor skills]. *Sport*, **24**, 144–161.

Ranger, P.L. (1978). *Le test collectif des figures cachées* [The collective embedded figure test]. Montréal: Institut de recherches psychologiques.

Rosenshine, B.V., & Berliner, D.C. (1978). Academic engaged time. *British Journal of Teacher Education*, **4**(1), 3–16.

Siedentop, D., Tousignant, M., & Parker, M. (1982). *Academic learning time: Physical education 1982 coding manual*. Columbus: Ohio State University, School of Health, Physical Education and Recreation.

Silverman, S. (1985). Student characteristics mediating engagement outcome relationships in physical education. *Research Quarterly for Exercise and Sport*, **56**(1), 66–72.

Stallings, J. (1980). Allocated academic learning time revisited, or beyond time on tasks. *Educational Researcher*, **9**(11), 11–17.

Telama, R., Varstala, V., Tiainen, J., Laakso, L., & Haajanen, T. (Eds.). (1983). *Research in school physical education*. Jyväskylä, Finland: The Foundation for Promotion of Physical Culture and Health.

Templin, T.J., & Olson, J.K. (Eds.). (1983). *Teaching in physical education* (Big Ten Body of Knowledge Symposium Series, Vol. 14). Champaign, IL: Human Kinetics.

Yerg, B.J. (1983). Re-examining the process-product paradigm for research on teaching effectiveness in physical education. In T.J. Templin & J.K. Olson (Eds.), *Teaching in physical education* (pp. 310–317). Champaign, IL: Human Kinetics.

Yerg, B.J., & Twardy, B.M. (1982). Relationship of specified instructional teacher behaviors to pupil gain on a motor skill task. In M. Piéron & J. Cheffers (Eds.), *Studying the teaching in physical education*. Liège, Belgium: University of Liège.

Student Responses as a Measure of Teacher Effectiveness

Judith E. Rink
Peter Werner

In the past few years literature on teaching effectiveness in physical education has primarily endorsed the notion of academic learning time as an indirect measure of effective teaching (Siedentop, 1983). As Siedentop has suggested, the theoretical support for this variable is quite high. Likewise, the research support for related time-on-task variables in classroom research is very convincing (Rosenshine & Berak, 1979). More recently, authors have called for category redefinitions as well as content specificity to resolve some of the inherent problems of using this variable in different settings. Settings without specific or clear learning goals pose a particular problem (Parker & O'Sullivan, 1983; Siedentop, 1983).

The validity of using ALT-PE (Siedentop, Tousignant, & Parker, 1982) or any measure of student responses as an indirect measure of teaching effectiveness is beginning to be questioned. The purpose of this chapter is to present a theoretical perspective on the problems inherent in using student responses to instructional tasks as a measure of teacher effectiveness in achieving a psychomotor learning goal.

The problem of using student response time as a measure of effectiveness was illustrated in an initial study of three teachers over a unit of instruction in volleyball (Rink, Werner, Hohn, Ward, & Timmermans, 1986). One of the teachers in a 15-lesson middle-school volleyball unit spent approximately 40% of the unit time on the overhead set and 38% of the time on the forehand pass. This teacher was the most effective of the three teachers studied in developing student skill in the set, and yet the teacher had no positive effect on skill in the forearm pass. Another teacher in the study spent less time on both skills and was very effective in the forearm pass but not in the set. All three teachers in the study were strong managers, were task-oriented, and had very high levels of ALT-PE motor easy time.

A second study followed four elementary physical education teachers through six lessons teaching jumping and landing skills to second-grade students (Werner & Rink, 1985). This time, practice trials were used to describe student contact with the content. Again student responses were not a predictor of student achievement. With the exception of Phillips and Carlisle (1983), little support exists for ALT-PE as an indirect measure of teacher effectiveness. A recent and rather extensive study by Godbout, Brunelle, and Tousignant (1987) adds support to the idea that ALT-PE does not have a high relationship with teacher effectiveness when more long-term process-product studies are conducted.

Why is ALT-PE alone not a predictor of teacher effectiveness when motor skill acquisition is the dependent variable? Part of the answer may lie in the theoretical assumptions made regarding how motor skills are learned. From a motor learning perspective several key ingredients must be present before learning can occur:

1. A task must be selected that is a proper match between learner needs and the content goal.
2. The motor task must be clearly communicated to give learners an accurate motor plan.
3. Learners must have adequate quality practice time with the task.
4. Learners must have feedback on their performance.

These variables are not new. Much of the model was described by Gentile (1972) in her model of motor skill acquisition and was used by Yerg (1981) as a basis for the model she developed for research on teacher effectiveness.

The relationships of these concerns are described in Figure 1 in a slightly different format: Learning goal represents the long-term goal for skill acquisition; task appropriateness, the selection of the en route learning tasks in an instructional setting; task presentation, the delivery of the task to the learner; and student responses represent the immediate responses of the student to the teacher task. The feedback loop is not meant to dictate any particular kind of feedback at this point.

The problem with using student responses to a teacher task as a measure of effectiveness is made clear in the model. Student responses may

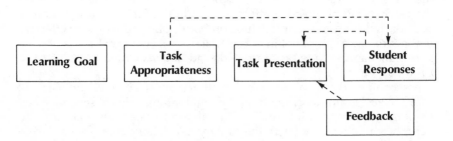

Figure 1 Instructional model of motor skill acquisition.

be appropriate to the teacher task, but the teacher task may not be appropriate to the learning goal. Indeed, teachers may not have a learning goal. Teachers may or may not select tasks that have the potential to effect student learning. Under the present ALT-PE system, if students are practicing with some degree of success motor appropriate time is given, in spite of the fact that the quality of practice may not be sufficient to improve performance or that the task may be unrelated to the learning goal.

The relationship we want to measure is the relationship between student practice and the learning goal. In some simple tasks that do not require much progression from simple to complex experiences we may be able to do this directly. For most of the complex motor skills involved in physical education programs, however, and, particularly in situations in which there are multiple desired outcomes, we do not have the ability to be able to measure this relationship directly.

The model also illustrates another problem. Task presentation, which functions to give the learner an accurate motor plan of the intended task, also lies between the learning goal and the responses of students. Even if the teacher selects an appropriate task, the delivery of that task to the learner represents another whole set of concerns. Student intent and teacher intent may not be the same.

The problem of identifying effectiveness through direct observation of instruction becomes one of identifying the ways in which teachers are likely to produce quality student responses toward a defined goal. The teacher's selection of an appropriate task and the characteristics of task presentation are beginning points for inquiry because they represent intermediaries between the learning goal and the responses of the student.

The authors sought to study the relationships between task appropriateness and task presentation to student learning in a study done on the teaching of jumping and landing skills to second grade students. The study involved extensive pre- and posttesting of all groups on jumping and landing skills. A major part of the study involved developing instrumentation to look at four instructional dimensions: task appropriateness, task presentation, student responses, and teacher feedback. A description of the categories for this instrument is provided in Figure 2. Task appropriateness was ultimately eliminated from data analysis because the researchers could not get reliability on stringent definitions of appropriateness, and the less stringent definition of both task appropriateness to previous student responses and task appropriateness to the learning goal was not discriminating in this study.

The design of the study used a teach/intervention/reteach format. In the initial teaching the four teachers studied varied a great deal in their effectiveness, with one teacher showing consistent effectiveness across measures and several teachers actually producing student regression in performance. The differences on instrument dimensions between the teacher found to be more effective and the teachers showing less consistency in effectiveness are graphed in Figure 3 (preintervention). The more consistently effective teacher had higher levels of recorded behavior

Figure 2   Task Analysis and a Teaching Appropriateness Scale

Task Appropriateness

1. *Task Appropriate to Objective*

   Was the task given appropriate to the unit of study? Was the task developmentally appropriate to improve the force production and force reduction capabilities of students?

   Yes: Example of appropriate: any task focusing on take-off/landing abilities or related to those abilities.

   No: Example of inappropriate: any task that focused outside of take-off/landing abilities or related to those abilities.

2. *Task Appropriate to Student Responses*

   Was new task a logical move in progression based on responses to previous task?

   Yes: Task increased or reduced complexity or difficulty when students were successful or unsuccessful at previous task or focused on refining problems students encountered in their performance.

   No: Task was (a) not related to previous task, (b) not logical in progression, (c) too complex for students based on previous responses, and (d) increased complexity before needed refinement.

Task Presentation

3. *Clarity*

   Teacher's verbal explanation/directions communicated a clear idea of what to do and how to do it. This judgment is confirmed on the basis of student movement responses to the presentation, and is relative to the situation.

   Yes: Students proceeded to work in a focused way on what the teacher asked them to do.

   No: Students exhibited confusion, questions, off-task behavior, or lack of intent to deal with the specifics of the task.

4. *Demonstration*

   Visual information modeling desired was executed by teacher, student(s), and/or visual aids.

   Yes: Full model of the desired movement.

   Partial: Incomplete model of task performance exhibiting only a part of the desired movement.

   No: No attempt to model the movement task.

5. *Appropriate Number of Cues*

   The degree to which the teacher presented sufficient information useful to the performance about the movement task without overloading the learner.

   Appropriate: Three or fewer new learning cues related to the performance of the movement task.

   Inappropriate: More than three new learning cues related to the performance of the movement or none given when needed.

   None given: No attempt at providing learning cues was given.

Figure 2 (Cont.)

6. *Accuracy of Cues*

The degree to which the information presented was technically correct and reflected accurate mechanical principles.

Accurate: All information presented was correct.
Inaccurate: One or more incidences of incorrect information.
None given: No cues given.

7. *Qualitative Cues Provided*

Verbal information provided to the learner on the process or mechanics of movement.

Yes: Teacher's explanation or direction included at least one aspect of the process of performance.
No: Teacher's explanation or direction included no information on the process of performance.

Student Responses

8. *Appropriate to the Focus*

The degree to which student responses reflect an intent to perform the task as stated by the teacher.

(All)   One – No more than two students viewed on the screen exhibited inappropriate responses.
(Partial) Two – Three students or more viewed on the screen exhibited inappropriate behavior.
(None)   Three – No students exhibited appropriate behavior.

Teacher Feedback

9. *Specific Congruent Feedback*

The degree to which teacher feedback during activity is congruent (matched) to the focus of the task.

Yes: More than two incidences were evident where teacher feedback was congruent with the task.
Partial: One or two incidences of congruent feedback were evident.
No: No congruent feedback given.

Figure 2 (Cont.)

in the most desirable categories of the instrument when compared with the other three teachers. The intervention program to improve teaching skills was developed on many of the constructs of the instrument. After the intervention the teachers taught the same content to a different group. Increases in teacher effectiveness were seen for the teachers less effective in the initial lessons. Teacher performance on the variables of the instrument in the postintervention phase of the study are described in Figure 3. Very clear and positive changes were noted in the dimensions of the instrument for the teachers who had previously scored considerably lower.

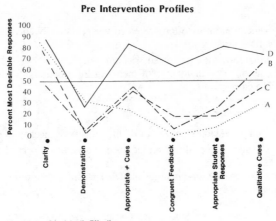

Pre Intervention Profiles

Teacher D = Consistently Effective
Teacher A, B, and C = Less Consistently Effective

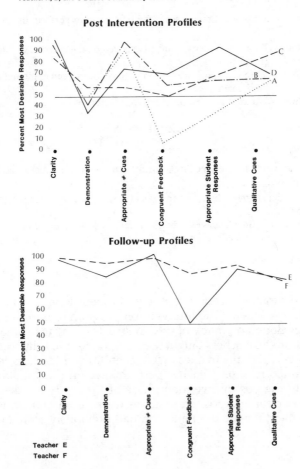

Post Intervention Profiles

Follow-up Profiles

Teacher E
Teacher F

Figure 3 Teaching appropriateness scale profiles of teachers A–F.

A third phase of the study involved the two researchers teaching two additional classes in the same manner as the first two phases of the study. Student achievement on posttests was consistently high for these two classes. Teacher performance on the variables of the instrument is also described in Figure 3 (follow-up). Again, teacher performance for these teachers was very high in the desirable categories of the instrument for all the dimensions.

Conclusion

The results of the study described suggest that task presentation characteristics in particular may be important dimensions of effective teaching. When coupled with a measure of student responses and congruent feedback (which reinforces the specifics of the task and may act as an accountability system for the task as presented), profiles of the effective teacher can be described. Task appropriateness remains an important dimension that may have to wait for more objective evidence on appropriate teacher moves in skill acquisition. We simply do not know enough about learning motor skills to be able to evaluate the appropriateness of teacher choice in progressions with any certainty.

The simple model presented suggests many other relationships that need to be studied to increase our knowledge of effective teaching. The arrows on the model indicate those used in some form in the instrumentation described. Other relationships have been studied in other research efforts and many have yet to be explored.

Although the search will continue for efficient ways to describe and measure teacher effectiveness, none of the relationships in and of themselves are likely to be accurate predictors of teaching effectiveness. They are interdependent, and each by itself is likely to provide nothing more than a limited perspective. The more information that is gathered on each of the dimensions described, the more accurate we are likely to be in establishing relationships between the teaching process and student learning.

References

Gentile, A. (1972). A working model for skill acquisition with application to teaching. *Quest* (Monograph No. 17), 3–23.

Godbout, P., Brunelle, J., & Tousignant, M. (1987). Who benefits from passing through the program? In G.T. Barrette, R.S. Feingold, C.R. Rees, & M. Piéron (Eds.), *Myths, models, and methods in sport pedagogy* (pp. 183–197). Champaign, IL: Human Kinetics.

Parker, M., & O'Sullivan, M. (1983). Modifying ALT-PE for game contexts and other reflections. *Journal of Teaching Physical Education* (Summer Monograph No. 1), **2**, 8–10.

Phillips, D., & Carlisle, C. (1983). A comparison of physical education teachers categorized as most and least effective. *Journal of Teaching Physical Education*, **2**(3), 55–67.

Rink, J., Werner, P., Hohn, R., Ward, D., & Timmermans, H. (1986). Differential effects of three teachers over a unit of instruction. *Research Quarterly for Exercise and Sport*, **57**(2), 132–138.

Rosenshine, B., & Berak, V. (1979). Content time, and direct instruction. In P. Peterson & H. Walberg (Eds.), *Research on teaching: Concepts, findings, and implications*. Berkeley, CA: McCutchan.

Siedentop, D. (1983). Academic learning time: Reflections and prospects. *Journal of Teaching Physical Education* (Summer Monograph No. 1), 3–7.

Siedentop, D., Tousignant, M., & Parker, M. (1982). Academic learning time: Physical education 1982 revision coding manual. Columbus: Ohio State University, School of Health, Physical Education and Recreation.

Werner, P., & Rink, J. (1985). *Identifying effective instructional skills for teaching jumping and landing*. Unpublished manuscript.

Yerg, B. (1981). Reflections on the use of R.T.E. model in physical education. *Research Quarterly for Exercise and Sport*, **1**, 38–47.

Specific Teacher Feedback's Effect on Academic Learning Time and on a Novel Motor Skill

Paul C. Paese

One variable that has been given much attention over the years in teaching research is feedback. Most of the supervision studies completed at Ohio State University during the 1970s relied on the setting of goals for student interns on various teaching skills/behaviors by a variety of change agents (Siedentop, 1981). One teaching behavior that was a part of almost every study and that was used as part of a package intervention that served as a dependent variable was teacher verbal feedback. Feedback as a teacher behavior has probably been the most targeted teaching behavior/variable by teacher educators over the last 15 years. During the 1980s much of the research on teaching studies in physical education (RTE-PE) has used teacher verbal feedback as a major dependent variable with a variety of subjects in a variety of settings (McKenzie, 1981; Paese, 1984).

The emergence of teacher effectiveness research has led to many investigations on teacher feedback's effect on student achievement both in the long and short term. Many teacher educators have felt over the years that feedback was as important, or possibly even more important, than actual skill practice in the learning of a motor skill. From the number of studies completed in teacher effectiveness research that investigated feedback's effect on student achievement, some doubts were cast on the earlier assumptions of the importance of feedback (Graham, Soares, & Harrington, 1983; Piéron, 1982; Yerg, 1977; Yerg, 1981b). These studies concluded that high amounts of teacher verbal feedback were not found to be significantly correlated with student achievement. In fact, some conclusions made stated that feedback impeded student achievement because it took away from actual skill practice. In spite of these findings many teacher educators have felt that teacher feedback is important. The importance of teacher feedback in the process of learning a motor skill seemed obvious when looking over the ALT Instructional Model (Metzler, 1982). There is little doubt that the opportunity to practice is the most important variable in the learning of a motor skill, but for certain students in certain skills continued practice would not make a difference without teacher feedback. A study by Yerg and Twardy (1982) seemed to conclude what many have felt over the years—that the less complex a skill the more important teacher feedback becomes. "Practice without feedback," they found, "not only is not helpful, but may even be detrimental to achievement" (p. 68).

Because of the many conflicting studies on the type and rate of feedback and its relationship to effective teaching (Paese, 1986; Yerg, 1981a) further research in this area seems warranted. One way to draw some firm conclusions on feedback's importance would be through the use of experimental teaching units (ETU). ETUs have been gaining in popularity over the past 5 years and have been used in many teacher effectiveness studies with the intent of investigating what effective teachers do when they teach. ETUs have also been used to investigate the rates/percentages of various teaching behaviors and criterion process variables in the classes of physical education teachers and how these variables correlate with student achievement (Graham et al., 1983; Paese, 1985; Yerg, 1981a). The purpose of this study was to assess the effect of teacher feedback on academic learning time and student achievement in a novel motor skill.

Method

Subjects and Settings

Ten preservice physical education majors were used as teachers for this study. Each intern was assigned to a public school in the central Texas area as a part of the field experience section of an intermediate elementary methods class (Grades 3 to 5) in physical education. The 10 interns were all in their junior year and were divided into two groups of 5 (4 females and 1 male). At the time of data collection each intern had been in field experience for 2 weeks, with approximately 2 weeks left. Each intern was in his or her second field experience in the public schools; their first experiences were in primary physical education (Grades K to 2). All interns were placed with fifth-grade classes and one cooperating teacher.

Experimental Teaching Unit

The modified experimental teaching unit used for this study was on a novel badminton skill. The objective was to drop the shuttle and attempt to continuously hit it as many times as possible. This skill was chosen because it has a medium level of difficulty, and none of the fifth-grade students who participated in the ETU had ever played badminton.

Observation and Data Collection

All 10 preservice interns taught one 20-minute lesson to their class in the gymnasium of the public school they were placed in for field experience. The 20-minute lesson was preplanned by the 10 interns and the major investigator of the study. The reason for preplanning the lesson was to have the same tasks for each teacher's lesson and to attempt to have equal amounts of management, instruction, and activity time within the lesson. Each intern used the same equipment (13 badminton rackets and 13 shuttles) and had the same class size of 12 fifth-grade students (6 boys and 6 girls). The reason for having the same class size, equipment, and lesson plan was to try to have each student/class involved in the same amount of individual skill practice (engaged motor). The only difference was that one group of teachers were to give as much specific verbal skill feedback as possible during class time, and the other group of teachers was to give no feedback at all.

The interns pretested their students one at a time on the novel badminton skill. Each student was given two attempts at hitting the shuttle as many times as possible without missing it or losing control of it. After all the students were pretested, one 20-minute lesson followed, adhering to the guidelines of the lesson plan. At the conclusion of the 20-minute lesson each student was posttested, following the same procedures as the pretest.

All lessons taught by the 10 interns were videotaped and coded for amounts of activity time (class time spent in skill practice), management time, instruction time, motor engagement (individuals actually doing a motor skill), and academic learning time (ALT, individuals doing a motor skill with a high rate of success). The coding system used was the Academic Learning Time Observation System (Siedentop, Tousignant, & Parker, 1982). Event recording (Siedentop, 1983) was used to record the amount of teacher verbal feedback to students by the teachers who were instructed to give verbal feedback to their students.

Reliability

Interobserver agreement was checked three times during the coding of the 10 videotapes. Both coders and the standard had several years of experience in coding and in the use of the ALT system. The scored interval method of calculation (Hawkins & Dotson, 1975) was used to assess the ALT system, and the formula described by Siedentop (1983, pp. 264–65) was used to assess reliability for event recording. Overall reliabilities were 0.92 for the event recording of feedback and 0.84 for the combined categories in the ALT interval system.

Analysis

Means were calculated for each group of teachers on activity time, instruction time, management time, engaged motor, and ALT. Feedback was only calculated on the group of teachers giving feedback. Means for feedback rate per minute, ratio of positive feedback to corrective, and percent of specific feedback were calculated.

A t test was computed on all variables to determine significance between the two groups. A t test was also computed within the two groups to determine significance on pretest/posttest results.

Results

Differences between the two groups in management, instruction, and activity time were not significant ($p < .10$). The feedback group of teachers had 12% of the allocated time (20 minutes) in their lessons devoted to management, 23% to instruction, and 66% to activity. The nonfeedback group of teachers had 13% in management, 22% in instruction, and 63% in activity. The feedback group of teachers had students engaged in motor activity for an average mean of 53%, compared to the nonfeedback group's 50%. The difference was also not significant ($p > .10$). Differences between the two groups of teachers in ALT was significant ($p < .02$). The feedback group of teachers had a mean average of 36% ALT for their students in comparison to the nonfeedback group's 30%.

There was no significant difference between the two groups on both the pretest and posttest scores ($p > .80$). The students in the classes of the teachers who gave feedback improved scores on the novel badminton skill from pretest to posttest by almost two hits compared to the students in the classes of the nonfeedback teachers, who improved by just over one hit. Still, the difference for the feedback group was not significant ($p > .08$). The data of the two groups of teachers are given in Table 1.

Table 1   Comparison of Selected Variables Between and Within Teacher Groups

Variable	Group[a]	M	SD	t	p
Management	1	12%	2.19	2.05	.74
	2	13%	1.26		
Instruction	1	23%	1.79	.420	.67
	2	22%	2.19		
Activity	1	66%	2.83	1.83	.12
	2	63%	3.16		
Engaged motor	1	53%	5.60	1.80	.10
	2	50%	5.76		
ALT	1	36%	7.42	2.82	.02
	2	30%	4.60		
Pretest	1	4.78	1.31	.130	.90
	2	5.20	.67		
Posttest	1	6.75	2.03	.137	.88
	2	6.25	.80		

Variable	Group	Net gain	r	t	p
Pre to post	1	1.97	.78	2.04	.08
within groups	2	1.05	.58	1.56	.16

[a]1 = Feedback teachers' group, 2 = Nonfeedback teachers' group.

The teachers in the nonfeedback group did average over four feedbacks per minute during the 20-minute lesson. They also had a ratio of a little over two positive feedback statements to one corrective statement. Of the total number of feedbacks given by the teachers, 51% was specific feedback.

Discussion and Conclusion

The data indicate that the attempt to control variables to assess feedback's effect on ALT and posttest results was successful. By having each teacher in the two groups have the same amount of students, equipment, and so forth, and by having all interns plan the 20-minute lesson together, management, instruction, activity, and engaged motor were almost equal among teacher groups. This allowed the investigator to assess feedback's effect on ALT and the posttest in the ETU.

Interns in the feedback group were very successful in giving feedback. Having over four feedback statements per minute, a 2-to-1 ratio of positive to corrective feedback, and approximately 51% of the total feedback specific is well within the criteria/goals set by teacher educators (Siedentop, 1983).

Because criterion process variables were controlled, the major conclusion of the study could be made. Students in the classes of teachers who gave feedback had higher rates of ALT during the time they were engaged in skill practice than the students in the nonfeedback-teachers' classes. Feedback in no way impeded student engagement or achievement in this particular medium-level skill. Although students in the classes of the teachers giving feedback had higher rates of ALT and did improve more on the posttest than students in the nonfeedback-teachers' classes, this increase was not significant.

A major hypothesis generated from this study is that more significant results would have occurred if the ETU lesson was 40 minutes (or two 20-minute lessons) instead of 20 minutes in length. Speculation is that in a longer ETU, engaged motor time would have dropped in the classes of the nonfeedback teachers. Feedback as it was given in this study, and in general, tends to reinforce and keep students on task. Students in the nonfeedback teachers' classes began to become more off-task toward the end of the 20-minute lesson, and this rate would probably have continued in a longer lesson due to the absence of feedback. This would have led to lower rates of engaged motor, ALT, and, subsequently, to lower posttest scores.

A major recommendation for further study besides a longer ETU would be to do a second posttest at least 1 to 2 months after the first. The reason for the second posttest is to assess long-term achievement. Another area neglected in this study was the cognitive perceptions of students. Students in the classes of both teacher groups could have been given a cognitive test on the skill and been asked what helped them the most in learning this skill.

Specific verbal feedback, when given along with high rates of student opportunity to practice a skill, does make a difference in the overall student learning of a motor skill. Teacher educators should continue to work with student interns on the teacher behavior of verbal feedback in both lab and field settings.

References

Graham, G., Soares, P., & Harrington, W. (1983). Experienced teachers' effectiveness with intact classes: An ETU study. *Journal of Teaching in Physical Education*, 2(2), 3–14.

Hawkins, R., & Dotson, V. (1975). Reliability scores that delude: An Alice in Wonderland trip through the misleading characteristics of interobserver agreement scores in interval recording. In E. Ramp & G. Semb (Eds.), *Behavior analysis: Areas of research and application* (pp. 359–376). New York: Prentice-Hall.

McKenzie, T. (1981). Modification, transfer and maintenance of the verbal behavior of an experienced physical education teacher: A single-subject analysis. *Journal of Teaching in Physical Education*, (Introductory Issue), 48–56.

Metzler, M. (1982). Adapting the academic learning time instructional model for teaching physical education. *Journal of Teaching in Physical Education*, 1(2), 44–55.

Paese, P. (1984). The effects of cooperating teacher interaction and a self-assessment technique on the verbal interactions of elementary student teachers. *Journal of Teaching in Physical Education*, 3(3), 51–58.

Paese, P. (1985). Assessment of a teacher education program based on student intern performance. *Journal of Teaching in Physical Education*, 5(1), 52–58.

Paese, P. (1986). Comparison of teacher behavior and criterion process variables in an experimental teaching unit (ETU) taught by preservice physical education majors at the entrance and exit levels. In M. Piéron & G. Graham (Eds.), *The 1984 Olympic Scientific Congress proceedings: Vol. 6. Sport pedagogy* (pp. 71–76). Champaign, IL: Human Kinetics.

Piéron, M. (1982). Behaviors of low and high achievers in physical education classes. In M. Piéron & S. Cheffers (Eds.), *Studying the teaching in physical education* (pp. 53–60). Liège, Belgium: University of Liège.

Siedentop, D. (1981). The Ohio State University supervision research program summary report. *Journal of Teaching in Physical Education* (Introductory Issue), 30–38.

Siedentop, D. (1983). *Developing teaching skills in physical education*. Palo Alto, CA: Mayfield.

Siedentop, D., Tousignant, M., & Parker, M. (1982). *Academic learning time–physical education: Coding manual* (1982 revision). Columbus: Ohio State University, School of Health, Physical Education and Recreation.

Yerg, B. (1977). Relationships between teacher behaviors and pupil achievement in the psychomotor domain. *Dissertation Abstracts International, 38,* 1981A. (University Microfilms No. 77-21,229)

Yerg, B. (1981a). The impact of selected presage and process behaviors on the refinement of a motor skill. *Journal of Teaching in Physical Education, 1*(1), 38–46.

Yerg, B. (1981b). Reflections on the use of the RTE model in physical education. *Research Quarterly for Exercise and Sport, 52*(2), 38–47.

Yerg, B., & Twardy, B. (1982). Relationship of specified instructional teacher behaviors to pupil given on a motor task. In M. Piéron & J. Cheffers (Eds.), *Studying the teaching in physical education* (pp. 61–68). Liège, Belgium: University of Liège.

Personalized Instruction: A Relief for Some and a Pain for Others

Marielle Tousignant
Jean Brunelle

The purpose of this study was to describe students' reactions in a course in which a personalized system of instruction was applied to a group of 80 students. The choice of a personalized system of instruction (PSI) was motivated by our desire to provide students with learning conditions most likely to produce high levels of achievement while allowing individual needs to be met. A significant amount of research has demonstrated that PSI generally produces superior student achievement and a good level of satisfaction (Castonguay-Leblanc, 1977; Keller, 1966; Kulik, Kulik, & Cohen, 1979; Siedentop, 1973).

During our 3 years of experimentation with this type of teaching strategy most of our students indicated that they had acquired a satisfactory level of knowledge and skill and that they found their learning experience rewarding. However, contrary to what might be expected, not all of them were pleased with a course in which the requirements were objectively specified in advance and in which each student received personal attention. Some of them were actually quite disturbed by this teaching strategy.

The major focus of the PSI literature was on product variables, not on process variables. We could not find descriptive studies of the participants' behavior in such teaching settings. On the other hand, the conclusions of research on the ecology of the teaching-learning process and the factors associated with the students' cooperation in the proposed activities provided the background information needed to state the problem underlying this study (Doyle, 1980, 1983; Noble & Nolan, 1976; Tousignant & Siedentop, 1983).

The data for this study, which explored a particular aspect of our teacher education program in physical education, were of two types. First, qualitative descriptions using techniques derived from ethnography were gathered by trained observers participating as tutors in the teaching situation. Second, quantitative data produced naturally during the course were collected.

The central objective of the study was to describe how students coped with the requirements in a course using a personalized system of instruction. A strategy of qualitative analysis was developed to describe students' behavior and the context in which it occurred naturally. As a result, we were able

- to develop a typology of student behavior;
- to qualify students' degree of cooperation; and
- to identify potential factors to explain the various types of students' reactions to the teaching strategy.

Method

Participants

The subjects of the study were 82 students (50 males and 32 females) who, in their second year of a preservice PE program, registered for a mandatory course in pedagogy. They were observed throughout the 15-week session. The teachers were three university professors and seven graduate students, previously trained as observers, who had taken the course earlier.

This pedagogy course was aimed at developing basic knowledge and skills in teaching physical activities. The teaching strategy was an adaptation of Keller's (1966) personalized system of instruction. The following features resemble the characteristics of PSI as summarized by Siedentop (1973):

- The content to be learned was broken into units that were small enough to master completely.
- The final performance for mastery was objectively and behaviorally specified.
- The student's performance was criterion referenced rather than norm referenced.
- The contingencies related to grading for the course were clearly specified in advance.
- Aversive consequences were minimized; failing a module was penalized only to the extent that it required more time for the student to prepare for another assessment.
- Each student was given personal attention in the form of a weekly meeting of a small group of 8 to 12 students with an assigned tutor and individual counseling when requested by the student. (p. 118)

The teaching strategy differed from the PSI in that:

- it did not rely uniquely on readings as a variety of learning conditions were used: attending lectures and small group discussions, observing teaching settings with various instruments, and participating in laboratories during practice teaching;
- learning was not assessed through recitation. The students had to produce an analytical report every week. In each paper, they had to demonstrate that they could use the concepts included in the readings of the module to describe a teaching situation, comment on its effectiveness, and suggest ideas for improving it; and

- the course had a touch of individualized instruction in the form of optional modules aimed at fulfilling each student's specific goals.

Quantitative Data Collection

Various data produced naturally during the session were gathered by the tutors (attendance records, students' scores, and information included in the students' reports). For instance, the data on presage variables such as age, teaching experience, and work experience were extracted from a report in which students had to produce their curriculum vitae.

Strategy to Collect Qualitative Data

The nine members of the teaching team who acted as tutors for small groups of students collected field notes throughout the semester. In the role of participant-observer they made detailed descriptions of as many events as possible related to the ways their students cooperated in the various activities proposed in the course: laboratories, lectures, small group encounters, and individual meetings. During the session, the nine observer-tutors met together once a week. They shared their data in order to ensure that they all had a clear understanding of the research questions and that they were gathering descriptions of all types of behavior relating to how their students behaved, namely, information on those who cooperated nicely as well as those who were experiencing difficulties coping with the class format.

Data Analysis

To develop a typology of student behavior, three members of the team began the process of reducing the qualitative data. A preliminary set of categories emerged after processing about 500 incidents contained in their field notes. They used a technique of semantic relations to identify cover terms (Spradley, 1980). Then the first draft of the typology was presented to the other observers, who were invited to analyze data from their field notes to saturate the categories. From this phase, category definitions were revised and refined. Then a reliability check was made by three independent observers, who coded 100 randomly selected incidents. Agreement of 83% was achieved, and instances of differences were discussed until a general agreement was reached, that is, when category definitions were made more mutually exclusive. The next step consisted of developing a five-level rating scale using the categories of behavior to qualify the students' degree of cooperation. Finally, an ex post facto analysis was done to explore the relations between students' degree of cooperation and various presage variables. The five phases of the strategy for analyzing the data are summarized in Table 1.

Table 1   Phases of Data Analysis

1. Development of a preliminary draft of a typology of student behavior
2. Saturation and refinement of the categories
3. Interanalysts' reliability check to render the definitions mutually exclusive
4. Development of a five-level rating scale to qualify student's degree of cooperation
5. Ex post facto analysis to explore the relations between the student's degree of cooperation and various quantitative data

Results and Discussion

An eight-category typology was developed inductively from the qualitative data. These categories of behavior summarized in Table 2 were associated with two sets of requirements:

1. The formal requirements were related to the *savoir faire* needed to pass the course, that is, weekly reports that students were expected to produce as evidence that they had mastered the material included in each module.
2. The *savoir être* was related to the "unwritten code of expected behavior" during teaching situations. This behavior did not influence students' scores, but it was noted by the tutors as manifestations of cooperation (e.g., facilitating behavior such as listening carefully during a lecture, proposing solutions to management problems, or non-facilitating behavior such as not attending a group session and asking for a private meeting to get a summary of the necessary information or reading during a group discussion).

Behavior ranged from (a) "doing even more than expected," "contributing to class management" (innovator and leader) to "having a hard time understanding and accepting the rules" (resister and deviant); and (b) from studious, disciplined behavior of students who "play by the book" to the careless, nonchalant behavior of those who "did not seem to care too much."

The various combinations of these observed behaviors allowed the development of a five-level rating scale to characterize students' patterns of cooperation (see Table 3).

Maximal Cooperation

Some students' behavior pattern was characterized by innovative, leadership behavior. They regularly introduced personal points of view

Table 2 Definitions of Eight Categories of Student Behavior Describing Patterns of Cooperation

Categories associated with *Savoir-Faire*	Categories associated with *Savoir-Être*
Innovator: To demonstrate one's ability to apply knowledge and skills by conducting recommended optional experiments.	*Leader:* To take initiative in order to enhance the effectiveness of teaching management.
Studious: To meet precisely the mandatory requirements as stated in the study guide.	*Disciplined:* To behave according to an explicit or tacit code of behavior.
Careless: To present reports that contained numerous mistakes and omissions.	*Nonchalant:* To show obvious lack of concern for the management of the teaching situations.
Resister: To criticize the course goals and requirements overtly.	*Deviant:* To behave in ways that hinder the effectiveness of teaching management.

Table 3 Identification of Students' Degree of Cooperation

Degree of cooperation	Corresponding categories of student behavior	Number of students ($N = 82$)	%
Maximal	Regularly innovative and leader	9	11
Optimal	Usually studious and disciplined	28	34
Uncertain	Mixture of facilitating and not-so-helpful behavior (e.g., studious but nonchalant and occasionally deviant; leader but careless in one's report)	23	28
Mediocre	Mainly careless and nonchalant	13	16
Minimal	Often emitting resister and deviant behavior but managing to meet the course requirements	9	11

into their weekly reports. Whenever possible they went out of their way to observe real teaching situations. Moreover, they occasionally contributed to the management of classes by suggesting solutions to a problem or volunteering for a task. For example, Nancy, who had observed her volleyball coach and discussed the results with him, agreed to share her impressions of this experience with her classmates.

Optimal Cooperation

A good percentage of students coped with the course requirements by conforming to the mandatory tasks outlined in the study guide. For instance, Jim showed his appreciation of the process by saying, "I like doing the compulsory reports and I will have plenty of chances to pursue the matter further during the field experiences." Most of the time, these students behaved according to the explicit or tacit rules. During teaching situations they listened carefully. They had read the written material and showed interest in the subject matter at group discussions. They eagerly took part in teaching observation and practice. This studious, disciplined behavior characterized the cooperation of students who were pleased with the subject matter and enjoyed the teaching strategy.

Minimal Cooperation

At the other end of the continuum, a small percentage of students disturbed with the method expressed their disagreement with the course's explicit and implicit rules. They resisted by questioning the purpose of the course or the relevance of the requirements, by criticizing the evaluation, and by seeking peer support to change the contingencies. However, it should be emphasized that none of the "resisters" adopted totally noncooperative behavior; they all managed to meet the compulsory requirements even if they contested their appropriateness. In addition to resisting, deviant behavior characterized the type of cooperation judged as minimal. On occasion, some students talked with friends during classes; made noisy, late arrivals; refused to participate in the teaching practice; or told jokes that were in poor taste.

Mediocre Cooperation

Among the "nonfacilitating, less obtrusive" patterns of cooperation were students who frequently adopted "careless" and "nonchalant" behavior. They appeared satisfied with incomplete and less-than-perfect reports. During the teaching situations, they did not seem to take the code of expected behavior seriously. They arrived late, missed courses for no reason, and remained silent during discussions. The general pattern of behavior of the student who failed the course was classified in this category.

Uncertain Cooperation

Whereas some students adopted generally predictable patterns of behavior, others followed rather changing patterns. For example, Sam regularly produced very adequate reports but frequently adopted nonchalant behavior that reflected his "cool student" mentality. Mary acted as if she enjoyed the course, but on occasion she did not seem to be motivated to write complete reports or to redo them when suggested.

It is important to stress the fact that the code of behavior applied in this class would appear quite severe if compared to observations made by teachers in a typical "lecture, recitations, and/or term papers" teaching setting. Only the close, frequent interaction between tutors and students allowed such direct observations of students' manifestations of uneasiness, boredom, and lack of consistency, as well as their high degree of satisfaction. Most of the behavior judged nonfacilitating in this personalized system of instruction (e.g., nonchalant) would have gone unnoticed in a traditional setting in which little personal exchange exists.

Search for Explanatory Factors

What could explain the fact that a strict set of rules and personal attention were very much appreciated by some students while abhorred by others? In our search for potentially explanatory factors, an ex post facto analysis of relations between the students' degree of cooperation and *presage variables* such as age, sex, past experience teaching physical activities, and cognitive style did not reveal any noticeable association.

Questioning Professional Orientation

One of the variables that appeared interesting to consider was the students' professional orientation. Although we did not possess quantitative data on the level of certainty of their career choice, we collected various critical incidents related to cases of students who seriously questioned their choice of a physical education career. The data tended to confirm Chu's (1984) theory that students who do not intend to become professionals in a particular domain do not appear motivated to learn the specific knowledge and skills needed to become one. However, in our class, some of those who indicated that they were questioning their choice needed good grades to go elsewhere, so they tended to conform to the specific requirements but did not care much for optional activities or personal attention to get an in-depth understanding of the science and the art of teaching.

A Need for Developing New Learner's Skills

A variety of incidents pointed to the difficulty students experienced in discriminating and interpreting the course requirements. Ecological research on how learning occurs had indicated that "competent" students learn to select the most relevant cues from the large amount of information given by the teacher (Doyle, 1979; Mehan, 1980). Learning to learn in a personalized system of instruction requires a shift in some students' study habits. It seemed as if some students, skilled at picking up cues from the teacher's lectures, were slow at getting information from the study guide, whereas others soon appreciated the "written, clearly outlined, presented-in-advance" requirements.

Also, the "busy students" who managed their lives according to a very tight schedule found various ways to let us know that they were upset by the weekly requirements, the deadlines, and our numerous offers to "enrich their learning experiences." What they meant was, "Just tell me what you really want and get off my back; I have other things to do!" Meanwhile, weekly reports and opportunities to discuss were welcomed by those who did not cope very well with the rush of producing term papers and studying for final exams, and who were not quite as successful at "guessing real requirements."

A Low Level of Risk but a Different Type of Ambiguity

Although university students have a great deal of experience in discriminating class requirements, the PSI course puzzled some of them. They acted as if they were inspecting the study guide to find "catches." For instance, once she trusted her tutor, Diane said, "We follow this and that is it! You aren't kidding, it is all there! This is a lot of work but I don't mind as long as I am sure of the results."

Doyle's (1983) concepts of risk and ambiguity were useful in helping to understand some reactions. Some students found it difficult to accept the fact that they did not have to negotiate. First, there was no risk involved because they could redo a report if they had failed or were not satisfied with the result. Also, they could get all the help they wanted if they felt ambiguity existed. Furthermore, on occasion, they could select optional ways to reach a goal if they thought it would better suit their needs.

This study made us realize that an individualized system of instruction tends to isolate learners from each other. It seemed to be a good news/bad news story. The good news is that students can select the tasks they prefer and do them at a pace that suits them. The bad news is that they no longer are able to compare their performance with their classmates. Students are accustomed to accountability systems in which as long as you keep up with the group you are doing all right, or at least you are not in trouble (namely, norm-referenced systems). In an individualized program, the absence of peer comparison seemed a source of ambiguity even when all requirements were spelled out from the beginning.

Conclusion

The findings about the ecology of a personalized system of instruction provided by this exploratory study allow us to state some working hypotheses for improving the learning conditions and the degree of students' cooperation.

- Use a variety of strategies to teach the contingencies as soon and as effectively as possible so that students will not waste too much time learning to discriminate the relevant cues but will learn the subject matter.
- In order to reduce the problem associated with a completely self-paced system, which runs the risk of becoming a no-paced system, we agree with Rainey (1981), who suggested providing students with specific deadlines to prevent procrastination.
- Continue with group lectures to provide guidance. Although this teaching method has been questioned as an effective means of conveying knowledge, lectures are an effective way of managing large groups and coordinating subgroups' activities. Moreover, Rainey (1981) hypothesized that "the lecture can provide necessary continuity in the learning process. Immature students need the role model provided by the professor—the professional with expertise in the subject matter. Further, the lecture can be used to motivate and inspire, and to instill pride and professionalism" (p. 156). The idea that lectures help to reduce the feeling of isolation associated with personalized instruction may be an "ecological" explanation for Keller's intuition about the motivational effect of lectures. It goes without saying that the style of communication of the professor giving the lecture will greatly influence its "motivational dimension."

To conclude, we would like to indicate that it required a great deal of humility to continue paying close attention to students' reactions, which are usually ignored by university teachers. On the other hand, teacher education, and any teaching for that matter, should not be viewed as a popularity contest. However, it is necessary to understand the various aspects of students' "mentalities" and their ways of coping with teachers, especially when one wants to implement effectively innovative teaching strategies such as a personalized system of instruction. We are convinced that to understand the complexity of students' lives we need to use more research methodologies derived from ethnography. Conventional tools such as end-of-session questionnaires could not possibly fill this need. It seems that the life of the university student is so full of unspoken and poorly received feelings that getting into what underlies them requires in-depth analysis of the natural setting.

Finally, we knew that being observed was no pleasure. However, this exploratory study made us even more empathetic and grateful toward all of those school PE teachers that so gracefully let us "bug" them for the purpose of advancing science. We advise all teacher educators and researchers to allow themselves to be put under the spotlight periodically. We believe that there are unsuspected benefits to be gained.

References

Castonguay-Leblanc, Y. (1977). L'enseignement personalisé au collège et à l'université [Personalized instruction in college and at the university]. *Canadian Journal of Education*, **2**(4), 37–54.

Chu, D. (1984). Teacher/Coach orientation and role socialization: A description and explanation. *Journal of Teaching in Physical Education*, **3**(2), 3–8.

Doyle, W. (1979). Classroom tasks and students' abilities. In P.L. Peterson & H.J. Walberg (Eds.), *Research on teaching: Concepts, findings, and implications* (pp. 183–209). Berkeley, CA: McCutchan.

Doyle, W. (1980). *Student mediating responses in teaching effectiveness.* Unpublished manuscript. (Available from the author at the R & D Center for Teacher Education, The University of Texas at Austin)

Doyle, W. (1983). Academic work. *Review of Educational Research*, **53**(2), 159–201.

Keller, F.J. (1966). A personal course in psychology. In R. Ulrich, T. Stachnik, and J. Mabry (Eds.), *The control of behavior*. Glenview, IL: Scott Foresman.

Kulik, J.A., Kulik, C.C., & Cohen, P. (1979). A meta-analysis of outcome studies of Keller's personalized system of instruction. *American Psychologist*, **34**(4), 307–318.

Mehan, H. (1980). The competent student. *Anthropology and Education Quarterly*, **11**(3), 131–152.

Noble, C.G., & Nolan, J.D. (1976). Effect of student verbal behavior on classroom teacher behavior. *Journal of Educational Psychology*, **68**, 342–346.

Rainey, G.L. (1981). How to survive instructional innovation. *Engineering Education*, **72**(2), 154–157.

Siedentop, D. (1973). How to use personalized systems of instruction in college teaching. In *NCPEAM Proceedings 77th Annual Meeting* (pp. 116–125). Reston, VA: American Alliance for Health, Physical Education, Recreation, and Dance.

Spradley, J.P. (1980). *Participant observation.* New York: Holt, Rinehart and Winston.

Tousignant, M., & Siedentop, D. (1983). Qualitative analysis of task structures in required secondary physical education classes. *Journal of Teaching in Physical Education*, **3**(1), 45–57.

An Ethnographic Study of One Teacher and Two Classes

Wilma M. Harrington

The study of one teacher and two classes provides a unique opportunity to observe how one teacher interacted with two different groups of students in the classroom and the gymnasium. Most of the research on teaching has been conducted in two settings, the classroom or the gymnasium. The situation observed also presented two classes that were grouped by academic abilities in contrast to physical education classes which are often a heterogeneous mix of students. Heterogeneous grouping makes it difficult to determine the influence, if any, academic ability might exert on a teacher's perceptions of students and his or her expectations regarding them. The work by Rosenthal and Jacobson (1968) has shown that teachers' perceptions regarding student abilities exert a very strong influence on their expectations and interactions with students.

Background

All the individuals discussed and the observation site have been identified using pseudonyms to comply with the ethical presentation of fieldwork. Plaid County High School is located in a rural area of northeastern Georgia. Sixty-six percent of the population is poor and black. The major sources of employment are a sock factory and a pulpwood processing plant. In general, there are not enough jobs to support the population, and a number of residents are financially dependent on some form of public assistance or welfare. Industry, local government, and the school board are controlled by a minority of affluent, white citizens.

The high school housed 1,075 students in Grades 7 through 12. Seventy-seven percent of these students were black. The majority of these aspired to graduating from high school. A high school diploma is a status symbol and is not viewed as the means for educational ends. A small minority will graduate and go on to college, the majority of these students will be white.

The two Grade 9 classes described here were comprised of two distinct groups of students. The first group contained "basic" students who represented the academic average for the school. The students in this school have consistently scored 187th out of 187 on the state minimum competency tests. The second group, the "smart kids," represented the academic minority who were classified as high achievers or gifted.

The basic class contained 27 students; 23 were black and four were white. The racial makeup for the "smart kids" was 12 black students and 10 white ones. They were enrolled in a required 15-week physical education class that met daily. On Monday, Wednesday, and Friday class was activity-based and conducted in the gymnasium. Tuesdays and Thursdays the classes met in a classroom. The content was physical fitness concepts and applications. A textbook, worksheets, and filmstrips were used in the classroom. Physical activities focused on applying the concepts of flexibility, muscle endurance, and cardiovascular endurance covered in written materials.

The teacher, Cathy Woods, was a white female with 18 years of teaching experience. Cathy had been at Plaid County High School for 8 years at the time of the study. Her previous experiences had been in an exclusive girls prep school, in an inner city school plagued by crime and violence, and in an urban middle class setting. She has a master's degree in counseling. Of all of her experiences she liked teaching in Plaid County best. Cathy was specifically chosen by me to observe because she was a distinctive teacher (Earls, 1981) who was respected by her colleagues in the field.

Data were collected using field notes, documents, an audiotaped interview, and informal interviews with the teacher. The focus of the observations was teacher behavior.

Results and Discussion

Early in the observation of Cathy Woods and the "basic" and "smart" kids, it became obvious that she interacted, reacted, and held different expectations for the two groups. The following are descriptors that Cathy used regarding the two classes:

- *The "basic" students:* "like, more receptive, more real, show feeling, free to be myself, feel different with them, [teaching them] is like teaching a group" (taped interview).
- *The "smart kids":* "aloof, cold, judgmental, behaved better, dressed out, did better on tests, on paper [I'm] more successful with them" (taped interview).

These two sets of descriptors give a good indication of Cathy's attitudes toward the two classes. The next step was to examine her teaching strategies and general behavior with the two classes to determine if there was differential treatment. The field notes describing classroom and gymnasium settings were analyzed separately to see if there were specific patterns of behavior for each.

Her classroom teaching style was lecture-discussion. This was consistent for both groups. The one exception was on the two occasions when she had students read a paragraph from the textbook and then discuss it. She used this method with the "basic kids" to help them learn the material better. She used it with the "smart kids" as a form of punishment. They hated to have class conducted this way. She told them, "Do you know why teachers have you do that? Because they know you're too lazy to do it yourself" (field notes, p. 92). On the whole, Cathy conducted both classes in the same manner.

In the gymnasium her style could best be described as a command style (Mosston, 1981). It was in the gym that two different ways of approaching the classes emerged. With few exceptions the "basic kids" all participated in the same activities led by Cathy. However, the "smart kids" were given choices. When Cathy believed that some would not like aerobic dance, which she used often for cardiovascular endurance, she allowed them to jump rope or run during that portion of the class. She felt that this group would participate if given a choice, and they did. However, there were also students in the basic group who did not like the dance sessions and displayed minimal to no participation. These students were not provided a choice.

This difference in treatment reflects Cathy's belief that teaching the basic students was "like teaching a group," and she viewed them as such. Because that was her perception she operated on it. Some of the "smart kids" were seen as judging the activity as unacceptable, so they were given an alternative to keep them active.

A further examination of Cathy's belief that the "basic kids" were like a group and the "smart kids" were not provides reinforcement of her perception regarding the two classes. When discussing the basic class she singled out only 1 student from the 27 as a separate case. This was a black female who was constantly acting out. Cathy referred to her as "the mouth of the South." She said if she excluded this student from the class she could deal with anything from them. In other words, with one exception she liked and enjoyed the group.

Her discussion of the "smart kids" was quite different. Three subgroups

Table 1 Failure Rate Calculated From Final Grades

Sample	Previous quarter (%)	Current quarter (%)
Overall	22	16
Basic class	32	18.5
Smart kids	7	13.6

emerged as Cathy talked about them. These were the "snobs"—white students whose parents were influential in the school and whom she perceived saw themselves as better than everybody else; the "real" students—who behaved consistently and did not appear to judge her; and the "quiet ones"—those students who did not speak out or draw attention to themselves. Cathy freely admitted that she ignored this group. When asked about the "snobs," Cathy identified three members of this group. She also indicated that they exerted a great deal of control over her interactions within this class. She stated that she "ran class in terms of one little group."

This was quite true. The "snobs" very much controlled Cathy's attitudes about the entire class. She did not adjust her teaching style on the basis of their perceived judgment, but she often changed from positive and happy to negative and down after meeting their class as a result of their behavior.

In order to apply the criteria Cathy used for successful teaching as a check on her consistency, she was asked to describe them. They were the descriptors she had used earlier for the "smart kids": good grades, good behavior, and dressing out. She also indicated that even though the "smart kids" met the criteria, she preferred the "basic kids."

To check how closely the two classes met the criteria, the final grades and participation patterns for the two groups were reviewed. At one point Cathy reported that 60% of the students who took physical education failed the class. The grades for the previous quarter for Grade 9 classes were reviewed for comparison. It was also interesting to note that even though the overall grades were higher for the "smart kids," there were more As and Bs awarded to the basic students (see Table 1).

A review of the participation patterns from the two groups yielded data in conflict with what Cathy believed. The number of students who received zeros for not dressing and taking class on 10 different days had been recorded. In the basic groups on most days one or two students took a zero. In the smart group an average of four students sat out, and the figure was as high as six to eight on some days. Therefore, more "smart kids" chose not to participate, although Cathy believed it was the basic kids who didn't take part.

It was difficult to determine better behavior because in the classroom Cathy tolerated a good deal of off-task behavior before attempting to control it. She would allow the noise level in the basic class to escalate to a point at which she had to shout to be heard. This group was more vocal, but she permitted it rather than modifying behavior. The "smart kids" were quieter and good at being unobtrusively off-task. In the gymnasium good behavior meant taking part. In reviewing those data there were no differences in incidences of "being slack," not being active.

Conclusion

An overall consideration of how well each group met the criteria of grades, behavior, and participation does not account for the differences that Cathy perceived as existing between the two groups. In fact, the participation patterns show that she was wrong. The grades did indicate the "smart kids" passed physical education more often, but more basic students earned higher grades. Cathy was in essence successful with both classes. Her basic students exceeded her expectations and she was unaware of it.

Rist (1973) and Lortie (1975) have both discussed teachers' tendencies to focus on an elite few who can succeed as a basis for gauging good teaching. Cathy Woods, however, did not seem very rewarded by her "smart kids." Her real satisfaction came from the "basic kids." The source of this attitude was not good grades, good behavior, or participation. The criteria for preferring one class over another was how she felt when interacting with them. In this instance, the good students were the "basic kids," and they were viewed as a group rather than an elite few. For Cathy Woods the elite few, "the snobs," proved to be a source of frustration and negative attitudes toward the class in general. It may be that Cathy's erroneous perceptions regarding the differences between the "basic kids" and the "smart kids" permitted her to feel more comfortable with the basic group. The nonthreatening atmosphere in the class allowed her to be herself.

One final observation about the expectations Cathy held for the basic group further confirms the feeling that she did not view their perceived differences as due to academic inferiority. In the exit interview Cathy was asked what her expectations had been for the basic class. She indicated that she wished some had done better on tests and that she had expected them to "get it" (i.e., the fitness concepts and applications). She did not attribute not "getting it" to academic problems. She felt that those who did not do well had not studied or were unaware of the relationship between fitness concepts and the activities in the gym.

References

Earls, N.F. (1981). Distinctive teachers' personal qualities, perceptions of teacher education and the realities of teaching. *Journal of Teaching in Physical Education,* **1**(1), 59–70.

Lortie, D.C. (1975). *School teacher: A sociological study.* Chicago: University of Chicago Press.

Mosston, M. (1981). *Teaching physical education* (2nd ed.). Columbus, OH: Charles & Merrill.

Rist, R.C. (1973). *The urban school: A factory for failure.* Cambridge, MA: The MIT Press.

Rosenthal, R.S., & Jacobson, L. (1968). *Pygmalion in the classroom.* New York: Holt, Rinehart and Winston.

Coaches' Interactions and Their High- and Low-skilled Athletes' ALT-PE: A Systematic Perspective

Victor H. Mancini
Deborah A. Wuest

Educational researchers have long been interested in the effects of teachers' expectancies on students' learning. A considerable body of knowledge indicates that expectancies function as self-fulfilling prophecies. Researchers interested in studying expectancy effects in physical education have used various systematic observation instruments. One interaction analysis system used is the Dyadic Adaptation of CAFIAS, or DAC. DAC was developed by Martinek and Mancini (1979) from CAFIAS. CAFIAS provided researchers with information on the teacher's interaction with the whole class. To study expectancy effects, Martinek and Mancini modified CAFIAS so that the teacher's interactions with individual students could be noted; DAC was the result of their efforts.

Another instrument that has been used is the Academic Learning Time–Physical Education (ALT-PE) (Siedentop, Tousignant, & Parker, 1982) instrument. The ALT-PE instrument provides information about students' activities and opportunities to learn. Because the instrument focuses on the actions of individual students, it can be used to assess expectancy effects.

The interest of researchers in the self-fulfilling prophecy has extended to the coaching realm. This chapter describes the procedures and results of 13 studies, using DAC and ALT-PE, that have focused on the effects of coaches' expectations on their high- and low-skilled athletes' behaviors, specifically their interactions and opportunities for motor engagement (see Table 1). Coaches and athletes of men's and women's basketball and lacrosse teams, men's American football teams, women's volleyball teams, women's soccer teams, and women springboard divers served as subjects for these studies. This chapter presents generalized findings with a view toward presenting practical applications.

Table 1 Investigations Focusing on Athletes of Different Abilities

Sport	Researchers	Year	Instrument
Basketball (men)	Mars, Mancini, Wuest, & Galli	1984	ALT-PE
	Wuest, Mancini, Frye, & Murphy	1985	ALT-PE
Basketball (women)	Hecklinger	1985	ALT-PE
Football	Boyes	1981	DAC
	Murray	1984	ALT-PE
	Schaffner	1985	ALT-PE
Lacrosse (men & women)	Hoffman	1981	DAC
	Thomas, Mancini, & Wuest	1984	ALT-PE
Soccer (women	Shields	1984	ALT-PE
	Goetcheus	1985	ALT-PE
Volleyball (women)	Wuest, Mancini, Mars, & Terrillion	1985	ALT-PE
	Ware	1985	DAC
Diving (women)	Rush	1985	DAC

Method

Selection of Subjects

To identify athletes of different abilities the athletes were first ranked on a continuum. With the exception of the football and diving studies, athletes were ranked on a continuum by their coaches at the end of the season. Specific criteria were given to coaches to assist them in the ranking process. In the football studies, athletes were ranked according to their status as starting and nonstarting athletes for the upcoming weekly competition. In the diving study, the average of the athletes' scores from all competitions during the season was used to rank the athletes.

Once the athletes were ranked, two processes were used to place the athletes into ability groups. First, where the number of members comprising a given team was small, all athletes from a given team were used and divided evenly into ability groups based on their rankings. The top athletes were designated as high-skilled, the lowest ranked athletes as low-skilled, and the athletes in between were designated as average-skilled. This procedure was used in the basketball, volleyball, and diving studies. A modification of this procedure was used in the football studies. The football studies looked at positional coaches and their athletes. Because only a small number of athletes were working with each coach, the athletes, once ranked, were divided evenly into high- and low-ability groups.

In the lacrosse and soccer studies, because the number of athletes on each team was greater, a different procedure was followed. The top 10 athletes on the team were classified as high-skilled athletes and the lowest 10 athletes as low-skilled.

Procedures

Two instruments were used in these investigations. DAC was used to describe the coach's interactions with the high-, average-, and low-skilled athletes. The revised ALT-PE instrument was used to record athletes' involvement and opportunities to learn.

In all studies, the coding procedures used for DAC and ALT-PE were consistent. The procedures to code DAC are similar to those used to code CAFIAS. However, rather than recording a behavior every 3 seconds or as often as they change, behaviors are recorded only when the coach is interacting with the target athletes.

For the ALT-PE coding, three target athletes were randomly selected to represent each ability group—high-skilled, low-skilled, and, in some cases, average-skilled. During each coding interval, one target player from each ability group was observed. A 6-second observe, 6-second record format was used.

For all studies randomly selected practices throughout the season were videotaped. Practices were videotaped in their entirety, and typically lasted from 1½ to 2½ hours. The number of practices videotaped varied from 10 to 24 practices. During the videotaping the coach wore a wireless microphone so as to not interfere with coaching functions.

The videotapes were coded by an expert coder. To determine DAC reliability, two to four videotapes were randomly selected to be coded using DAC on two independent observation sessions. The top 10 interaction patterns were ranked, and the Spearman-rank order correlation technique was applied to the rankings. Mean reliability for all DAC studies was .98.

To determine ALT-PE reliability, intraobserver agreement (IOA) was calculated. Two to four videotapes were randomly selected to be coded during two independent observation sessions. IOA was calculated using the scored-interval method and on an interval-by-interval basis. Mean IOA for all ALT-PE studies was 94.2%.

For both DAC and ALT-PE, descriptive statistics were calculated. Visual comparisons were used to determine whether differences existed between the different ability groups.

Results

DAC Results

The DAC data indicated that differences existed in the behaviors of the coaches as they interacted with athletes of differing abilities. During the practice sessions the coaches praised and accepted their high-skilled athletes' efforts more than those efforts put forth by the lesser skilled athletes. They also asked more questions of the high-skilled athletes. Furthermore, coaches provided their high-skilled athletes with more information and demonstrations about skill techniques and strategies than they presented to their lesser skilled teammates. In contrast, the coaches responded to the efforts of the lesser skilled athletes with more criticism.

They gave these athletes directions specifying the behaviors desired, rather than giving them information like they gave the high-skilled athletes. The high-skilled athletes exhibited more interpretive responses in the form of live situation drilling, scrimmaging, or game play, whereas the lesser skilled athletes exhibited more predictable responses (e.g., mechanical drilling). The only exception to these results occurred in the diving study; in this study, the amount of predictable responses exhibited by both the high- and low-skilled athletes was similar. Predictable athlete behavior was the most predominant athlete behavior exhibited during all diving practices.

The predominant interaction patterns of the coaches with their differing-ability athletes revealed that the coaches interacted more and exhibited more varied behaviors toward the high-skilled athletes. They provided their high-skilled players with more feedback to improve their performance and tended to give the athletes feedback while they were practicing. In contrast, not only did the lesser skilled athletes receive less feedback, but the coaches tended to observe these athletes' performance without comment for extended periods of time.

ALT-PE Results

Few differences were found in the context level categories between the skill groups for all studies. Each coach did, however, devote different amounts of time to the various practice activities. The greatest differences between the ability groups were found at the learner involvement level, both in the not-motor-engaged and in the motor-engaged categories. The lesser skilled athletes spent considerably more time inactive, waiting for a chance to participate in an activity, than did the high-skilled teammates. Subsequently, these lesser skilled athletes had less opportunity to perform during practices and to improve their skills. The high-skilled athletes spent more time actively participating during practices. The most pronounced difference between skill abilities was observed in the motor-appropriate category reflecting the amount of ALT-PE accrued. The high-skilled athletes were more successful and effective in performing motor skills, accruing more ALT-PE than their lesser skilled teammates.

Discussion

The DAC and ALT-PE data indicated that coaches favored their high-skilled athletes in their interactions as well as in the practice opportunities they provided. The high-skilled athletes enjoyed more advantageous practice conditions than their lesser skilled teammates. The DAC data revealed clear demarcation between coaches' behaviors and interactions with their athletes of different skill abilities.

When examining the results of these studies, several practical applications are available for consideration by coaches. First, coaches should make an effort to equalize both the nature of the feedback and the manner in which it is given to their athletes. Generally, the coaches provided their high-skilled athletes with concurrent feedback so that these athletes could use this information to improve their skills while continuing to perform. Coaches were more responsive to their high-skilled athletes' actions and used significantly more praise, acceptance, and encouragement both during and after their efforts. Conversely, coaches tended to give their lesser skilled athletes more criticism and directions that tended to restrict their behaviors, discouraging initiative and interpretive behavior on their part.

It is likely that the praise and other motivating behaviors exhibited toward the high-skilled athletes encouraged them to put forth more effort during practice as well. As sport psychologists remind coaches, the role of motivation in achieving high-level performance is a critical one. Shouldn't coaches make a more concerted effort to motivate athletes of all ability levels, not only the highly skilled?

Coaches should also ask their athletes, regardless of skill ability, more questions to check their comprehension of the material being presented. High-skilled athletes were asked more questions than their lesser skilled teammates. The coach should make a conscious effort to ask the low-skilled athletes more questions so that if they are having difficulty understanding the material the coach can provide further information. If the athletes' responses to the coach indicate lack of comprehension, the coach can reinstruct the players. This reinstruction prior to the athletes' attempting the skill may alleviate some of the criticism directed their way following their performance.

Another discrepancy between players of different abilities was the amount of interpretive behavior in the form of live situation drilling, scrimmaging, or game play that occurred. High-skilled athletes engaged in interpretive behavior more often than their lesser skilled teammates. If coaches want to teach athletes to "think on their feet" just as they would in the throes of the game, interpretive behavior on the part of all players should be encouraged and planned for during each practice.

Analysis of the ALT-PE data revealed several disparities in the opportunities to learn provided to the athletes by the coaches. Low-skilled athletes were not actively engaged more often and, for the most part, this difference was accounted for in the longer time that they spent waiting. The longer waiting time resulted in the lesser skilled athletes' having fewer opportunities to practice skills. This lack of opportunity hinders the skill development of these athletes and further widens the gap between the ability groups. The use of smaller groups for drills, more equipment and activity stations, and elimination of the practice of providing the lesser skilled athletes with fewer trials would enhance the development of the lesser skilled players.

High-skilled athletes were more actively engaged in relevant motor activities during the practice sessions and were more successful and effective, as evidenced by the accrued ALT-PE. Coaches should try to provide the lesser skilled athletes with similar opportunities to experience success and to learn. Results from several of the studies revealed that the ratio of inappropriate behavior to appropriate behavior was close to 1:1.

How motivating is it for a lesser skilled athlete to fail so frequently, and how much is learned in the process? Coaches should consider designing practices so that some segments of practice can be used to work with the lesser skilled athletes in small groups, focusing on the skills that they have not mastered. The use of appropriate progressions for skill development warrants mention as well.

Conclusion

Both the DAC and ALT-PE data substantiate that the "Pygmalion effect" is alive and well in the coaching environment. Coaches provide their high-skilled players with more advantageous practice conditions and offer them more support and encouragement than they offer their lesser skilled teammates. How can this preferential treatment be overcome?

At the risk of being simplistic, coaches need to become aware of the behaviors they and their athletes are exhibiting during practice. Although a coach may be reluctant to spend the time learning how to use various systematic observation instruments, the coach should at least make the effort to videotape one or two of his or her practices. Advances in videotape equipment and the increased availability of this equipment make it easy for the coach to assign a manager to this function. In viewing the videotape, the coach could then follow one or two high- and low-skilled players, making notes of what they do and what was said to them. From the intervention studies conducted of teachers and coaches, researchers know that the experience of seeing oneself in action can be eye-opening; the phrase "I didn't know I did that or I said that" is an apt description of teachers' and coaches' initial reactions to seeing themselves at work. To promote equal opportunities for all athletes in order for each to reach his or her fullest potential, the coach must make a concerted effort to motivate and to teach both the high-skilled and low-skilled athletes and provide them with equal chances for success.

References

Boyes, J. (1981). *The interaction behavior patterns of college football coaches with their starting and nonstarting athletes.* Unpublished master's thesis, Ithaca College, Ithaca, NY.

Goetcheus, C. (1985). *The ALT-PE of high- and low-skilled intercollegiate female soccer players.* Unpublished master's thesis, Ithaca College, Ithaca, NY.

Hecklinger, T. (1985). *A comparison of the academic learning time-physical education of high-, average-, and low-skilled female intercollegiate basketball players.* Unpublished master's thesis, Ithaca College, Ithaca, NY.

Hoffman, A.F. (1981). *The interaction patterns of collegiate lacrosse coaches with high-skilled and low-skilled athletes.* Unpublished master's thesis, Ithaca College, Ithaca, NY.

Mars, H. van der, Mancini, V., Wuest, D., & Galli, G. (1984, July). *The ALT-PE of high- and low-skilled basketball players.* Paper presented at the Olympic Scientific Congress, Eugene, OR.

Martinek, T.J., & Mancini, V.H. (1979). CAFIAS: Observing dyadic interaction between teacher and student. *Journal of Classroom Interaction, 14*(2), 18–23.

Murray, D. (1984). *A comparison of the academic learning time-physical education of high-skilled and low-skilled intercollegiate junior varsity football players.* Unpublished master's thesis, Ithaca College, Ithaca, NY.

Rush, D. (1985). *Coach's interactions with his high- and low-skilled female intercollegiate divers.* Unpublished master's thesis, Ithaca College, Ithaca, NY.

Schaffner, P. (1985). *The ALT-PE of starting and nonstarting football players.* Unpublished master's thesis, Ithaca College, Ithaca, NY.

Shields, F.J. (1984). *A comparison of the academic learning time-physical education of high- and low-skilled female intercollegiate soccer players.* Unpublished master's thesis, Ithaca College, Ithaca, NY.

Siedentop, D., Tousignant, M., & Parker, M. (1982). *ALT-PE coding manual* (rev. ed.). Columbus: The Ohio State University.

Thomas, J., Mancini, V., & Wuest, D.A. (1984, April). *A comparison of the ALT-PE of high- and low-skilled male and female collegiate lacrosse players.* Paper presented at the American Alliance for Health, Physical Education, Recreation, and Dance National Convention, Anaheim, CA.

Ware, J. (1985). *Interactions of an intercollegiate volleyball coach with female players of different abilities.* Unpublished master's thesis, Ithaca College, Ithaca, NY.

Wuest, D.A., Mancini, V.H., Frye, P.A., & Murphy, J.A. (1985, April). *A comparison of the academic learning time of high-, average-, and low-skilled basketball players during a unit of instruction.* Paper presented at the American Alliance for Health, Physical Education, Recreation, and Dance National Convention, Atlanta, GA.

Wuest, D.A., Mancini, V.H., Mars, H. van der, & Terrillion, K. (1985). The ALT-PE of high-, average-, and low-skilled intercollegiate volleyball players. In M. Piéron & T. Templin (Eds.), *The 1984 Olympic Scientific Congress proceedings: Vol. 6. Sport pedagogy* (pp. 123–129). Champaign, IL: Human Kinetics.

Learning Behavior in PE Lessons and Physical and Psychological Responses to PE in High-Skill and Low-Skill Pupils

Risto Telama
Väinö Varstala
Pilvikki Heikinaro-Johansson
Jari Utriainen

In several countries, including Finland, physical education in schools is expected to teach basic motor skills. Very different approaches have been chosen in order to handle the problem caused by the heterogeneity of pupils in the teaching of skills. In mastery learning theory, the meaning of equality was in a way emphasized because it tried to promote the skills of all or a large number of pupils (Bloom, 1971). Also Dodds (1986) starts from the principle of equality when she speaks about "motor elitism." Among other things, motor elitism refers to using only one learning task for a whole class when it is obvious that some students will be unable to perform the task.

According to the Pygmalion theory, the teacher develops preconceptions about his or her pupils, for instance on the basis of their skills; such preconceptions in turn guide the pupils' behavior and learning (Martinek, Growe, & Rejeski, 1982). This, too, introduces inequality into teaching. In Pygmalion theory, more emphasis is put on the teacher's attitude toward the pupil, whereas motor elitism pertains more to the general nature of teaching.

According to the Pygmalion theory, research findings on teachers' attitudes toward low-skill and high-skill pupils are conflicting. Some studies have found that teachers have a more favorable attitude to high-skill pupils as compared to low-skill pupils (Martinek et al., 1982, p. 19; Martinek & Johnson, 1979). Other studies have found differences in the behavior of low-skill and high-skill students but none in the teachers' behavior (Piéron, 1982; Shute, Dodds, Placek, Rife, & Silverman, 1982). No differences in teacher behavior were observed when pupils who were either passive or active in their free time were compared (Telama, Varstala, Heikinaro-Johansson, & Paukku, 1986).

The conflicting research findings may be due to the fact that only the teacher-pupil interaction has been studied, in which interaction the teacher's attitude toward motor elitism, for instance, does not necessarily surface. Therefore, it is important to study the problem in as wide a context as possible and to pay attention to how teaching is arranged, including differentiation and design of learning tasks.

As part of the larger Research Project on School Physical Education Classes, the present study attempts to find out how pupils with different motor skill levels participate in physical education teaching, how they experience it physically and psychologically, and to what extent teaching has been differentiated in order to account for interpupil differences.

Method

The data were collected during 406 physical education classes. Pupil behavior in physical education classes was observed in terms of a system of 10 categories (reclassified into six categories in this study, see Table 1) using 6-second time units; at the same time, the intensity of the physical activity was assessed in a 5-point scale (1 = doesn't move; 5 = moves a lot). After every minute of observation, emotional involvement in the lesson was assessed along a 5-point scale (1 = misbehavior; 5 = very much involvement). At the end of the lesson, the observer also made overall trait ratings on 12 traits. After the class, the students were interviewed about such points as how strenuous they perceived the physical education class to have been and whether they had sweated and become breathless. In the systematic observation of pupil behavior, the nominal agreement of two coders reached the level of 81%.

From among the 812 students observed, three groups were selected—high-skill, average, and low-skill—on the basis of three variables: physical education grade, student's own estimation of his or her skills, and the observer's estimation of the student's skills. In the high-skill group ($N = 54$) were included those whose physical education grade was 9 or 10 on a grading scale of 4 to 10 and whose personal and observer skill estimation was above average (on a scale of lower than average, average, and above average). In the average group ($N = 52$) were included those with a PE grade of 8 and at least one average skill estimation. In the low-skill group ($N = 43$) were included those with a PE grade of 7 or lower and at least one below-average skill estimation.

Case study material was used as supporting evidence for the statistical data. One high-skill and one low-skill pupil were observed through the whole school year during a total of 30 classes. The pulse rate of these pupils was recorded and their activity measured on a pedometer. In the observation, the category system referred to above was used.

Results

Category findings obtained by systematic observation showed that generally, when all classes were taken into account, no statistically significant differences existed between the participation in teaching of pupils in different skill level groups (see Tables 1 and 2). In ball game classes, in which pupils have more freedom to regulate their activity level, in girls the low-skill group followed the teaching more than the other groups did (see Table 1). In boys' ball game classes, the time-on-task of the low-skill group was lower than that of the high-skill group. The low-skill group

Table 1 Girls' Activity in All Lessons and Ball Game Lessons by Skill Groups (%)

Behavior categories	All lessons				Ball game lessons			
	Low %	Average %	High %	p	Low %	Average %	High %	p
Organizing	18.3	18.2	14.5	—	19.0	17.9	14.4	—
Following teaching	13.8	14.0	10.5	—	14.0	7.8	5.6	**
Getting feedback	3.2	3.6	1.9	—	1.4	3.8	1.7	—
Time-on-task	49.9	47.9	52.0	—	51.5	50.9	54.9	—
Waiting for turn	9.6	9.2	15.5	—	10.5	10.3	19.0	—
Other activities	3.7	7.0	2.9	—	3.9	9.2	1.6	—
	100	100	100		100	100	100	
N	27	37	26		12	12	14	

$**p < .01.$

Table 2 Boys' Activity in All Lessons and Ball Game Lessons by Skill Groups (%)

Behavior categories	All lessons				Ball game lessons			
	Low %	Average %	High %	p	Low %	Average %	High %	p
Organizing	11.2	16.6	14.4	—	14.0	17.2	16.3	—
Following teaching	6.9	9.1	6.2	—	6.7	5.3	4.9	—
Getting feedback	1.1	3.9	0.4	—	1.4	4.4	0.3	*
Time-on-task	55.6	55.5	64.3	—	48.6	60.5	69.0	*
Waiting for turn	17.6	12.9	9.5	—	25.7	11.8	7.2	*
Other activities	5.8	0.9	5.2	—	3.4	0.8	2.2	—
	100	100	100		100	100	100	
N	16	15	28		9	11	18	

$*p < .05.$

used more time waiting for their turn than did the high-skill group. The high-skill group received the least amount of feedback (see Table 2).

In the total scores given by the observer for physical activity, no significant differences existed between the different skill-level groups in girls (see Figure 1). In boys, the difference was such that the activity of the high-skill group was higher than that of the other groups (see Figure 2).

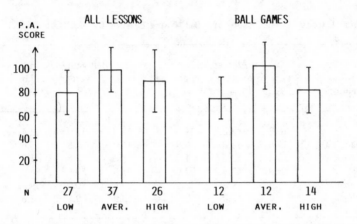

Figure 1 Means and standard deviations of the girls' physical activity (P.A.) score in all lessons and ball game lessons by skill groups.

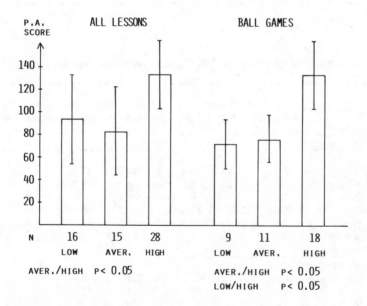

Figure 2 Means and standard deviations of the boys' physical activity (P.A.) score in all lessons and ball game lessons by skill groups.

The purpose of the case study of two students was to find out how two different pupils experience physically different learning contents and classes in the PE curriculum during a whole academic year. Student 1 is above average in his motor skills and condition, whereas Student 2 is lower than average. In terms of the observational categories, there were no differences between the students in teaching participation. Pedometer counts showed that the high-skill student moved more during PE classes, yet according to heart rate averages the low-skill student found the classes as strenuous and, in spring term, more strenuous than did the high-skill pupil (see Figure 3). Naturally, there are substantial differences between lessons with different content both in heart rates and pedometer counts (see Figure 4). As shown in Figure 4, there is a large difference between Students 1 and 2 in the amount of movement, particularly in soccer, although there is little difference in heart rate levels.

The clearest differences between the different skill-level groups were recorded in the variables of the affective domain. Participation motivation, as estimated by the observers, increased linearly from the low-skill group to the high-skill group, the differences being very significant (see Figure 5). A corresponding difference was recorded in the students' enthusiasm, which was estimated after the class. The students in the high-skill group were also estimated to be less anxious and more self-assured than the low-skill students (see Table 3). The boys in the high-skill group had more social interaction than low-skill boys.

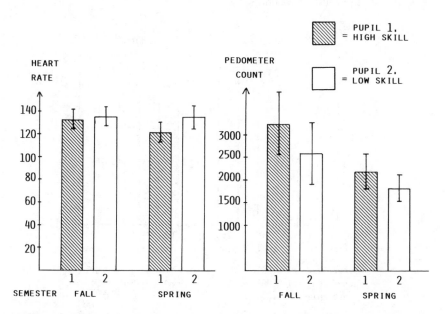

Figure 3 Means and standard deviations of heart rate and pedometer count of one high-skill and one low-skill pupil during fall and spring semester.

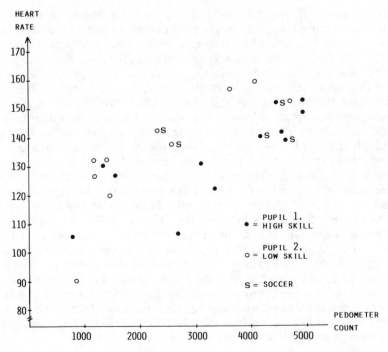

Figure 4 Average heart rates and pedometer counts of one high-skill and one low-skill pupil during 22 physical education lessons.

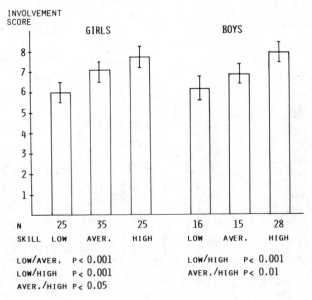

Figure 5 Means and standard deviations of pupils' involvement motivation by sex and skill groups.

Table 3 Frequency Distribution of Trait Rating Anxiety—Ease by Sex and Skill Groups

	Girls			Boys		
	Low	Average	High	Low	Average	High
Anxious or average	14	11	4	13	7	1
At ease	10	25	20	3	9	25
Total	24	36	24	16	16	26

$\chi^2 = 9.58, df = 2$ $\chi^2 = 25.83, df = 2$
$p < 0.01$ $p < 0.001$

Table 4 Grouping of the Class in Physical Education Lessons (%)

Class as a whole	33.0
Pupils in groups	54.2
Pupils in pairs	9.7
Pupils individually	3.1
	100
N (periods) (406 lessons)	1,532

Table 5 Differentiation by Subject Matter (%)

The whole class has the same task	66.7
The group has the same task	31.2
Individual tasks	2.1
	100
N (periods) (406 lessons)	1,526

Estimation and analysis of teaching methods used in PE classes showed that there was little in the way of differentiation in PE classes. Usually, the class performed either as one unit or in groups (see Table 4). Groups are usually not formed on the basis of pupils' skills. In the majority of lessons, the whole class had the same task; individual tasks were very rare (see Table 5). According to observer estimation, 83% of the periods observed did not have any differentiation at all (see Table 6).

Table 6   Differentiation of Teaching in Physical Education Lessons (%)

No differentiation	82.9
Differentiation of subject matter	11.6
Differentiation of pupils	5.5
	100
N (periods)	1,531

Discussion

According to the findings pertaining to the observational categories used in this study, pupils with different skill levels seem to participate in teaching in much the same way. In ball games, though, in low-skill boys the time-on-task is lower and the time spent by them waiting for their turn is higher than in boys with better skills.

In boys, estimated physical intensity of movement was higher in the high-skill group than it was in the low-skill group. In girls, this difference did not exist, and it seems that in the teaching of girls, on the level of manifest behavior, low-skill pupils are better included than in the teaching of boys.

The case studies done on two boys lent support to the notion that a high-skill student moves more during PE lessons, especially in ball games. However, no clear differences were recorded in heart rate levels, or else the heart rate averages of the low-skill student were higher. On an average, heart rates were moderately high. What this may indicate is that although the low-skill student moved less than the high-skill one, his cardiovascular system was being subjected to proportionally the same or a higher load than that of the high-skill student. Thus, the goal of physical fitness, particularly that of endurance, would not seem to be a problem for the low-skill student. Because this was a case study, however, all it can supply is hints to help set up hypotheses.

The clearest differences between the skill level groups were recorded in variables associated with the affective goals of physical education. Both in girls and boys clear differences were seen in participation motivation, enthusiasm, and in attitudes to physical education, such that high-skill pupils were the more enthusiastic and had the more favorable attitudes. High-skill pupils also were less anxious and more self-assured. In boys, the high-skill group also had more social interaction.

One reason for the differences mentioned is teaching methods. Although skill level differences between students are large, teaching has been insufficiently differentiated in terms of learning content and pupil skill levels. Teaching is mostly carried out the same way for all pupils and mainly in accordance with the skill level of average or high-skill students. Although low-skill students somehow manage to participate in the instruction, they do not find it as psychologically interesting or pleasant as do high-skill students. In view of the circumstances, low-skill students probably do not benefit as much as high-skill students from the teaching.

In the Finnish physical education curriculum, there is much ball game playing, especially for boys. In teaching, ball games can be assumed to represent a differentiated situation in which all pupils can participate according to their individual skill level. According to the findings, in boys in particular, the participation of low-skill pupils, as measured, for instance, as time-on-task, is proportionally less than in other types of lessons. Further, participation motivation and enthusiasm in ball games were lower in low-skill students than in high-skill ones. One must add, however, that the time-on-task in ball game lessons was rather high in low-skill pupils as well (48%).

A ball game could also be a situation to enhance a pupil's skills. In regular game playing, however, game performances (throwing, hitting, kicking, etc.) tend to be done mostly by high-skill students (Laakso, 1985). This, of course, affects both skill acquisition and participation motivation.

Conclusion

In summary, one can say that although teachers may try to treat pupils with different skill levels equally, a certain inequality may make itself apparent on the level of the pupil's behavior and experiences. This may be due above all to the fact that in nondifferentiated teaching low-skill pupils have inadequate opportunities for participation on their own terms. The findings suggest that no such differences exist in the teachers' behavior toward students, as maintained in the Pygmalion theory. If, however, low-skill students do not have adequate learning opportunities available for them, the end result is the same as that caused by the Pygmalion effect: High-skill students benefit most and are most motivated by the teaching.

In the way of a practical recommendation for solving the problem discussed, the following is suggested: The starting point of teaching should be checked with a view to the principle of equality, and more philosophy in accordance with the principle of mastery learning should be applied to teaching. Also, the role of teaching methodology should be increasingly emphasized by applying teaching methodology that systematically takes into account aspects such as differentiation. (For this purpose, *Spectrum of Teaching Styles* [Mosston, 1981] is recommended.)

References

Bloom, B. (1971). Mastery learning and its implications for curriculum development. In E.W. Eisner (Ed.), *Confronting curriculum reform* (pp. 17–32). Boston: Little, Brown.

Dodds, P. (1986). Stamp out the ugly "isms" in your gym. In M. Piéron & G. Graham (Eds.), *The 1984 Olympic Scientific Congress proceedings: Vol. 6. Sport pedagogy* (pp. 141-150). Champaign, IL: Human Kinetics.

Laakso, L. (1985). Pelitilanteen systemaattinen arviointi palloilun didaktiikan apuna [Systematical observation of teaching ball games]. *Liikunta ja Tiede,* **22**(4), 168-175.

Martinek, T.J., Growe, P.B., & Rejeski, W.J. (1982). *Pygmalion in the gym: Causes and effects of expectations in teaching and coaching.* Champaign, IL: Leisure Press.

Martinek, T.J., & Johnson, S.B. (1979). Teacher expectations: Effects of dynamic interactions and self-concept in elementary age children. *Research Quarterly,* **50**(1), 60-70.

Mosston, M. (1981). *Teaching physical education.* Columbus, OH: Charles E. Merrill.

Piéron, M. (1982). Behaviors of low and high achievers in physical education classes. In M. Piéron & J. Cheffers (Eds.), *Studying the teaching in physical education* (pp. 53-60) (Proceedings of the AIESEP 1982 World Convention). Liège, Belgium: University of Liège.

Shute, S., Dodds, P., Placek, J., Rife, F., & Silverman, S. (1982). Academic learning time in elementary school movement education: A descriptive analytic study. *Journal of Teaching in Physical Education,* **1**(2), 3-14.

Telama, R., Varstala, V., Heikinaro-Johansson, P., & Paukku, P. (1986.) The relationship between pupil's leisure-time physical activity and motor behavior during physical education lessons. In M. Piéron & G. Graham (Eds.), *The 1984 Olympic Scientific Congress proceedings: Vol. 6. Sport pedagogy* (pp. 57-62). Champaign, IL: Human Kinetics.

Participant Engagement and Teacher's Feedback in Physical Education Teaching and Coaching

Maurice Piéron
Carlos Gonçalves

To better understand the context in which this study was completed it should be understood that distinctive differences exist between coaching functions in Europe (in this case, in Portugal) and those in the United States. Unlike those of a coach in the American sport scene, the duties of a coach in Europe are generally not related to or based in school or university communities.

Often, in Europe the same individual provides teaching duties in a school setting and coaching duties in the sport club setting. It can be hypothesized that teachers and coaches behave differently within these two different contexts and are influenced by the individual characteristics of the participants. The purpose of this study was to describe and analyze participant engagement and teacher/coach feedback in physical education (instructional program) and coaching (sports competition) contexts.

Time variables (time-on-task, ALT-PE) and augmented feedback have emerged as seemingly important variables related to pupil achievement based on the classroom process-product research (Bloom, 1979; Rosenshine, 1980) and on physical education studies based on experimental teaching units (Piéron & Graham, 1984).

Teacher augmented feedback and student motor engagement or ALT-PE have been frequently compared with respect to several context variables and analyzed in specific descriptive studies using multidimensional observation systems (Dodds, Rife, & Metzler, 1982; Piéron, 1983). On the other hand, studies of coaches' behaviors are much less numerous, and studies analyzing the same individual in both functions are even more rare.

Coach-athlete interaction and the teacher-student interaction within groups directed by the same individual in both settings have focused on recording the direct and indirect interaction approaches (Kasson, 1974; Mancini & Agnew, 1978). Differences in the overall interaction patterns were observed in the two different situations. Overall, coaches exhibited a greater variety of behaviors in the coaching sessions but less variety of teacher-pupil interaction in the physical education classroom (Mancini & Agnew, 1978).

Method

Teacher's feedback has been observed and recorded using the category system FEED/ULg devised by Piéron and Delmelle (1981). The system has been simplified to be applicable in "live" conditions. Feedback is categorized according to three main dimensions: the intent (evaluation, description, prescription, and questioning), the form (verbal, visual, and kinesthetic) and the direction (class, group, and student).

A modification of the OBEL/ULg observation schedule (Piéron & Cloes, 1981) was used to describe how the coach-teacher organized practices and how the players/students spent their time during the practice session. In the system, major dimensions (setting and engagement) are each sub-divided in coding categories (see Table 1). Coach/teacher behaviors and players/students were not recorded simultaneously.

Reliability determined by percentage of agreement between coders was 88.3% for augmented feedback and 86% for player/student behaviors. These percentages were within acceptable standards for direct observation.

Six male teachers were observed six times: three times in a physical education class setting and three times during coaching practice sessions in basketball. All the teachers were experienced both in teaching physical education (3 to 15 years) and in coaching basketball (3 to 16 years). Analysis of data focused on the feedback intervention rate, on the feedback profile according to the categories of the multidimensional system used for the observation, and on the time spent in different types of engagement.

Results

Clear behavior differences were observed in the respective settings. A greater use of situational play (scrimmage) was observed in the coaching setting than in the school setting (19.2% vs. 4.6% of the observation time). This difference was balanced by a larger amount of time spent in the full game situation (coaching 21.1% vs. teaching 14.9%) and by a larger portion of the time providing information to the participants (27.8% vs. 23.0%) in the teaching context. Time differences in the "drill" category were negligible.

Direct motor engagement was significantly higher (Wilcoxon Matched-Pairs Signed-Ranks Test, $T = 0$, $p = .05$) in coaching (37.2%) as compared to teaching (23.9%). Duration differences in favor of the coaching context were also observed for the category "player in contact with the ball" (when the player is taking part in an action closely related to the ball), whereas in direct engagement comparisons were almost identical. Waiting periods (31.5 to 23.3%) and cognitive engagement (28.3 to 23.1%) were higher in teaching than in coaching, whereas the intervention rates did not differ significantly in the teaching and coaching situations.

Table 1   Motor Engagement of Participants: Comparison of Teaching and Coaching (Data in % of Observation Time)

	Teaching			Coaching		
	M	Min.	Max.	M	Min.	Max.
Setting						
Drill	40.2	17.7	53.0	39.8	28.3	48.3
Scrimmage	4.6	0.0	14.2	19.2	12.8	27.5
Full game	21.1	4.4	31.5	14.9	5.5	36.3
Cognitive engagement	27.8	17.6	39.5	23.0	13.4	39.6
Nonspecific motor activity	6.3	0.0	21.2	3.0	0.0	7.7
Participation						
With the ball	13.9	8.6	23.2	18.4	12.1	26.7
Without the ball	10.0	8.5	12.2	18.8	14.8	21.7
Indirect engagement	6.7	2.3	9.1	6.6	2.5	11.4
Cognitive engagement	28.3	17.7	39.4	23.1	13.4	39.6
Waiting	31.5	20.0	47.3	23.3	11.0	30.5
Organization	3.0	0.0	7.9	6.9	3.2	12.0
Nonspecific motor activity	6.3	0.0	21.2	3.0	0.0	7.7

Table 2   Augmented Feedback: Comparison of Teaching and Coaching

Type of feedback	Teaching			Coaching		
	M	Min.	Max.	M	Min.	Max.
Approbatory evaluative	10.3	0.0	22.2	15.4	3.7	34.5
Disapprobatory evaluative	2.5	0.0	11.1	2.7	0.0	8.8
Positive prescriptive	45.1	21.2	71.4	57.4	37.9	85.2
Negative prescriptive	17.7	5.8	39.4	11.4	4.2	17.6
Positive descriptive	10.6	0.0	28.9	7.2	0.0	14.9
Negative descriptive	3.2	0.0	7.1	1.9	0.0	6.4
Positive affective	0.2	0.0	1.9	0.1	0.0	0.1
Negative affective	2.2	0.0	17.9	1.0	0.0	5.9
Interrogative	8.3	0.0	32.0	3.0	0.0	9.4

Moderate arithmetic differences emerged in the feedback functions. A tendency was observed to use evaluative and prescriptive feedback more frequently in coaching than in teaching, whereas descriptive and interrogative feedback were more frequent in teaching than in coaching (see Table 2).

More striking differences were identified when dealing with specific feedback functions. In the coaching situation, approbative feedback and positive prescriptive feedback were used more frequently, whereas in the teaching setting negative prescriptions and negative affective feedback were more prevalent.

Discussion

The percentage distribution of the different activities selected to be practiced by players and students showed that the time devoted to the full game was higher in teaching than in coaching. Conversely, the time allocated to gamelike situations was higher in coaching than in teaching. Student involvement and opportunities to learn within these two settings differed. In gamelike situations (2 × 2, 3 × 3, etc.) players (coaching context) had greater opportunities than students (teaching context) to be directly involved in the main actions and to be in contact with the ball. One might argue that this vehicle is a unique source of progress for beginners as well as for more advanced players. Moreover, scrimmage or gamelike situations are often used by teachers/coaches to facilitate the motor engagement of the participant and to reduce the number of failures in taking part in the game.

Student waiting time during full-game participation was twice as high in teaching (31.5%) than in coaching (16.0%). It seemed as if the major concern was to keep the students "busy and happy" by choosing a less demanding and more attractive situation. The higher motor engagement time of players may be partially explained by presuming higher motivation in players. However, strategies used in coaching and the perceived higher intensity and energy of the coaches seemed to facilitate the maximizing of time spent in practicing specific learning tasks. Comparison to other reported teaching and coaching context studies revealed that waiting time (23.3%) was similar to that of the elite volleyball players reported by McKenzie (1985). In teaching, waiting time (31.5%) was similar to data reported by Costello and Laubach (1978). The rate of feedback was within the range of rates reported in the literature, only slightly higher than those reported for teachers (Arena, 1979; Fishman & Tobey, 1978) but lower than in teachers involved in their special area of expertise (Brunelle & Carufel, 1982; Piéron & Delmelle, 1981).

It has been suggested that coaches rely almost exclusively on direct style of communication with players (Lombardo, Faraone, & Pothier, 1982; Sherman & Hassan, 1985; Smith, Smoll, & Curtis, 1979). The data gathered in this study on feedback confirmed this directive coaching style. In addition, prescriptive feedback was the most frequently occurring category and was substantially higher in coaching than in teaching. The reason for directness (prescription) may be due to the nature of the objectives set forth by the coach. One might argue that objectives in the coaching context are more precise and less ambiguous in the direct approach and thus can be used with great effectiveness. Direct instruction has also been considered to be an effective teaching style in academic classroom settings (Rosenshine, 1980). Furthermore, the emphasis on direct instruction in coaching may not, as some might argue, create problems related to the interactive climate. It may very well be that coach/athlete interaction is inherently warmer due to the larger amount of approbatory evaluative feedback and of positive prescriptive feedback. This finding is consistent with that of Mancini and Agnew (1978), who found that coaches used more praise and acceptance in their interaction with athletes.

Teachers, on the other hand, tended to induce more participant reflection by asking more questions, as in guiding the students to discover their errors, or by giving a larger amount of descriptive feedback. With this type of feedback, the participant receives performance information that is as accurate as possible, compares it to the performance model, and is directly responsible for subsequent performance decisions.

Conclusion

Although in this study the same individual was in control of both the decision-making process and interventions, several differences were observed in the practice setting and in coach/teacher behaviors. As expected, the participants' engagement time and distribution were different in the coaching and teaching contexts. In coaching, motor engagement of players was higher and seemed to be more specific and more appropriate to long-term objectives. In the teaching context student learning can be enhanced by more carefully designing the educational setting in order to maximize student engagement time and to create a more positive classroom climate.

References

Arena, L. (1979). *Descriptive and experimental studies of augmented instructional feedback in sport settings.* Unpublished doctoral dissertation, Ohio State University, Columbus.

Bloom, B. (1979). *Caractéristiques individuelles et apprentissages scolaires.* [Human characteristics and school learning]. Brussels: Editions Labor.

Brunelle, J., & Carufel, F. de (1982). Analyse des feedbacks émis par des maîtres de l'enseignement de la danse moderne [Analysis of feedback emitted by master teachers of modern dance]. *La Revue Québécoise de l'Activité Physique,* 2(1), 3–9.

Costello, J., & Laubach, S. (1978). Student behavior. In W. Anderson & G. Barrette (Eds.), *Motor skills: Theory into Practice: Monograph No. 1. What's going on in gym* (pp. 11–24). Newton, CT: A.L. Rothstein.

Dodds, P., Rife, F., & Metzler, M. (1982). Academic learning time in physical education: Data collection, completed research and future directions. In M. Piéron & J. Cheffers (Eds.), *Studying the teaching in physical education* (pp. 37–51). Liège, Belgium: University of Liège.

Fishman, S., & Tobey, C. (1978). Augmented feedback. In W. Anderson & G. Barrette (Eds.), *Motor skills: Theory into practice: Monograph No. 1. What's going on in gym* (pp. 51–62). Newton, CT: A.L. Rothstein.

Kasson, P. (1974). *Teaching and coaching behaviors of university physical educators.* Unpublished doctoral dissertation, University of Wisconsin, Madison.

Lombardo, B., Faraone, N., & Pothier, D. (1982). The behavior of youth sport coaches: A preliminary analysis. In M. Piéron & J. Cheffers (Eds.), *Studying the teaching in physical education* (pp. 189–196). Liège, Belgium: University of Liège.

Mancini, V., & Agnew, M. (1978). An analysis of teaching and coaching behaviors. In W. Straub (Ed.), *Sport psychology: An analysis of athlete behaviors* (pp. 402–409). Ithaca, NY: Mouvement Publications.

McKenzie, T.L. (1985). Analysis of the practice behavior of elite athletes. In M. Piéron & G. Graham (Eds.), *The 1984 Olympic Scientific Congress proceedings: Vol. 6. Sport pedagogy* (pp. 117–121). Champaign, IL: Human Kinetics.

Piéron, M. (1983). Teacher and pupil behavior and the interaction process in P.E. classes. In R. Telama, V. Varstala, J. Tiainen, L. Laakso, & T. Haajanen (Eds.), *Research in school physical education* (pp. 13–30). Jyväskylä, Finland: The Foundation for Promotion of Physical Culture and Health.

Piéron, M., & Cloes, M. (1981). Interactions between teachers and students in selected sports activities: The student as a starting point. *Artus* (Rio de Janeiro), **9**(11), 185–188.

Piéron, M., & Delmelle, R. (1981). Descriptive study of teacher's feedback in two educational situations. *Artus* (Rio de Janeiro), **9**(11), 193–196.

Piéron, M., & Graham, G. (1984). Research on physical education teacher effectiveness: The experimental teaching units. *International Journal of Physical Education*, **21**(3), 9–14.

Rosenshine, B. (1980). How time is spent in elementary classrooms. In C. Denham & A. Liebermann (Eds.), *Time to learn* (pp. 107–126). Washington, DC: National Institute of Education.

Sherman, M.A., & Hassan, J.S. (1985). Behavioral studies of youth sport coaches. In M. Piéron & G. Graham (Eds.). *The 1984 Olympic Scientific Congress proceedings: Vol. 6. Sport pedagogy* (pp. 103–108). Champaign, IL: Human Kinetics.

Smith, R., Smoll, B., & Curtis, B. (1979). Coach effectiveness training: A cognitive-behavioral approach to enhancing relationship skills in youth sport coaches. *Journal of Sport Psychology*, **1**, 59–75.

The Study of Active Learning Time: Profile of Behavior

Claude Paré
Michel Lirette
Fernand Caron
Pierre Black

To assert that the physical education teacher must take students into account when preparing the physical education lesson makes sense for everybody. Furthermore, it is impossible to be wrong by suggesting that teachers will change their way of teaching according to the subject matter and that they will not teach the same way when teaching kindergarten and high school students. Are teachers really that flexible, or do they prepare their lessons in the same way for all their students? What are the effects of these preparations on real class time management? What is the students' engagement time, and is there any significant difference between primary and high school students' time distribution in physical education classes?

Literature

Gentile (1972) presents a theoretical teaching model in which major teaching components are identified. Gentile's model adopted by Arnold (1981) reports on the presentation of three series of parallel motor learning activities: student activities, teacher activities, and those of the researchers. This model is closely related to the concepts identified in Dunkin and Biddle's (1974) classification of variables. Dunkin and Biddle (1974) identify the following concepts: presage, context, process, and product whereas Gentile (1972) deals with the teacher variable, identifying the following: goals clarification, tasks selection, direction of performance, observation, feedback, adjustments, and practice. Although each model uses different terms, it is possible to find similar concepts within the two models that should guide teachers in their professional activities. It should be noted that Dunkin and Biddle's classification (1974) was used in physical education research by Graham and Heimerer (1981), Piéron (1982a, 1982b, 1984) and Tousignant and Brunelle (1982), in which the program variable was included.

One might hypothesize that all teaching activities are continued within the parameters of these models and that teachers utilize these concepts, consciously or not, to manage their teaching activities. The question then arises, How pertinent are these variables to the everyday teaching of physical education? Are any of these factors more important than others in the management of teaching? Considering the exactness of the proposed models, it appears that the experimental control of some variables could help to demonstrate their impact on teaching. This impact should be measured by the student learning rate or by the student achievement of program objectives.

Within this study the following variables were taken into account: student grade level, the different subject matter of the program, and the teacher. Although time on task serves as an indicator of pupil learning, other researchers have investigated this line of inquiry. Siedentop, Birdwell, and Metzler (1979); Piéron and Haan (1979); Piéron and Forceille (1983); Brunelle, Godbout, Drouin, Desharnais, Lord, and Tousignant (1980); and Paré, Lirette, and Caron (1983) have reported that the cultural context causes no substantial difference in the proportion of class time or in the distribution of student engagement time.

Differences, however, could come from intrinsic teaching variables or elements closely related to class management. Consequently, the following is hypothesized:

- Class time distribution will show significant differences according to the subject matter being taught, to the student grade level, or to the teacher.
- Student engagement time distribution will show significant differences according to the subject being taught, the student grade level, or the teacher.
- Student motor engagement time distribution will show significant differences according to the subject being taught, to the student grade school level, or to the teacher.

Method

This study included 17 experienced physical education teachers; eight came from primary schools and nine from high schools. Each teacher taught four lessons, twice the same lesson to two different classes and two different lessons to the same class. The subject matter of the lesson was determined by the teacher according to the program objectives. No specific instructions were given to teachers except to conduct their classes in a normal fashion.

Student time on task was measured using a modified form of the Siedentop's ALT-PE instrument as modified by Paré et al. (1983). Coders for the study had an interjudge coefficient of reliability of 0.92.

Descriptive techniques were used to gather data from all physical education classes, and data were analyzed using ANOVA with Fischer arcsine to correct for errors in the distribution of scores.

Results

Class time distribution among categories for each grade level is shown in Table 1. These results are consistent with those present in similar studies. Studies conducted by Metzler (1979), Brunelle et al. (1980), and Godbout, Brunelle, and Tousignant (1983) show percentages from 73.6 to 81.2%.

Table 1 also shows pupil engagement time distribution for both the primary and high school settings. It is noteworthy that students were motor engaged in the primary setting 28% of the time and 25% at the high school level. Cognitive was 22% primary and 15% high school, whereas waiting and nonengagement measures were 21% for primary and 22% for high school. Finally, the total engagement time varies slightly from 53% for primary classes to 52% for high school classes. These results are quite similar to results reported in the studies above. On the other hand, the results are slightly higher than those reported by Piéron and

Table 1 Percentages of Class Time Distribution for High School and Primary School Lessons

Category	High school	Primary school
Waiting	4.47	7.11
Transition	6.79	9.47
Organization	1.49	0.78
Rest	0.03	1.27
Personal subjects	0.69	0.49
Total	13.47	19.12
Skill practice	31.43	38.41
Lead-up games	0.05	2.82
Match	37.51	7.74
Physical exercises	2.14	4.73
Other physical activities	0.19	2.28
Cognitive development	12.39	20.56
Individual activities	2.34	2.62
Social development	0.48	1.72
Total PE	86.52	80.88
Motor engagement	24.54	27.83
Indirect engagement	12.90	3.04
Cognitive engagement	14.73	21.72
Total engagement time	52.17	52.59
Not engaged + waiting	22.24	21.24
Not engaged + organize	10.37	5.53
Not engaged + disturb	1.74	1.52

Table 2 ANOVA of Percentages of Time Distribution in All Groups

Sources	Physical education time			Engagement time			Motor engagement time		
	Mean square	df	F	Mean square	df	F	Mean square	df	F
Groups	0.0015	1	0.19	0.0029	1	0.46	0.0013	1	0.20
Error	0.0080	16		0.0064	16		0.0067	16	
Lessons	0.0029	1	0.11	0.0097	1	1.56	0.0029	1	1.53
Error	0.0026	16		0.0062	16		0.0086	16	
Groups/lessons	0.0001	1	0.04	0.0012	1	0.37	0.00002	1	0.01
Error	0.0012	16		0.0033	16		0.0020	16	
Mean	46.446	1	1872.9	18.007	1	537.1	4.8819	1	162.67
Error	0.0249	16		0.0336	16		0.0300	16	

Haan (1979) and Piéron and Forceille (1983), who show 23.6% (primary) and 19.5% (high school).

No significant differences are reported in Tables 2 and 3; consequently, all three research hypotheses were rejected.

Discussion and Conclusion

The total absence of any significant difference raises several questions. Do physical education teachers really consider their students when they prepare lessons for them? Our results based on the variables measured suggest they do not. It seems that other forces control class time/management; results point out that the management time model used here is very hermetic to change. This opposition to progress can come from different origins. First, it may result from the type and quality of professional preparation that teachers received at their university. Perhaps teachers receive the same training in all programs. Perhaps cultural models for teaching are carried to the younger staff by the veteran teachers, and thus change is difficult to effect. Finally, does the ignorance or lack of knowledge of factors leading to good time management explain the observation reported here, or are there other explanations that are more plausible?

Answers to these questions are not easy. In the final analysis it is clear that we must carry out studies that involve much greater numbers of

Table 3 ANOVA of Percentages of Time Distribution for High School and Primary School Groups

Sources	Physical education time			Engagement time			Motor engagement time		
	Mean square	df	F	Mean square	df	F	Mean square	df	F
High school groups									
Groups	0.0002	1	0.04	0.0007	1	0.17	0.0058	1	1.15
Error	0.0049	8		0.0043	8		0.0051	8	
Lessons	0.0016	1	0.55	0.0081	1	0.81	0.0054	1	2.18
Error	0.0029	8		0.0099	8		0.0025	8	
Groups/lessons	0.0016	1	1.65	0.00001	1	0.00	0.00001	1	0.00
Error	0.0009	8		0.0033	8		0.0030	8	
Mean	26.214	1	1085.2	8.762	1	221.7	2.25	1	61.6
Error	0.0241	8		0.0395	8		0.0365	8	
Primary school groups									
Groups	0.0050	1	0.41	0.0116	1	1.39	0.0008	1	0.09
Error	0.0121	7		0.0084	7		0.0087	7	
Lessons	0.0003	1	0.12	0.0028	1	0.87	0.0000	1	0.00
Error	0.0026	7		0.0026	7		0.0016	7	
Groups/lessons	0.0010	1	0.74	0.0030	1	0.86	0.0001	1	0.10
Error	0.0013	7		0.0035	7		0.0016	7	
Mean	20.48	1	912.8	9.342	1	354.2	2.6565	1	113.85
Error	0.0224	7		0.0263	7		0.0233	7	

teachers and that teachers must become more aware of their teaching behavior and the theoretical and conceptual constructs that provide the basis for their actions.

References

Arnold, R. (1981). Developing sport skills: A dynamic interplay task, learner and teacher. In *Motor skills: theory into practice: Monograph No. 2*. Newton, CT: A.L. Rothstein.

Brunelle, J., Godbout, P., Drouin, D., Desharnais, R., Lord, M., & Tousignant, M. (1980). *Rapport de recherche sur la qualité de l'intervention en education physique* [Research report on the quality of intervention in physical education]. Québec: Université Laval.

Dunkin, M.J., & Biddle, B.J. (1974). *The study of teaching.* New York: Holt, Rinehart, and Winston.

Gentile, A. (1972). A working model of skill acquisition with application to teacher. *Quest, 17,* 3–23.

Godbout, P., Brunelle, J., & Tousignant, M. (1983). Academic learning time in elementary and secondary physical education classes. *Research Quarterly for Exercise and Sport, 54*(1), 11–19.

Graham, G., & Heimerer, E. (1981). Research on teacher effectiveness: A summary with implications for teacher. *Quest, 33*(1), 14–25.

Metzler, M. (1979). *The measurement of academic learning time in physical education.* Unpublished doctoral dissertation, Ohio State University, Columbus.

Paré, C., Lirette, M., & Caron, F. (1983). L'ahalyse du temps de pratique active chez les élèves du secteur adaptation scolaire [Analysis of students' active learning time in the scholarly adaptation sector]. *Revue des Sciences de l'Education, 9*(3), 401–417.

Piéron, M. (1982a). Contribution de l'observation des enseignants à la methodologie des activités physiques et sportives [Contribution of teacher observation to the methodology of physical and athletic activities]. *Révue de l'Education Physique, 22*(2), 13–18.

Piéron, M. (1982b). L'Observation des enseignants [Teacher observation]. *Education Physique et Sports, 173,* 14–18.

Piéron, M. (1984). *Pedagogie des activités physiques et sportives: Methodologie et didactique* [Pedagogy of physical and athletic activities: Methodology and didactic]. Liège, Belgium: University of Liège.

Piéron, M., & Forceille, C. (1983). Observation du comportement des élèves dans des classes de l'enseignement secondaire: Influence de leur niveau d'habilété [Observation of high school students' behavior: Influence of their ability level]. *Révue de l'Education Physique, 23*(2), 9–16.

Piéron, M., & Haan, J.M. (1979, July). *Interactions between teacher and students in physical education settings: Observation of student behaviors.* Paper delivered at the International Council for Health, Physical Education, and Recreation Congress, Kiel, Germany.

Siedentop, D., Birdwell, D., & Metzler, M. (1979, March). *A process approach to measuring teaching effectiveness in physical education.* Summary of paper delivered at the American Alliance for Health, Physical Education, and Recreation research symposium, New Orleans, LA.

Tousignant, M., & Brunelle, J. (1982). What we have learned from students and how we can use it to improve curriculum and teaching. In M. Piéron & J. Cheffers (Eds.), *Studying the teaching in physical education* (pp. 3–22). Liège, Belgium: University of Liège.

A Characterization of
Recreational Dance Classes

Madeleine Lord
Bernard Petiot

Very little knowledge is available on the dance-teaching process. Few descriptive studies have been conducted in the actual dance class setting. These studies have mainly focused on teacher behaviors in classes of modern dance technique (Brunelle & De Carufel, 1982; Lord, 1982; Piéron & Delmelle, 1983; Piéron & Géoris, 1983), ballet (Gray, 1983), and choreography (Lord, 1981–1982).

Descriptive data on modern dance classes are starting to show how the behavior of dance teachers differs from teacher behavior occurring in other physical activity. Like most such teachers, dance instructors use the direct teaching approach, relying mainly on "guiding the performance of motor activity," "preparing for motor activity," and "providing feedback." Dance teachers tend, however, to use more demonstration in the preparation and guidance of the activities and to use verbal and nonverbal skills to accompany and guide student performance (Lord, 1982; Piéron & Géoris, 1983). Their feedback behaviors tend to be quantitatively more predominant, very brief (less than 3 seconds), and highly specific (Brunelle & Carufel, 1982; Piéron & Delmelle, 1983).

Little attention has been paid in dance settings to student behavior. Results in this regard, although limited, indicate a tendency on the part of dance students to spend more time on task than students of other types of activity (O'Sullivan, 1985; Piéron & Delmelle, 1983; Piéron & Géoris, 1983).

Due to the generally small number of teachers and classes involved in these investigations, and due also to the differences or uncertainty surrounding the contexts (academic, recreational, and professional training) in which they were conducted, the results can hardly be considered representative of teaching practices in general. More descriptive studies are needed to develop a better knowledge and understanding of what specifically is involved in the dance teaching-learning environment, in both academic and nonacademic contexts.

A study conducted by Telama, Paivi, Varstala, and Paananen (1982) revealed some differences in pupil behavior in physical education classes that were oriented toward recreation, fitness training, learning, or other goals. The present study focused on the recreational teaching process.

It was believed that the prime importance of immediate enjoyment as a major goal of recreational activity would favor development of a teaching process that would feature specific characteristics of student as well as teacher behavior.

The purpose of this study was to identify some of these characteristics. This portion of the research was prompted by the following two questions:

- What are the major context and student involvement conditions in recreational dance classes?
- What are the major teacher behaviors operative in recreational dance classes?

In addition, to contribute to the general store of descriptive data on dance classes, it was hoped that the study would provide basic data on the learning environment encompassing "pleasurable" activities.

Method

The study was conducted during the fall of 1984 in the municipal recreational services of the cities of Laval and Montreal in the Province of Quebec. Thirteen dance teachers acknowledged as successful in their field and 126 dance students served as our subjects. Two lessons of the same jazz class given by each of the 13 teachers were observed "live" by two analysts. Thirty minutes were recorded from each lesson for a total of 780 minutes. The two analysts shared a common 5-second interval of observation and recording, each one using a different observation instrument. In each class, one focused on the participants while the other focused on the teacher.

Observations of participants were made using the revised ALT-PE Instrument (Siedentop, Tousignant, & Parker, 1982). It was used in its original form except for the motor context categories, which were adapted to the case of dance. Table 1 provides the definitions of the motor context categories for dance.

Dance teachers were observed using an adaptation of Anderson and Barrette's categories of physical education teachers' professional functions (1978). A summary of the categories is provided in Table 2.

Interrater reliability proved to be high: Over 80% agreement was reached between the two analysts in live observations of teacher behaviors and over 90% in their observations of the participants, prior to data collection.

A questionnaire based on 3-point and 5-point rating scales was completed by the participants at the second observation of each class. This questionnaire contained 17 questions, 4 of which pertained to the amount of immediate pleasure experienced by the participants during the class. The data obtained from the (5-point) satisfaction scale for these 4 "pleasure" questions were compiled to yield a mean coefficient of satisfaction with the "pleasantness" conditions experienced in each class.

Table 1 Summary of ALT-PE System Subject Matter Motor Categories Developed for Dance

Category	Definition
Skill practice (P)	Time devoted to practice of technical dance movements, outside an applied context[a], with the primary goal of skill development
Dance combination (C)	Time devoted to the execution and refinement of chains of dance skills or dances, outside or in an applied context with the primary goal of connecting movement, and during which there is frequent instruction and feedback for the participants
Structured improvisation (SI)	Time devoted to the invention or variation of movements, outside of an applied context, initiated by a task providing specific movement limitations for the participants
Free improvisation (FI)	Time devoted to spontaneous and continuous creation of movements, in or outside an applied context, initiated by a task that provides a stimulus and no movement limitation for the participants
Composition (Co)	Time devoted to the selection and organization of the movement material of a dance into a whole outside of an applied context
Performance (Per)	Time devoted to the performance of dances created by the students themselves, the teacher or any other choreographer, in an applied context, without intervention from the teacher
Fitness (F)	Time devoted to activities whose major purpose is to alter the physical state of the individual in relation to dance (strength, flexibility, cardiovascular endurance, etc.)

[a]Applied context in dance involves a performance before an audience (teacher, classmates, parents and friends, or general public).

Results and Discussion

The satisfaction, or "pleasure," coefficients obtained for each teacher were first examined to yield a measure of the degree to which the teaching processes under investigation constituted a "pleasant" learning environment.

Pleasure coefficients ranged from 11.6 to 18.1, with a standard deviation of 2. A mean of 14.8 out of 20, or 73.6%, was obtained for the 13

Table 2 Summary of the Categories to Describe Teacher Behaviors

Category	Definition
1. Preparing for motor activities	
a. Demonstrating[a]	Providing information to students about activity by demonstrating the movement exactly as it should be performed by the students
b. Explaining[a]	Providing information to students about activity by explaining the movement to be performed
c. Illustrating[a]	Providing information to students about activity by illustrating it through a partial demonstration or other nonverbal means
d. Organizing	Providing information to students about their location, position, grouping, role, order of performance, and so forth
2. Guiding the performance of motor activities	
a. Serving as a model	Demonstrating the movements in front of the group performing the activity
b. Guiding with cues	Providing instruction to students while they are performing the activity
3. Providing feedback	Reacting to students' behaviors or motor responses
4. Observing the performance of motor activities	Silently attending to student(s) who are performing motor activities
5. Participating in motor activities	Participating in a motor activity (not leading or demonstrating)
6. Interacting: dance related	All other interactions directly related to dance which do not fall into the above categories
7. Interacting: dance unrelated	All other interactions not related to dance which do not fall into the above categories
8. Noninteracting	Periods during which no interactive function is being carried out
9. Nondiscernible intervals	Periods during which you cannot determine whether the teacher's behavior is interactive or noninteractive

[a]These categories can be used in combination.

teachers. On the basis of these data, the teaching processes in evidence could not be considered ideal, but they were nevertheless adequate for the purpose of this study.

Major Context and Student Involvement Conditions

Results pertaining to the first of the two questions mentioned were based on the mean percentage of occurrence of each ALT-PE category obtained over the total 26 classes. They are represented in Figures 1 and 2.

With the percentage of ALT-PE means at 41.6% for the first observation of all the classes and 41.8% for the second, the ALT-PE data were considered fairly stable over time.

A glance at Figure 1 reveals that recreational dance classes were, like academic dancing classes, mostly centered on content (81.4%). Indeed,

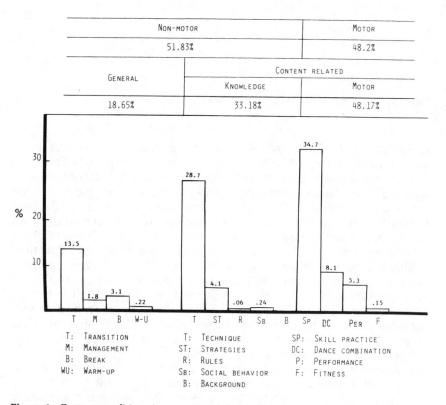

NON-MOTOR		MOTOR
51.83%		48.2%

GENERAL	CONTENT RELATED	
	KNOWLEDGE	MOTOR
18.65%	33.18%	48.17%

T: TRANSITION   T: TECHNIQUE   SP: SKILL PRACTICE
M: MANAGEMENT   ST: STRATEGIES   DC: DANCE COMBINATION
B: BREAK   R: RULES   P: PERFORMANCE
WU: WARM-UP   SB: SOCIAL BEHAVIOR   F: FITNESS
                  B: BACKGROUND

Figure 1 Context conditions in recreational dance classes.

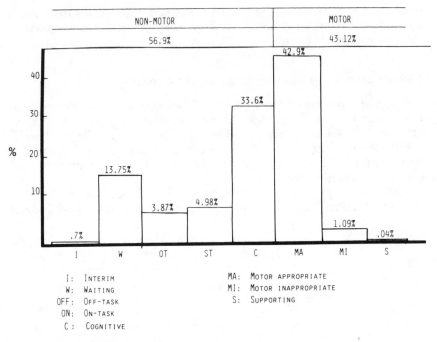

Figure 2 Involvement conditions in recreational dance classes.

O'Sullivan (1985) found that 80.4% of dance class time was devoted to content in secondary schools. This proportion is slightly higher than the 78% Tousignant and Brunelle (1982) found in secondary school physical education (PE) classes. More than half the class time in our study exhibited a nonmotor context (51.8%). The great majority of this time was devoted to cognitive activities related to jazz technique, with the remaining nonmotor time mainly consisting of transitions (13.5%) and breaks (3.1%).

Forty-eight percent of the class time was motor in context. This time mainly consisted of students' practicing jazz skills (34.7%) and combinations of dance movements (8%). Only 5% of the time was devoted to the actual performance of dances. Considering that interpretation is the ultimate and most playful of dance activities, this proportion of time was considered low for the recreational dance context. Participants were not given much opportunity to just get out there and "dance."

Results for learner involvement are presented in Figure 2. They show that participants were involved in dance activities 76.7% of the time, that 43% of that involvement was motor, and that 97% of that motor activity was appropriate or successful, to the extent that students successfully performed the movements required of them. These participation percentages are much higher than the mean percentages of 39% and 18% found in PE classes (Tousignant & Brunelle, 1982), but the percentage of motor activity is much lower than the 73% found in high school dance classes

(O'Sullivan, 1985). These results confirm the tendency of dance classes to offer more "academic learning time" than other physically oriented classes but also suggest that recreational dance classes are less intensive physically than academic instruction. Indeed, when not performing dance movements participants spent a great deal of time listening to explanations of dance movements and just waiting.

In spite of the high success rates found in the PE classes (Tousignant & Brunelle, 1982), the rates obtained in this study were even higher, indicating a level of difficulty that almost perfectly matched students' existing skill levels. Such results argue against any strong emphasis on skill development's being a major teaching goal in the recreational education sphere.

Major Teacher Behaviors

Results pertaining to the second research question mentioned above were based on the mean percentage of occurrence obtained for each of the teacher behavior categories over the total number of classes. They are illustrated in Figure 3.

The stability of teacher behavior data over time was investigated before the data were used to shed light on the characteristics of the recreational teaching process. The data from the 13 teachers taken as a group yielded a coefficient of .62 (Spearman rho correlation coefficient between the rank each category of teacher behavior earned during the first and second observations). This correlation was considered acceptable.

Characteristics of teacher behavior were related to the quantitative importance of the pedagogical functions assumed by the teachers during the classes. An examination of Figure 3 reveals that "Guiding the performance of the activity" was the dominant function, indicating a teacher's strong concern for the participants' active motor involvement. Although dance is a form of internally motivated movement, it did not require any greater amount of guidance behavior than other forms. The amount found in this study compares with that found in PE classes (Anderson & Barrette, 1978). "Modeling" was the main guidance strategy.

"Preparing for the dance activity" was the second most important function. The amount of time teachers devoted to presentation of the dance task is much greater than what Piéron and Géoris (1983) found for modern dance classes and what Anderson and Barrette (1978) reported for high school PE classes. "Explained demonstration" was clearly the dominant strategy used for the preparation function in our study. These results corroborate the dance teachers' tendency to use more demonstration than do other physical activity teachers in preparing and guiding activities. They also indicate a strong concern for clear student understanding of the dance task in their performance of these two functions, along with perhaps some lack of efficiency in their presentation of the task.

"To provide feedback" was the third function performed by the teachers. If we consider that teacher reactions both to student behavior

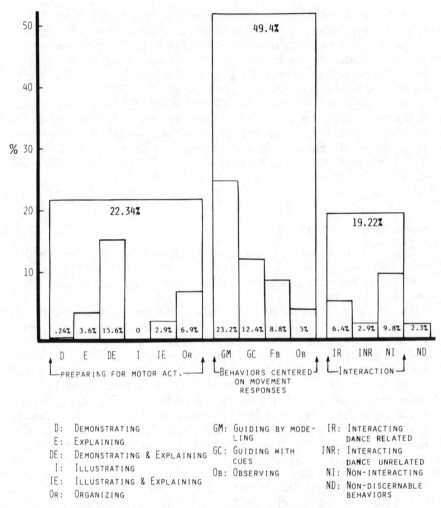

Figure 3 Teacher behaviors operative in recreational dance classes.

and motor responses were recorded as feedback, the percentage we found (8.8%) is much lower than the 20% found in modern dance classes (Piéron & Géoris, 1983). This rather low percentage was probably influenced by the small amount of time teachers spent in observation (5%), which in turn was influenced by the extent and nature of the guidance behavior. Teachers of recreational classes in our study gave priority to guidance rather than to observation and feedback and by doing so did not therefore exhibit a strong concern with the development of dance skills as a major goal.

Provision of general information about dance and interactions with participants on subjects unrelated to dance appeared to be minor functions in our study, but their nature is as yet unclear. They most likely did have the effect of curtailing students' motor participation but could also have had a strong leavening impact on the climate by injecting humor, esthetic stimulus, or the like into it. A more extensive observation of these functions would be necessary to yield a better understanding of their role in creating a pleasurable dance environment.

Conclusion

On the basis of the results obtained, the context of the recreational dance classes under investigation was observed to be primarily, but flexibly, centered on dance, to involve dance tasks that matched participants' abilities, and to offer eight times more opportunities to practice dancing skills and combinations than opportunities just to "dance." Participant involvement in the classes was seen to be mostly nonmotor and consequently not physically intensive, as well as highly "successful" or appropriate.

Results support the idea that successful motor participation in dance movement is a basic ingredient of the pleasant dance environment. This finding would tend to suggest that the quality of the motor participation might, in recreational classes, be more important than its quantity. Increasing the amount of time devoted to performance of dances might be a way to provide participants with an even more pleasurable motor experience.

The description of teacher behaviors in relation to the context and student participation conditions in evidence showed little emphasis on the development of dance skills as a teaching goal. The successful involvement of the participant seemed to be the main concern. This description of observed teacher behaviors would suggest development of a teaching strategy that might be characteristic of the process of teaching recreational dance. It would go like this. Teachers tend to do what is necessary to ensure a successful response by the participants to the dance movements. To that end, they therefore very clearly present dance tasks to match the participants' skill levels and then lead student performance along by providing a clear model to follow.

Being limited in scope and intent, the present study makes no claim to be a definitive description of the phenomenon of recreational dance teaching. More descriptive studies of recreational dance classes are necessary in order to confirm the present findings.

References

Anderson, W.G., & Barrette, G.T. (1978). Teacher behavior. In W.G. Anderson & G.T. Barrette (Eds.), *Motor skills: Theory into practice: Mono-*

graph No. 1. What's going on in gym (pp. 25–39). Newton, CT: A.L. Rothstein.

Brunelle, J., & Carufel, F. de (1982). Analyse des feedback émis par des maîtres de l'enseignement de la danse moderne [Analysis of feedback emitted by master teachers of modern dance]. *La Revue Québécoise de l'Activité Physique*, **2**(1), 3–9.

Gray, J. (1983). The science of teaching the act of dance: A description of a computer-aided system for recording and analyzing dance instructional behaviors. *Journal of Education for Teaching*, **9**(3), 264–278.

Lord, M. (1981–1982). A characterization of dance teacher behavior in choreography and technique classes [Double issue]. *Dance Research Journal*, **14**(1),(2), 15–24.

O'Sullivan, M.M. (1985). A descriptive analytical study of student teacher effectiveness and student behavior in secondary school physical education. In B.L. Howe & J.J. Jackson (Eds.), *Teaching effectiveness research physical education series*, University of Victoria, **6**, 22–31.

Piéron, M., & Delmelle, V. (1983). Les réactions à la presentation de l'élève étude dans l'enseignement de la danse moderne [Teachers' reaction to student execution in teaching modern dance]. *Revue de l'Èducation Physique*, **23**(4), 35–41.

Piéron, M., & Géoris, M. (1983). Comportements d'enseignants et interactions avec leurs élèves. Observation dans l'enseignement de la "Modern Dance" [Teaching behaviors and teacher-student interaction. Observation of modern dance instruction]. *Revue de l'Èducation Physique*, **23**(4), 42–46.

Siedentop, D., Tousignant, M., & Parker, M. (1982). *Academic learning time–physical education—1982 revision coding manual.* Columbus: Ohio State University, School of Health, Physical Education and Recreation.

Telama, R., Paivi, P., Varstala, V., & Paananen, M. (1982). Pupils' physical activity and learning behavior in physical education classes. In M. Piéron & J. Cheffers (Eds.), *Studying the teaching in physical education* (pp. 23–37). Liège, Belgium: University of Liège.

Tousignant, M., & Brunelle, J. (1982). What we have learned from students and how we can use it to improve curriculum and teaching. In M. Piéron & J. Cheffers (Eds.), *Studying the teaching in physical education* (pp. 3, 23). Liège, Belgium: University of Liège.